P9-DXF-748

Character Rigging and Animation

TABLE OF CONTENTS

HOW TO USE THIS BOOK

Learning Maya 6 | Character Rigging and Animation will teach you what you need to know to achieve effective character set-up in Maya. This book is designed to help you comprehend Character Rigging and animation in Maya, regardless of your current skill level.

However, before you start this book, you should already have some beginner level knowledge of working in Maya. As an added bonus, we have included the *Maya Beginner's Guide | Animation DVD*, where you will complete seven easy-to-follow, step-by-step exercises to get you comfortable when using some of the most common animation tools available in Maya.

Theoretical discussions

Each section of this book is introduced by a theoretical discussion explaining the concepts at play when working with various features. These sections will help you understand why and how Maya works so that you are better equipped to resolve challenges as your skills improve.

Project-based tutorials

Each chapter includes step-by-step tutorials to help you improve your skills when working with tools and features in Maya. Complete the full project for a broader understanding of the workflows or focus on specific tools to understand how they work.

Instructor overviews

View the instructor overviews on the accompanying DVD-ROM for additional discussions and demonstrations to complement the lessons in this book. Instructor overviews are provided by Alias Certified Instructors in QuickTime format and are intended to act as your virtual trainer.

Index

Expert users may skip to the index in order to find quick answers and solutions to production challenges without working through every lesson.

Updates to this book

In an effort to ensure your continued success through the lessons in this book, please visit our web site for the latest updates available: www.alias.com/maya/learningtools_updates/

Installing tutorial files

To install the tutorial scene files, copy the *support_files* directory from the DVD-ROM found at the back of this book onto your local hard drive.

Introducing Melvin

Animating digital characters is a growing field that is being incorporated into commercial and feature projects. The demands put on today's characters are growing at a rapid pace. Thanks to Maya®, the job of setting up and animating a character to meet these demands is made possible and fun.

This book explores the setup and animation of Melvin. As you setup Melvin, you will explore methods for creating skeletal and muscular systems, enabling the animation of this character in Maya.

Melvin

By completing the exercises in this book, you will learn the following:

- How to build and operate a complex hierarchy of joints and deformers that have been applied to a character-based model;

- How to create custom controls that streamline your workflow to allow for more creative and direct animations;

- How to animate Melvin to perform in typical animation scenarios such as walking and talking.

Melvin's bones

You will first learn how to set Melvin up. Here are examples of two different techniques that have been used when setting up Melvin's skeletal controls:

- **Foot and leg** - Single chain solved IK chain for leg with Pole Vector constraint determining knee direction. Foot controls for rotating ankle and bending toe controlled by selecting one object at the ankle.
- **Hand** - Instead of using Inverse Kinematics, Set Driven Key is used to drive Forward Kinematics of the finger joints. You will create a custom interface to ease the keyframing process for the hands.

Melvin's skin

Melvin will be skinned using three different methods:

- **Feet, legs, arms, hands** - traditional methods of adding skin to the joints.
- **Upper and lower torso** - lattices (deforming skin) and wrap deformers bound to the joints.
- **Complete body** - Smooth Skinned with influence objects parented to the joints.

Melvin's muscles

Many of the different flexor and deformers that Maya provides to create realistic control of both muscles and clothing are incorporated into this book.

- **Bicep muscle** - influence objects setup with Set Driven Key.
- **Elbows** - cluster, lattice flexors, and influence objects.
- **Face** - blendShape targets created using lattices, flexors, clusters, and Wire Deformers.

Set Driven Key is used in some cases to control the behavior of some of these deformers.

Animating Melvin

Once you've worked through character setup techniques, you'll take Melvin through several animation scenarios to test out both his construction and the controls that you create. These include:

- Walk cycle;
- Kicking the can;
- Facial animation/lip-sync.

You'll explore several techniques to aid in animating Melvin more efficiently and realistically:

- Motion studies;
- Keyframe techniques;
- Using Breakdown keys to keep positional relationship between standard keyframes;
- Using image planes for motion study;
- Using Character Sets to make attributes centrally located and easily keyed;
- Using sets to simplify selection for skinning and weighting;
- Make animating convenient by setting up attributes accessible through the Channel Box;
- Shelf buttons;
- Utilizing Pick Masks;
- Using layers for display, hiding, and templating;
- Scene organization.

Character optimization

In the coming projects, all the modeling work has been done for you. For reasons of efficiency, you should be aware of the geometry and its properties of construction at specific spots on the character. Pay attention to areas that are undergoing extreme deformation and thus require special consideration.

Also, note where the character may seem limited for specific applications. Generally a character is designed to perform specific actions and has been optimized for those needs. To make a character that will perform in all situations flawlessly could be a waste of time that could otherwise be spent animating. When designing your characters, keep a specific list of abilities in mind that are required by the script. This will go a long way in keeping the character from being overbuilt and too cumbersome to operate.

THE DEPENDENCY GRAPH

While creating characters, it is a good idea to have a basic knowledge of how Maya's system architecture works. Maya's system architecture uses a procedural paradigm that lets you integrate traditional keyframe animation, Inverse Kinematics, dynamics, and scripting on top of a node-based architecture that is called the Dependency Graph. If you wanted to reduce this graph to its bare essentials, you could describe it as nodes with attributes that are connected. This node-based architecture gives Maya its flexible procedural qualities.

Below is a diagram showing a primitive sphere's Dependency Graph as shown in the Hypergraph view. A procedural Input node defines the shape of the sphere by connecting attributes on each node.

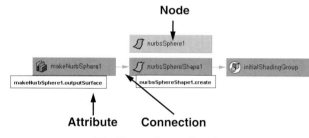

The Dependency Graph

Nodes

Every element in Maya, whether it is a curve, surface, deformer, light, texture, expression, modeling operation or animation curve, is described by either a single node or a series of connected nodes.

A node is a generic object type in Maya. Different nodes are designed with specific attributes so that the node can accomplish a specific task. Nodes define all object types in Maya including geometry, shading, and lighting. Shown below are three typical node types as they appear on a primitive sphere.

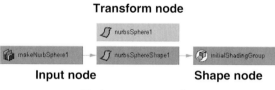

Node types on a sphere

Transform node - Transform nodes contain positioning information for your objects. When you move, rotate or scale, this is the node you are affecting.

Input node - The Input node represents options that drive the creation of your sphere's shape such as radius or endsweep.

Shape node - The Shape node contains all the component information that represents the actual look of the sphere.

Maya's user interface presents these nodes to you in many ways. Below is an image of the Channel Box where you can edit and animate node attributes.

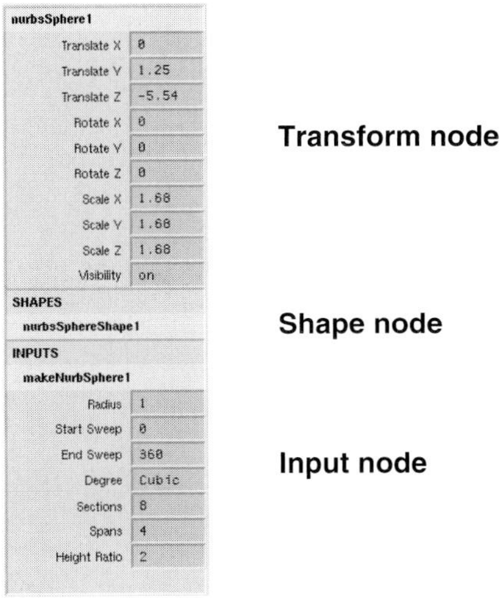

Transform node

Shape node

Input node

Channel Box

Attributes

Each node is defined by a series of attributes that relate to what the node is designed to accomplish. In the case of a Transform node, X Translate is an attribute. In the case of a shader node, Color Red is an attribute. It is possible for you to assign values to the attributes. You can work with attributes in a number of user-interface windows including the Attribute Editor, the Channel Box and the Spread Sheet Editor.

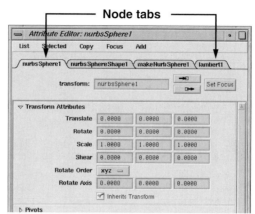

The Attribute Editor

One important feature in Maya is that you can animate virtually every attribute on any node. This helps give Maya its animation power. You should note that attributes are also referred to as channels.

Connections

Nodes don't exist in isolation. A finished animation results when you begin making connections between attributes on different nodes. These connections are also known as dependencies. In the case of modeling, these connections are sometimes referred to as construction history.

Most of these connections are created automatically by the Maya user interface as a result of using commands or tools. If you desire, you can also build and edit these connections explicitly using the Connection Editor, by entering MEL™ (Maya Embedded Language) commands, or by writing MEL-based expressions.

Hierarchies

When you are building scenes in Maya, you can build dependency connections to link node attributes. When working with Transform nodes or joint nodes, you can also build hierarchies which create a different kind of relationship between your objects.

In a hierarchy, one Transform node is parented to another. When Maya works with these nodes, Maya looks first at the top node, or root node, then down the hierarchy. Therefore, motion from the upper nodes is transferred down into the lower nodes. In the diagram below, if the *group1* node is rotated, then the two lower nodes will rotate with it. If the *nurbsCone* node is rotated, the upper nodes are not affected.

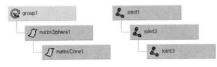

Object and joint hierarchy nodes

Joint hierarchies are used when you are building characters. When you create joints, the joint pivots act as limb joints while bones are drawn between them to help visualize the joint chain. By default, these hierarchies work just like object hierarchies. Rotating one node rotates all of the lower nodes at the same time.

When you are working with characters, you can use Inverse Kinematics to reverse the flow of the hierarchy.

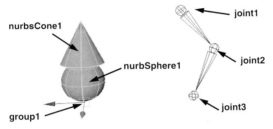

Object and joint hierarchies

The Hypergraph

In Maya, you can visualize hierarchies and dependencies using the Hypergraph. The following steps demonstrate how to work with various node types in the Hypergraph.

Working with hierarchies and dependencies

If you understand the idea of nodes with attributes that are connected, then you will understand the Dependency Graph. You can see what this means in Maya by building a simple primitive sphere.

1 **Setup your view panels**

To view nodes and connections in a diagram format, the Hypergraph panel is required along with a Perspective view.

- Select **Panels → Layouts → Two Panes Side by Side**.
- Setup a Perspective view in the first panel and a Hypergraph view in the second panel.
- Dolly into the Perspective view to get closer to the grid.

2 Create a primitive sphere

- Go to the Modeling menu set.

- Select **Create → NURBS Primitives → Sphere**.

- Press **5** to turn on smooth shading and **3** to increase the surface smoothness of the sphere.

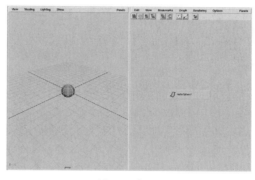

New sphere

3 View the Shape node

In the Hypergraph panel, you are currently looking at the Scene Hierarchy view. This Scene Hierarchy view is focused on Transform nodes. This node lets you set the position and orientation of your objects.

Right now, only a *nurbsSphere* node is visible. In actual fact, there are two nodes in this hierarchy but the second is hidden by default. At the bottom of most hierarchies, you will find a Shape node which contains the information about the object itself.

- In the Hypergraph panel, select **Options → Display → Shape Nodes**.

  You can now see the Transform node which is, in effect, the positioning node and the Shape node which contains information about the actual surface of the sphere. The Transform node defines the position of the shape below it.

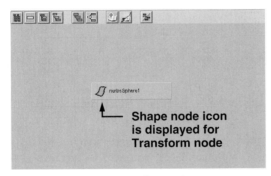

Transform and Shape nodes

- In the Hypergraph panel, select **Options** → **Display** → **Shape Nodes** to turn these **Off**.

  You will notice that when these nodes are expanded, the Shape node and the Transform node have different icons. When collapsed, the Transform node takes on the Shape node's icon to help you understand what is going on underneath.

Transform node on its own

4 View the dependencies

To view the dependencies that exist with a primitive sphere, you need to take a look at the input and output connections.

- Click on the sphere with the **RMB-select Inputs** → **Make Nurb Sphere** from the marking menu.

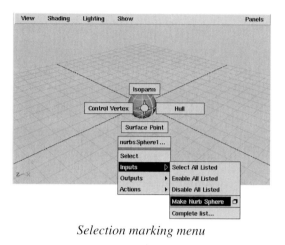

Selection marking menu

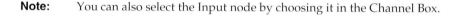

| Note: | You can also select the Input node by choosing it in the Channel Box. |

- In the Hypergraph panel, click on the **Input and Output Connections** button.

  See the original Transform node which is now separated from the Shape node. While the Transform node has a hierarchical relationship to the Shape node, their attributes are not dependent on each other.

  The Input node called *makeNurbSphere* is a result of the original creation of the sphere. The options set in the Sphere Tool's option window have been placed into a node that feeds into the Shape node. The Shape node is dependent on the Input node. If you change values in the Input node, the shape of the sphere changes.

Sphere dependencies

5 Edit the attributes in the Channel Box

In the Channel Box, you can edit attributes belonging to all of the node types. This lets you affect both hierarchical relationships and dependencies.

If you edit an attribute belonging to the *makeNurbSphere* node, then the shape of the sphere will be affected. If you change an attribute belonging to the *nurbSphere* Transform node, then the positioning will be changed. Using the Channel Box will help you work with the nodes.

- For the Transform node, change the **Rotate Y** value to **45**.

- For the Input node, change the **Radius** to **3**.

  You can set attribute values to affect either the scene hierarchy or the Dependency Graph.

Animating the sphere

When you animate in Maya, you are changing the value of an attribute over time. Using keyframes, you set these values at important points in time, then use tangent properties to determine how the attribute value changes between the keys.

The key and tangent information is placed in a separate Animation Curve node that is then connected to the animated attribute.

1 Select the sphere

- In the Hypergraph panel, click on the **Scene Hierarchy** button.

- Select the *nurbsSphere* Transform node.

2 Return the sphere to the origin

Since you earlier moved the sphere along the three axes, it's a good time to set it back to the origin.

- In the Channel Box, change the **Rotate Y** attribute to **0**.

3 Animate the sphere's rotation

- In the Time Slider, set the playback range to **120** frames.
- In the Time Slider, go to frame **1**.
- Click on the **Rotate Y** channel name in the Channel Box.
- Click with your RMB and select **Key Selected** from the pop-up menu.

  This sets a key at the chosen time.

- In the Time Slider, go to frame **120**.
- In the Channel Box, change the **Rotate Y** attribute to **720**.
- Click with your right mouse button and select **Key Selected** from the pop-up menu.
- Playback the results.

  The sphere is now spinning.

4 View the Hypergraph dependencies

- In the Hypergraph panel, click on the **Input and Output Connections** button.

  You see that an Animation Curve node has been created and connected to the Transform node. The Transform node is now shown as a trapezoid to indicate that it is connected to the Animation Curve node. If you click on the connection arrow, you will see that the connection is to Rotate Y.

  If you select the Animation Curve node and open the Attribute Editor, you will see that each key has been recorded along with value, time, and tangent information. You can actually edit this information here, or use the Graph Editor where you get more visual feedback.

Connected Animation Curve node

Parenting in the Hypergraph

So far, you have worked a lot with the dependency connections but not with the scene hierarchy. In a hierarchy, you always work with Transform nodes. You can make one Transform node the parent of another node, thereby creating a child which must follow the parent.

You will build a hierarchy of spheres that are rotating like planets around the sun. This example is a helpful way to understand how scene hierarchies work.

1 Create a new sphere

- In the Hypergraph panel, click on the **Scene Hierarchy** button.
- Go to the Modeling menu set.
- Select **Create** → **NURBS Primitives** → **Sphere**.
- **Move** the sphere along the Z-axis until it sits in front of the first sphere.
- Press **3** to increase the display smoothness of the sphere.
- Go to the Rendering menu set.
- Apply a checkered shader to both spheres.

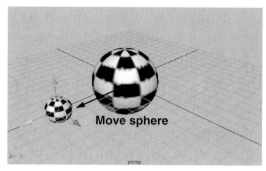

Second sphere

2 Parent the sphere to the first sphere

- In the Hypergraph, drag the node icon with the **MMB** for the second sphere onto the first sphere. Now they are parented together.

- Playback the scene.

  The second sphere rotates along with the first sphere. It has inherited the motion of the original sphere.

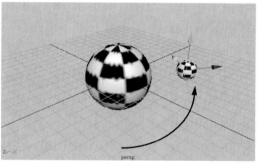

Rotating hierarchy

Summary

Creating a character for use in 3D is one of the most challenging tasks you will face. It is also one of the most rewarding. This book will stress the importance of building a foundation of understanding Maya in a broad sense. This will allow you to draw upon Maya's entire toolset to solve the problems that you encounter. Understanding how Maya's hierarchy and Dependency Graph work, for example, is core to understanding the why and how of building complex and interactive character rigs. The techniques utilized in this book are intended to teach an approach to character rigging much like that of building a marionette or puppet.

1 Skeleton Setup

To begin, you are going to set up the Melvin character. To help you organize your character's movement and provide a framework for applying deformations, you must first build a skeleton chain by creating a series of joint nodes.

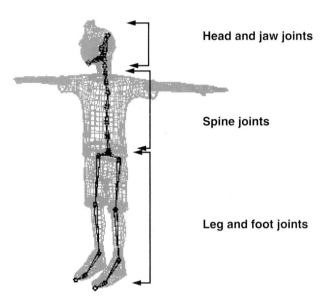

Head and jaw joints

Spine joints

Leg and foot joints

Melvin's bones

In an ideal world, you would create the skeleton perfectly the first time you create the joints. Realistically, you may want to later update or correct how your character is setup. To create the most flexibility for animating, you will setup the character's skeleton by combining several techniques.

In this chapter, you will learn the following:

- How to use layers and templating;
- How to create joints for the legs, feet, back, and neck;
- How to connect and parent joints.

CREATING THE LOWER BODY SKELETON

You will start work on Melvin by constructing the leg using existing geometry as a guide. To build the leg, you will complete the following:

- Import Melvin's body geometry;
- Add this geometry to layers;
- Template the geometry;
- Build the skeleton.

LAYERS AND TEMPLATES

A good tool for organizing the various parts of a character is the Layer Editor. This tool provides an easy way to separate all the parts of Melvin – geometry, skeletons, IK, etc. into logical groups. In the Layer Editor, you can hide, show, and/or template selected layers to speed up interactivity by reducing the visible elements in the scene.

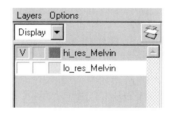

A view of the Layer Editor

Show or hide groupings of elements

The more elements you can hide in your scene, the quicker you can interact with your scene.

Select objects or groupings of elements

Sometimes it is difficult to select objects and groups of objects efficiently in the interface. If you find yourself picking the same object or group of objects, make a layer for them.

Template or untemplate groupings of elements

By templating objects, you will still see a transparent representation of them, but they are not selectable. This enables you to pick some types of objects and not pick the same type of others, but still see them.

Selecting and displaying only the elements of the scene that you are working on is crucial to successfully operating in a complex scene.

Layers can also be used to logically break down your scene. You can make your background elements a separate layer and your foreground elements another layer. Characters and effects can be on a layer that you may want to render separately as compositing passes.

Creating a layer and templating geometry

You are going to use Melvin's body to help position the skeleton properly, but you don't want to accidentally modify it, so you will create a separate layer just for the geometry, allowing you to template it. Templating is a means of inactivating something without necessarily hiding it.

1 Open a file

- Open the file called *Melvin_01.geometry.mb* from the support_files directory found on the DVD-ROM.

2 Create a new layer for Melvin's deforming geometry

- Press the **Create a New Layer** button in the Layer Editor to create a new layer.

  A new layer should appear in the Layer Editor.

Tip: To see the Layer Editor, check the **Channel Box/Layer Editor** button under **Display → UI Elements**.

- **Double-click** on the *layer 1* box to open the **Edit Layer** window.
- Name the layer *melvinDeform*.
- In the Outliner, **Select** the following group nodes:

    leftArm, rightArm, shirt, shorts, head, leftLeg, and rightLeg.

- **RMB-click** on the *melvinDeform* layer and select **Add Selected Objects**.

  The selected objects are now a part of the layer.

3 Create a new layer for Melvin's non-deforming geometry

- Repeat the above process to create a new layer named *melvin_nonDeformed*.
- In the Outliner, Select the following group nodes and add them the to the new layer:

    glasses, leftEye, rightEye, lowerTeeth, and *upperTeeth.*

4 Template both layers

- **LMB-click** on the middle box next to the *melvinDeform* layer until a "**T**", representing **template,** appears.

- Repeat for the other layer.

  Now you can see Melvin's geometry but you cannot select it using the default select modes. Later, you will learn how to select templated geometry.

BUILDING SKELETON JOINTS

In Maya, a skeleton chain is made up of joint nodes that are connected visually by bone icons. A skeleton chain creates a continuous hierarchy of joint nodes that are parented to each other. The joint and bone icons help you visualize the character's hierarchy in the 3D views but will not appear in your final renderings. The top node of the hierarchy is known as the Root joint.

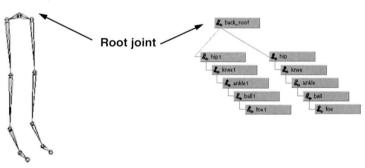

Joints and bones showing nodes in Hypergraph

Joint hierarchies let you group or bind geometry. You can then animate the joints, which in turn, animates the geometry. When you transform the joints you will most often use rotation. If you look at your own joints you will see that they all rotate. Generally, joints don't translate or scale unless you want to add some squash and stretch to a character's limbs.

When you rotate a joint, all the joints below it are carried along with the rotation. This behavior is called Forward Kinematics and is consistent with how all hierarchies work in Maya. In the next chapter, you will learn how to use Inverse Kinematics to make it easier to animate joint rotations.

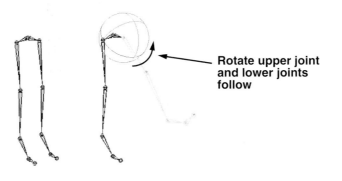

Rotate upper joint
and lower joints
follow

Joints rotations

To build Melvin's skeleton, you will first create joints for his legs and feet. Later you will build his back and neck, then this system will be connected to the legs at the hip joints.

Creating the leg skeletons

You will start by creating the left leg skeleton, then duplicating it to create the right leg skeleton.

1 In the side view, draw five joints for the left leg

- Select the **Skeleton → Joint Tool** – ❐.

- In the Option window, set the following options:

  Auto joint orient to **None**.

  (Joint Orientation will be discussed later in this book.)

- Starting with the hip, place **5** joints for the leg as shown below.

Note: Be sure to draw the knee in a bent position. This will make it easier to apply an IK solver to the chain in the next chapter.

- Rename the joints *hip, knee, ankle, ball,* and *toe.*

Traversing hierarchies

Use the up, down, left, and right arrow keys to quickly traverse through the joints in a hierarchy.

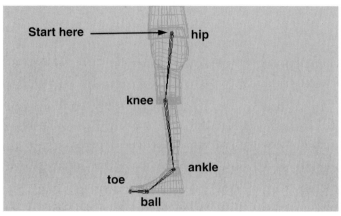

Left leg joints

2 Move the joint chain to Melvin's left side

The *hip* joint is now the root node of the leg's joint chain hierarchy. If you pick this node you can move the whole chain together.

- Select the *hip* joint and move it along the X-axis so it fits inside the geometry of Melvin's left leg.

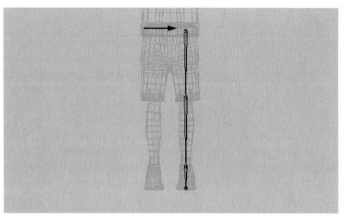

Moving the joint chain to Melvin's left

3 Duplicate the leg to create the right leg

- Select the *hip* joint.
- Select **Edit → Duplicate – ▢**.
- Press **Reset** under the duplicate window's **Edit menu**.
- **Move** the new leg over to the right.

If you look at the X translate of the left hip, you can put this value on the right hip and make it negative so that the skeleton is symmetrical.

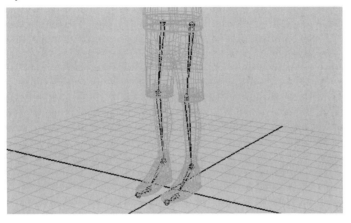

Duplicated leg

4 Rename your joints to include left_ and right_ prefixes

- Select the root joint of the left leg.

- Select **Modify → Prefix Hierarchy Names…**

- Enter *left_* in the text field. Click **OK** to validate.

- Repeat, using *right_* for the right leg joints.

- Edit the right leg joint names to remove the **1** that was appended in the duplicating step.

Tip: It is important to take the time now to name your objects so that later they'll be easy to select and replace.

---

5 Save your work

You will want to save your work in a way that makes it easy to access later. For this book, it is recommended that you save your files using the following convention:

- Select **File → Save As**.

- Enter the name *lesson1a.mb*.

    Rather than saving as *lesson1* then overwriting your work with a **File → Save**, it is recommended that you always use the **File → Save As** command and rename your file as *lesson1a.mb*, *lesson1b.mb* etc. This way you have many files that represent different stages in your work. This is useful if you need to go back a step or two to review some steps.

The first part of the file name represents the lesson you are working on and the second part indicates the file type. The *.mb* suffix represents **Maya binary**.

Maya offers two file types – **Maya binary** (*.mb*) and **Maya ascii** (*.ma*). The binary format is more compact and loads faster, making it better for larger files. The ascii format allows you to open the file in a text editor and tweak the file. You will be using **Maya binary** throughout this book.

Note: From now on, you will be prompted at key points to save your work. Saving frequently is always a good idea.

Creating the backbone, neck, and head

You will now create another skeleton hierarchy for the backbone, neck, and head. Start drawing joints from the base of the backbone. This will make the base joint the root joint of the skeleton hierarchy. The root joint is important since it represents the top of the hierarchy, even though it might be the bottom joint in the 3D view. Using the backbone as the root, the upper body and the legs will branch off from this node. You can then move the whole skeleton hierarchy by simply moving the root.

1 Place the first joint of the backbone just above the hips

- Select **Skeleton → Joint Tool** – ❐.
- Make sure that **Auto Joint Orient** is set to **XYZ**.

  By creating the joints with **Auto Joint Orient** set to **XYZ** and **World Axis Orient** set to **+X**, the X-axis will always point towards the child joint and the Y axis will point in the world +X direction. You set the orientation to **XYZ** so that the local rotation axis of the joints will be aligned in the direction of the backbone. This topic will be covered in more detail at the end of this chapter and throughout the book.

- **LMB-click** just above the hip joints to place the first joint.

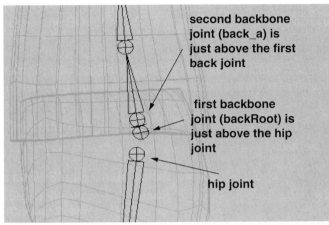

second backbone joint (back_a) is just above the first back joint

first backbone joint (backRoot) is just above the hip joint

hip joint

First two backbone joints

2 Draw more joints in the back to complete the backbone

- Draw six to twelve more joints until you reach the base of the neck.

- Rename the joints according to the illustration below:

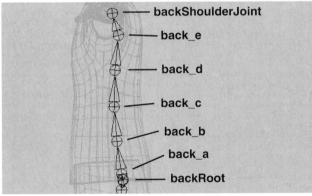

backShoulderJoint

back_e

back_d

back_c

back_b

back_a

backRoot

Joint names for spine

3 Continue drawing joints for the neck and skull

- Continue creating joints for the neck and head skeleton. From the last joint in the back, place approximately 9 joints through the neck and head.

- Rename the back joints as follows:

Placing joints

While placing joints, you can use the **MMB** to move the last joint that was placed.

The **Move Tool** will move the selected joint and any joints below it in the hierarchy.

The **Move Pivot Tool** (while in move mode press the **insert** key to toggle into this mode) will only move the selected joint.

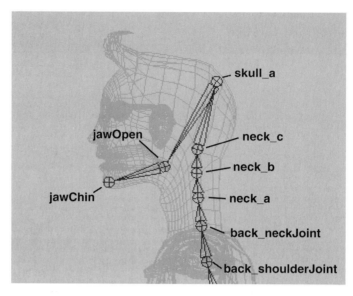

Joint names for neck and skull

Tip: There are no strict rules about how many joints are needed to create a backbone; it really depends on how you want to animate the motion in the back. You will be using an IK Spline solver for the back to simplify the control of such a large number of joints. Here are some guidelines for determining the number of joints to use in a typical biped character:
• backbone (6 - 12 joints)
• neck and head (6 - 9 joints)

4 Save your work

PARENTING SKELETONS

You now have three separate skeletons: one for each leg and the backbone/neck/head skeleton. These represent three different hierarchies. To create one branching hierarchy, you need to connect the three hierarchies using the parent command. You will start connecting these skeletons by connecting the hip joints to the backbone. Remember that although you are using the term connect, you are parenting joints. Connecting joints in Maya is a different operation that moves the joint to a position on top of the connected joint. This is much different than parenting which connects the joints together with an intermediary bone segment.

Attaching hips to the spine

There are several approaches to the hip/spine relationship. The method you use depends on what the animation requires and how much control you need.

For Melvin, you will create a simple setup that provides easy control and a natural pelvis/backbone motion.

1 Parent the hip joints to the spine

- Select the *left_hip* joint, then **Shift-select** the *right_hip* and *back_root* joint.

- Select **Edit** → **Parent** or press the **p** key.

Tip: You may want to open up a Hypergraph view so that you can see how the skeleton hierarchy is developing. You may also want to use the Hypergraph's freeform mode to create a more intuitive layout of the nodes, making it easier to review them.

Tip: You may want to explore using the Hypergraph view to parent these joints. **MMB-drag** the child node onto the intended parent.

---

2 Test the legs

- Test each leg's behavior by rotating their joints.

3 Reset the leg

- When you are finished testing the leg, select the *back_root* joint.

- Select **Skeleton** → **Assume Preferred Angle**.

4 Save your work

Summary

This project introduced the use of joints in Maya for building skeletal structures. Joints are special objects in Maya that are specially designed to live in hierarchies and maintain the parent-child relationship that is important for character design and operation. Joints, as you will see, can be animated using special controls such as Inverse Kinematics and Set Driven Key. Joints contain special attributes that maintain and control their orientation, which is important for character animation. You will see in coming sections the importance of knowing how joints operate with respect to their orientation, specifically their local rotation orientation.

Inverse Kinematics

In order to make it easier to animate Melvin's skeleton, you will use Inverse Kinematics to help drive the motion of your joint chains. Inverse Kinematics can place your character's feet on the ground and keep them planted there while you move the hips. This kind of control is very difficult with Forward Kinematics.

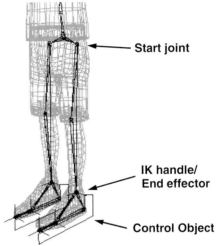

Melvin's legs with IK handles and foot controls

Set up Melvin's legs starting with simple IK solvers that are then parented into another separate skeleton chain used for manipulating the foot. The goal is to create a simple control mechanism for driving the action of the leg and foot.

In this chapter, you will learn the following:

- How to set up Single Chain IK solvers on Melvin's legs and feet;

- How to build an Inverse Skeleton Chain to control the foot;

- How to parent the IK handles into the control skeleton;

CHAPTER 2

- How to drive the Inverse Skeleton with a convenient control object;
- How to add attributes and set limits to the control object.

FORWARD VS. INVERSE KINEMATICS

In the last chapter, you learned that you can use Forward Kinematics to rotate joints one at a time. The resulting poses can be keyframed by setting keys on the joint rotation channels.

While the use of Forward Kinematics is very powerful, it has some limitations when animating a character. Since all of the animating is accomplished using the rotation of joints, it is not possible to take a joint lower down in the hierarchy and fix it in space. For instance, if you were to rotate a character's foot so that it sits on the ground, any movement in the pelvis area would move the foot out of place.

Inverse Kinematics solves this problem. Inverse Kinematics lets you control a series of joints using an IK handle. Moving either the handle or an upper start joint evokes an Inverse Kinematic solver that calculates the joint rotations for you.

Maya contains three main IK solvers that are covered in this book:

- **IK Single Chain solver** - This solver provides the simplest solution. By moving the IK handle, the chain will update so that the joints lie along a fixed plane. You will use the IK Single Chain solver in this chapter to set up Melvin's legs.

- **IK Rotate Plane solver** - This solver gives you more control over the position of the intermediate joints. You can use the IK handle so that the joints lie along a plane and then you can rotate the plane using a Twist attribute or by moving a Pole Vector handle. The IK Rotate Plane solver will be explored to set up Melvin's arms.

- **IK Spline Solver** - This solver lets you control the joint rotations using a spline curve. You can either move the chain along the curve or update the shape of the curve using its CVs. The IK Spline solver will be discussed in to set up Melvin's back.

A simple leg example - Forward Kinematics

The following example shows a simple leg being controlled by Forward Kinematics. Be sure to note what happens to the feet as you move the hip.

1 Create 3 joints to represent a hip, knee, and ankle

- In the side view panel, draw 3 joints.

- In front of the joints, place and scale 2 Primitive Cubes to act as positioning markers for the joints. These will help you visualize what is happening as you work with the joints.

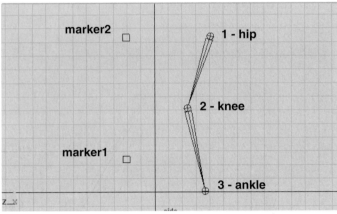

Three skeleton joints and positioning markers

2 Rotate the joints

- **Rotate** the hip and knee joints so that the ankle joint is positioned at *marker1*.

  With Forward Kinematics, you must rotate the joints into place to position the ankle.

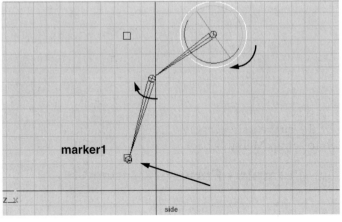

Positioned skeleton

3 Move the hip joint

- **Move** the *hip* joint forward to place it on *marker2*.

Set key hotkeys

In Maya, there are default hotkeys for all the active channels and for the translate, rotate and scale channels on their own:

Set key

Press s to set keys on all active channels displayed in the Channel Box.

Translate only

Press **Shift+w** to set keys on all the translation channels.

Rotate only

Press **Shift+e** to set keys on all the rotation channels.

Scale only

Press **Shift+r** to set keys on all the scale channels.

You may notice that the last three hotkeys correspond to the hotkeys for Move (w), Rotate (e), and Scale (r).

You will see how the knee and ankle joints also move. Now the ankle joint is no longer pointing towards the first marker. You would have to rotate the joints back to put the ankle back into its previous position.

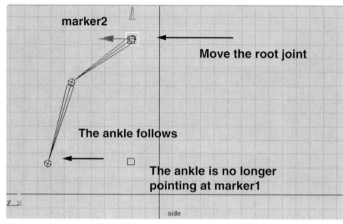

Moving the hip joint

Compare this to the IK solution outlined below:

A simple leg example - Inverse Kinematics

The following example shows a simple leg being controlled by the IK Single chain solver. Be sure to observe what happens both when you move the leg and when you move the foot.

1 Create 3 joints to represent a hip, knee, and ankle

- Draw another three joints as shown:

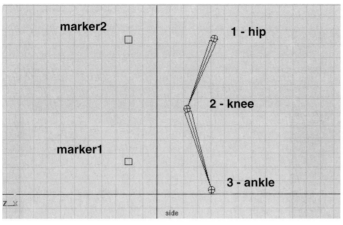

Three skeleton joints

2 Add a Single Chain IK Handle

- Select **Skeleton** → **IK Handle Tool** – ❑. In the option window, set the following:

     Current Solver to **ikSCsolver**.

- Press **Close**.

- Click first on the *hip* joint to establish the root of the solver.

- Click next on the *ankle* joint to place the IK handle.

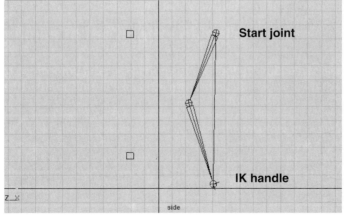

IK handle applied to leg

3 Move and key the IK handle

- Move the IK handle to the right so that it is placed on *marker1*.

Notice how the knee and hip joints rotate so that the end effector, currently at the ankle, is always at the ankle. This is a very easy way to control the leg.

- Press **Shift+w** to set keys on the translation channels of the IK handle.

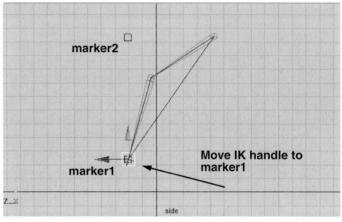

Moved IK handle

4 Move the hip

- Select the *hip* joint.
- Move the *hip* joint to the right to place it at *marker2*.

The IK handle keeps the ankle joint at the first marker as you move the hip forward. The ankle will remain with the IK handle until you pull the hip too far. Then the ankle joint will pull away from the IK handle.

Note: The IK handle at the ankle is staying in place because it has been keyframed. Later in this chapter, you will learn how to set the stickiness of the IK handle so that it will stay in place without requiring keyframes.

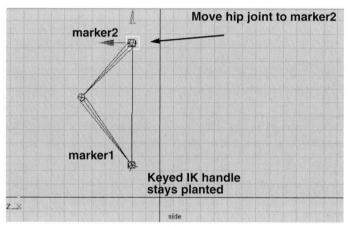

Moved hip joint

Snapping hotkeys

To help you accurately place points in 3D, you can press and hold on the following hotkeys:

- For **Grid snap** press **x**.
- For **Curve snap** press **c**.
- For **Point snap** press **v**.

Once you release the hotkey, the snapping is turned off.

PREFERRED ANGLE

A joint's preferred angle establishes the direction a joint will bend when driven by an IK solver. It's sort of like a default bend direction. For example, if you create a knee joint straight up and down, then run IK through that joint and try to manipulate it, the solver will not be able to bend the joint. By setting the preferred angle, the solver has a guideline to follow.

Working with preferred angle

In the following example, you will explore a situation where the preferred angle must be altered.

1 Create 3 joints to represent a hip, knee, and ankle

- Draw 3 joints in a straight line using grid snap so that there is no bend in the knee.

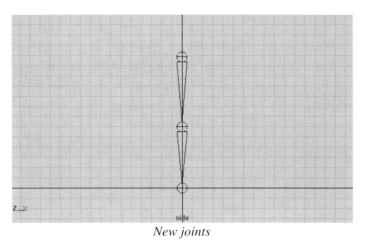

New joints

2 Add a Single Chain IK Handle

- Select **Skeleton** → **IK Handle Tool**.

- Select the *hip* joint as the root and then the *ankle* joint to place the IK handle.

3 Move the IK handle

- **Move** the IK handle to affect the chain.

    You should see that the knee does not bend. This is because there is no bend in the bones on either side of the knee. The solver is therefore not able to figure out which direction to bend.

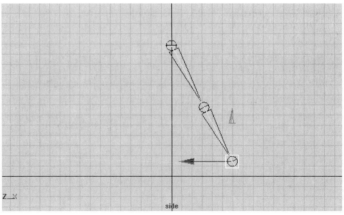

Moved IK handle

4 Undo

- Undo the last move on the IK handle to return the chain to its original position.

- Delete the IK handle.

5 Edit the preferred angle on the knee

- Select the *knee* joint.

- Rotate the joint so that the knee is bent back. Leave the *knee* joint selected.

- Select **Skeleton** → **Set Preferred Angle** – ❑. In the option window, turn **Selected Joint** to **On**.

- Press **Set**.

- Rotate the knee joint back to **0**.

RMB marking menu

You can use the **RMB** on a selected joint to access the **Set** and **Assume preferred angle** commands.

6 Add another IK Handle

- Select **Skeleton** → **IK Handle Tool.**

- Select the *hip* joint as the root and then the *ankle* joint to place the IK handle.

  The reason that you deleted the IK handle and created it again after you set the preferred angle is that the preferred angle will not be validated if an IK handle is present through the selected joints.

7 Move the IK handle

- **Move** the IK handle to affect the chain.

  Now the knee should be bending since the preferred angle gives the solver a clearer idea of which direction to bend.

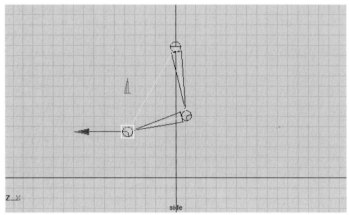

Moved IK handle

8 Assume Preferred Angle

You can also use the preferred angle to return a skeleton to its starting pose.

- Select the *hip* joint.

- Select **Skeleton** → **Assume Preferred Angle**.

    The leg skeleton chain should reorient itself to its default position.

Tip: Assume Preferred Angle can be used as a tool to quickly set your character back to its default position.

STICKINESS

By default, an IK handle will move when you move the root joint of the chain. Stickiness will help you keep the IK handle in one place. With a leg, the foot should stay planted on the ground and not move if the person moves their hips.

Setting stickiness

1 Move the top joint from the simple leg just created

The IK handle moves as if it were a child of the hip. If you look in the Hypergraph, you will see that this is not true.

2 Turn on stickiness

- Select the IK handle.

- Open the Attribute Editor.
- Under **IK Handle Attributes**, set **Stickiness** to **Sticky**.

3 Move the hip joint again

You should see that the IK handle stays in one place, as you would expect the foot to do.

Tip: Stickiness can be on when you create the IK handle if you turn the option to On in the IK handle option window. Also remember that once keys are set on an IK handle then it will behave in a similar manner.

IK PRIORITY

IK priority is the order in which IK solvers are evaluated. A solver with a priority of 1 is evaluated before a solver with a priority of 10. This is important to keep in mind as you build up the controls for a character. An IK solver in the hand or fingers should be evaluated after the IK solver in the arm. The joints in the finger are lower in the skeleton hierarchy so they depend on the joints in the arm for their placement.

If it seems that an IK chain is not updating properly in the interactive display or you notice differences between your interactive and your final rendering, you should check the IK priority of the solvers.

IK priority can be set at the time of creation or can be changed later through the Attribute Editor.

Changing IK priority

To change IK priority for an individual handle:

- Select an IK handle.
- Open the Attribute Editor. IK priority is found in the **IK Handle Attributes** section.

Tip: To see and change the priority of more than one IK handle at a time you can use the Attribute Spread Sheet.

IK priority can be changed for an entire character in one pass with a MEL command.

- Select all the IK handles for the character.

- Enter the following command:

  ```
  ikHandle -edit -autoPriority;
  ```

  edit will put the command into edit mode.

  autoPriority will automatically prioritize the selected IK handles based on their position in the hierarchy.

ADDING IK TO MELVIN'S LEGS

You will now use Inverse Kinematics to set up Melvin's legs. Several IK Single Chain solvers will help define the motion between the hip and the ankle of each leg as well as the ankle and ball and the ball and toe.

It seems like a good idea to create a skeleton with a single IK handle that flows from the hip to the toe as a quick way to set up a leg. The problem is that this kind of setup makes it hard to control the joints in the feet, since you are relying on the IK solver to calculate all the rotations.

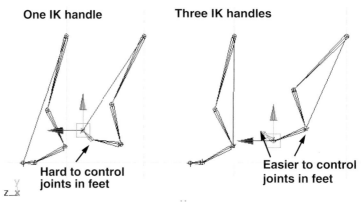

Different IK chains

A better way of setting up Melvin's legs would be to use several IK handles to control different parts of the leg. One chain will work from the hip to the ankle and two more will help define Melvin's foot.

The foot IK handles can then be grouped into a more complex hierarchy to create a heel to toe motion. You will be able to use Set Driven Key to make a single attribute to drive the roll of the feet.

Create the IK handles

You will start building Melvin's leg controls using three Single Chain IK solvers on each leg.

1 Open the scene

- Open the file *Melvin_02_legs.mb* from the scenes directory.

2 Hide Melvin's right leg

You will temporarily hide his right leg so that you can work on his left leg in the side view without worrying about accidentally selecting the wrong leg.

- Select the *right_hip* joint.
- Hide it by selecting **Display → Hide → Hide Selection**.

3 Set up an IK Single Chain solver on Melvin's legs

- Select **Skeleton → IK Handle Tool – ❏**. In the Option window, set **Current Solver** to **ikSCsolver**.

- Select the *left_hip* to establish the start joint of the IK chain and then the *left_ankle* to establish the end effector of the IK chain.

    Notice that an IK handle with end effectors is automatically created. The end effector is the transform position of the IK handle.

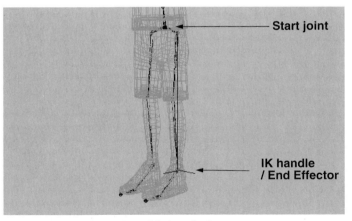

Start joint

IK handle / End Effector

IK added to the legs

4 Create IK chains for the foot

- Hit the **y** key to reinvoke the **IK Handle Tool**.
- Now click on the *left_ankle* joint, then the *left_ball* joint, to create your next IK chain.
- Repeat the process to run an IK handle from the *left_ball* joint to the *left_toe* joint.

- Rename the IK handles to:

    ankle_IK, ball_IK, toe_IK.

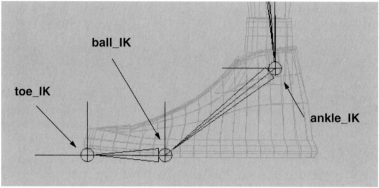

Foot IK handles

Create the inverse control system

You will now create the skeleton chain that will control the IK handles.

The control skeleton will be controlled by simple joint rotation, so it's important that they have predictable joint orientations. It is also important, for reasons that will be covered later in this chapter, that the root node of this skeleton match world space. To these ends, the skeleton chain will be created with **Auto Joint Orient** set to **None**.

1 Draw the inverse chain

- Open the option window for the **Joint Tool** and set **Auto Joint orient** to **None**.

- In the side view, place the first joint by holding down the **v** key (point snapping) and clicking near, but not right on, the *ankle_IK* handle. A new joint should be created in exactly the same world space position as the *ankle_IK* handle.

- Continuing in the side view, place another joint near the heel of Melvin's foot.

- The rest of the joints will be snapped to the other IK handles in Melvin's leg. Holding down the **v** key to invoke point snapping, click near the *toe_IK, ball_IK,* and finally the *ankle_IK* handles.

- Check in your Perspective view to make sure that the new joint chain is perfectly lined up with Melvin's foot.

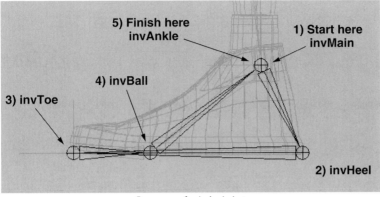

Inverse chain's joints

Note: If the chain is not lined up, delete it and start again, making sure that the right leg chain is hidden.

---

2 Name the joints in the inverse skeleton

- Starting at the root node of the inverse skeleton, rename the joints:

    invMain, invHeel, invToe, invBall, invAnkle.

3 Parent the IK handles to the inverse skeleton

- Parent each of the IK handles to the joints in the inverse foot by selecting an IK handle in the Outliner, **Ctrl-selecting** a joint in the inverse foot, then selecting **Edit → Parent** (or by hitting the p key).

- Parent the following:

    ankle_IK under *invAnkle;*

    toe_IK under *invToe;*

    ball_IK under *invBall.*

4 Save your work

Using curves as control objects

One of your goals in setting up Melvin is creating a system of puppet-like controls that will be easy to identify and select, and provide logical centralized controls for all aspects of Melvin's behavior. All of the control objects used in Melvin should be easy to recognize and select by the animator, and when possible, clearly indicate what the control is used for just by its appearance.

While the inverse skeleton chain could be used as the selected control object for Melvin's left leg and foot, in order to keep the selection process consistent, and ultimately easier, the inverse skeleton will be Point and Orient constrained to a curve.

1 Create a control curve for Melvin's foot and leg

- In the side view, draw a first degree CV curve to match the illustration below.

- Name it *leftFootControl*.

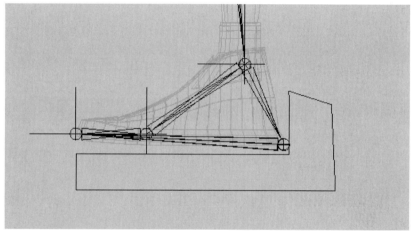

Control Curve for left foot

2 Move the control curve into position

- In the front view, move it into position relative to Melvin's left foot.

3 Move the pivot to the invMain joint

- With *leftFootControl* still selected, and the **Move Tool** still invoked, press the **Insert key** on the keyboard.

- The manipulator will change to indicate that you are editing the pivot instead of the object.

- Press the **v** key to invoke point snapping, then move the pivot by **MMB-dragging** towards the *invMain* joint. As you get closer, the pivot will snap to the *invMain* joint.

- Press the **Insert key** again to switch back to **Edit Object** mode.

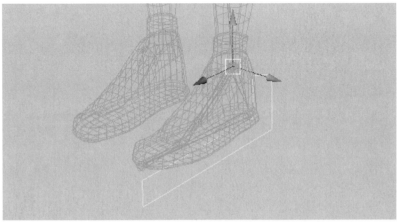

Control Curve's pivot snapped to invMain joint

4 Freeze the transformations

Now that *leftFootControl* has been translated, and had its pivot moved, it's a good idea to freeze its transformations. Freezing transformations has the benefit of "zeroing out" the transformations that have been applied to this object, now that it's in its user defined default position.

- Select *leftFootControl* then select **Modify → Freeze Transformations**.

5 Parent Constrain the *invMain* skeleton chain to the *leftFootControl* object

- Select the *leftFootControl* object, **Shift-select** the *invMain* joint, now select **Constrain → Parent**.

  Parent Constraints constrain both translation and rotation channels of an object. Parent Constraints are particularly useful when setting up characters because they do not cause constrained objects to transform to the current position of the constraining object the way that Point or Orient Constraints do. Rather, they behave more like a parent/child hierarchical relationship where the child follows the parent but retains its original position relative to the parent.

6 Test the control

- Select the *leftFootControl* and try translating and rotating it. The foot and leg should follow the *leftFootControl* object.

- When you're done, move and rotate the *leftFootControl* object back to zero.

Adding custom attributes to the control object

For *leftFootControl* to be an effective control object, it should provide control for all aspects of Melvin's foot and leg. To this end, you will now add a series of custom attributes to the *leftFootControl* curve.

1 Add a Heel_Rot_X attribute to the leftFootControl node

- Select the *leftFootControl* node.
- Select **Modify** → **Add Attribute...**
- In the Add Attribute window, set the following:

   Attribute Name to *heel_Rot_X*;

   Data Type to **Float**.

- Click **Add**.

   You should see a new attribute in the Channel Box called *Heel_Rot_X*. Right now the attribute is not connected to anything. The Connection Editor will be used to make it functional.

Even though you entered an attribute name of *heel_Rot_X*, it appears capitalized in the Channel Box. The Channel Box can show words in three different ways: Nice, Long, and Short. If the attribute translateX was displayed in the "Nice" setting, it would look like "Translate X." In the Long setting, it would look like "translateX" and the short setting would display it as "tx." You can change these settings within the Channel Box by selecting **Channels** → **Channel Names** and selecting one of the three.

Note: Minimum and maximum values could be added at this time, but since you don't know what your minimum and maximum values will be, attribute limits will be set later.

---

2 Add additional attributes

As long as the **Add** button is pressed in the **Add Attribute** window, the window will remain open. Pressing the **OK** button will add an attribute and close the window.

- Add the following attributes to the *leftFootControl* node:

  Heel_Rot_Y;

  Heel_Rot_Z;

  Ball_Rot;

  Toe_Rot_X;

  Toe_Rot_Y;

  Toe_Rot_Z.

3 Lock and hide channels

Now that you have added a series of custom attributes to this object, it's a good idea to lock, and make non-keyable, any attributes on this object which will not be used by the animator.

- Select *leftFootControl*.

- In the Channel Box, **LMB-select** the **Scale X, Y, Z**, and **Visibility** channels.

- **RMB-click** on one of the attributes and select **Lock and Hide Selected** from the menu. These channel's values are now locked and therefore can't be changed accidentally and have been removed from the Channel box.

In general, you should lock and make non-keyable all channels on your control object which you don't want the animator changing. This will reduce the amount of Static Channels that Maya creates every time you set a keyframe, and it will make creating efficient Character Sets much easier.

4 Save your work

Connecting the control object's custom attributes

Now that you have created a control object and equipped it with custom attributes, it's time to connect those attributes to their corresponding channels throughout Melvin.

1 Connect *leftFootControl*'s Heel_Rot_X Attribute to invHeel's Rotate X attribute

- Open the Connection Editor by selecting **Window → General Editors → Connection Editor**.

- Select *leftFootControl* and click the **Reload left** button, then select the *invHeel* joint and click the **Reload right** button.

- In the left hand column, select the *Heel_Rot_X* attribute, then in the right hand column select the *Rotate X* attribute.

The two channels are now connected with a direct, linear relationship. Changing the value of *leftFootControl:Heel_Rot_X* will also change the value of *invMain:RotateX*.

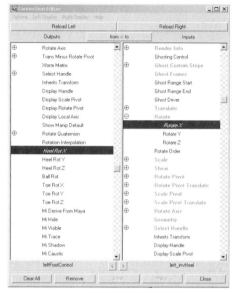

Heel_Rot_X connected to RotateX

2 Connect the rest of the custom attributes

Use the Connection Editor to connect the rest of the custom attributes:

> *Heel_Rot_Y* to *invHeel:rotY;*
>
> *Heel_Rot_Z* to *invHeel:rotZ;*
>
> *Ball_Rot* to *invBall:rotX;*
>
> *Toe_Rot_X* to *invToe:rotX;*
>
> *Toe_Rot_Y* to *invToe:rotY;*
>
> *Toe_Rot_Z* to *invToe:rotZ.*

3 Test the connections

At this point, it is a good idea to make sure that the connections are made properly, and the foot is behaving the way you expect.

- Select *leftFootControl* and try **Translating** and **Rotating** it to test the basic leg action.

- **Undo** back to the original setting, or simply enter values of zero for all of *leftFootControl*'s channels.
- Test each of the custom attributes in the Channel Box.

  You should notice that some of them behave properly within a certain range of values, but cause unwanted actions outside of that range.

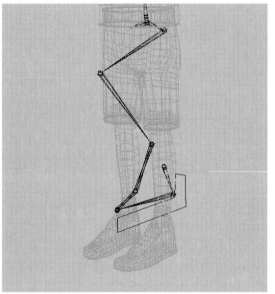

Testing the foot's behavior

Adding limits to the control object's custom attributes

In order to control the internal actions of the foot, it will be necessary to add limits to *leftFootControl*'s custom attributes.

Note: It would also be possible to set limits on the rotations of the joints themselves, but that would result in the joints stopping at a given value while the custom attribute's value continued to change. Setting limits on the control object's attributes will make for a more predictable control system.

---

1 Find Ball_Rot's proper range of motion

- Select *leftFootControl*.
- **LMB-click** on the *Ball_Rot* channel.

- **MMB-click** and drag in the Perspective view to invoke the virtual slider.

  Note that the foot acts properly as long as the *Ball_Rot* value is greater than zero, but once it goes below zero the foot acts unacceptably.

- Reset *Ball_Rot* back to **0**.

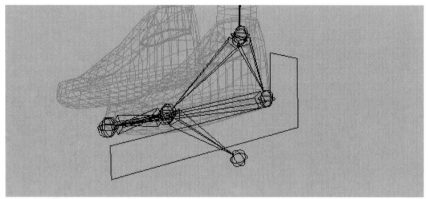

Ball Rotate outside of acceptable range

2 Set a minimum value for Ball_Rot

- Select **Modify** → **Edit Attribute...**
- In the **Edit Attribute** window, select *Ball_Rot*.
- Check **Has Minimum** to **On** and set the minimum value to **0**.

3 Set limits for the other attributes

- Test each of the other custom attributes and set limits accordingly.
- Note that for some attributes, you may not find it necessary to set limits.
- These values should work reasonably well:

  Heel_Rot_X Min **-45**, Max **0**;

  Heel_Rot_Y Min **-90**, Max **90**;

  Heel_Rot_Z Min **-90**, Max **90**;

  Ball_Rot Min **0**;

  Toe_Rot_X Min **0**, Max **85**;

  Toe_Rot_Y Min **-90**, Max **90**;

  Toe_Rot_Z Min **-90**, Max **90**.

4 **Save your work**

Final Touches

Now that you have set up the control system for Melvin's foot, it's time for a couple of finishing touches.

1 **Add prefix hierarchy names to the inverse foot**
- Add the prefix hierarchy name *left_* to the *invMain* chain.

2 **Hide unnecessary items**

In order to keep the selection of Melvin's various control objects as simple as possible, it's a good idea to hide anything that the animator does not need to pick.

- Create a new layer named *untouchables* and add all of the IK handles to it.
- Set the layer to **Reference** mode, then make it **Invisible**.

3 **Save your work**

4 **Repeat this process for the right leg**
- Now that the left leg is set up, unhide the right leg and repeat the whole process.

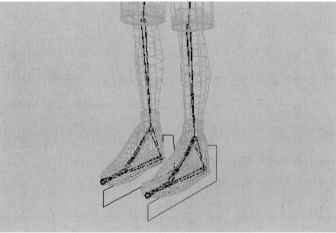

Melvin's right foot control

5 **Organize your controls into left and right layers**

You will now color code your control objects into "left" and "right" layers to help make them more visually distinctive.

- Create a new layer named *leftControls*.
- In the Edit Layer window, select the green color swatch.
- Create a new layer named *rightControls* and make it red.
- Select *left_footControl* and *left_knee_PV* and assign them to the *leftControls* layer. They should turn green.
- Select *right_footControl* and *right_knee_PV* and assign them to the *rightControls* layer. They should turn red.

6 Save your work

Test the setup

Now it's time to test your setup. You have three main controls:

- **leftFootControl** - controls the left leg and foot's heel to toe motion.

- **rightFootControl** - controls the right leg and the foot's heel to toe motion.

- **backRoot** - controls the root joint of the skeleton.

Go ahead and explore how these three controls work. Move Melvin forward and begin working with the action of the feet. You even may want to set keys on the controls and begin animating Melvin. Later you will be creating a walk cycle, but it doesn't hurt to get familiar with the setup now.

Summary

Inverse Kinematic animation of joint hierarchies requires understanding of the different types of IK Solvers available in Maya and their benefits and limitations. Some animators will prefer to use Forward Kinematics for some situations and IK for others. In this section, you created a foot setup that uses a NURBS curve as a control object to drive the actions of the foot and leg.

The appendix of this book also contains several other popular foot setups. Foot setups are a very debatable and contentious topic for most character riggers. You should keep your eyes open to all types of solutions as no clear standard for the "best" foot setup exists today and usually depends on the situation the character is placed in.

Arms and shoulders

In order to animate Melvin's arms and shoulders, you are going to use the IK Rotate Plane solver to help create the desired motion. This solver is necessary to give you more control over how the elbows are working.

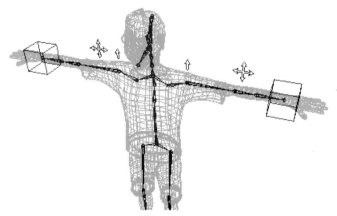

Melvin's arms and shoulders

Maya provides many ways of building characters. While three joints would be the easiest way of setting up Melvin's arm, you will explore a more complicated setup that uses an extra forearm joint. This setup will introduce several issues that will be dealt with throughout this book.

In this chapter, you will learn the following:

- How to use an IK Rotate Plane solver for arms;

- How to constrain the solver's Pole Vector to help aim the elbow;

- How to work with the solver's end effectors.

IK ROTATE PLANE SOLVER

In the last chapter, you set up the legs using the IK Single chain solver. This lets you easily control the forward motion of the leg, but if you wanted to rotate Melvin's legs out, you would find it difficult to control the position of the knee. For Melvin's arms, you want to be able to rotate the elbows out from the body. To do this, you will need the IK Rotate Plane solver which has extra manipulator controls to help you define how the whole arm will work.

When you set up an IK Rotate Plane solver, the whole length of the chain is controlled by a plane that is defined by the handle vector which runs between the start joint and the end effector, and a secondary vector that is called the Pole Vector. The plane acts as the goal for all the joint rotations. By default, the IK handle will manipulate the chain so that it works within this plane. You can then rotate the plane by either editing a twist attribute or by moving the Pole Vector handle.

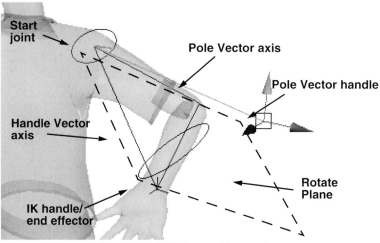

Diagram of IK Rotate Plane solver

Working with the IK Rotate Plane solver

The following example shows an arm being controlled by the IK Rotate Plane solver.

1 Create 3 joints to represent the shoulder, elbow, and hand

- In the Side view panel, draw 3 joints as shown in the following illustration.

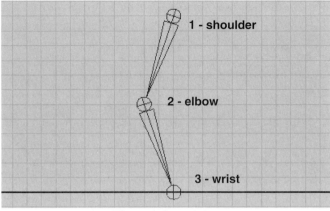

Three skeleton joints

2 Add a Rotate Plane IK handle

- Select **Skeleton** → **IK Handle Tool** – ❑. In the Option window, set the following:

  Current Solver to **ikRPsolver**.

- Click on the shoulder joint to set the start joint of the IK handle.

- Click on the wrist joint to place the IK handle.

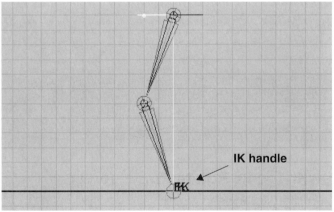

RP IK handle added to chain

Note: With the IK handle selected, Maya will display a secondary joint chain that represents the position of the joint chain if it were being manipulated with FK.

---

3 Move the IK handle

- Select the **Move Tool**.

- Move the IK handle to the right.

  The IK handle is now working in a similar manner to the IK Single chain solver. Basic IK handle manipulation is the same for both solvers.

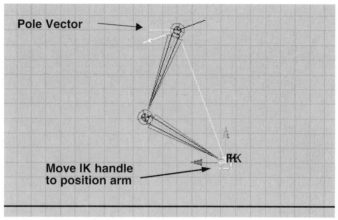

Moving the IK handle

4 Control the handle's Pole Vector

- Select the **Show Manipulator Tool**.

  A series of manipulators appear to let you control the IK handle's Pole Vector and twist.

- In the Perspective view, **Click-drag** on the **Pole Vector's** X-axis handle to rotate the IK solver's plane. For an arm, this lets you control how the elbows will animate in relation to the body.

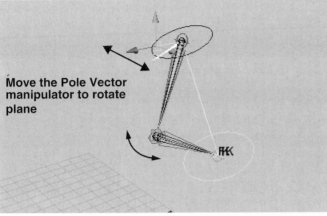

Pole Vector manipulator

5 Manipulate other Rotate Plane solver controls

- In the Channel Box, click on the IK handle's twist attribute to highlight it.

- **Click-drag** with your **MMB** to twist the IK solution away from the rotate plane.

  This is a sort of a rotation offset from the actual plane as defined by the Pole Vector location. You could use this attribute to rotate the elbows if you don't want to move the Pole Vector.

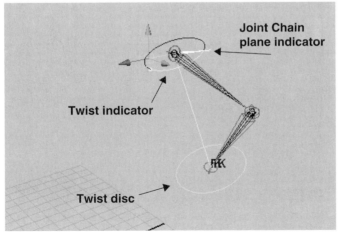

The IK handle's Twist attribute at -120

How to avoid flipping in the arm

Flipping occurs when the end effector is moved through the plane. If you experience flipping, you can use the Pole Vector axis handle to move the plane out of the way. You may need to set keys on this handle to control flipping in a more complex arm motion.

Pole Vector constraints

To give you easy access to the Pole Vector, you can constrain it to an object. In this way, you won't have to use the Show Manipulator Tool in order to edit the Pole Vector location. For Melvin, you will use constrained Pole Vectors to animate his elbows.

Working with IK/FK blending

While IK animation of a skeleton chain is an excellent way to control goal-oriented actions like a foot planting on the ground, or a hand picking something up, simple actions like an arm swinging as a character walks are typically easier to accomplish with FK animation.

Maya's IK/FK Blending makes it easy to seamlessly switch between IK and FK control of a skeleton chain.

In this exercise, you will animate a skeleton chain using IK, switch to FK animation for a few poses, then switch back to IK animation.

1 Open an existing scene file

- Open the scene file *IK_FK_Blending_01.mb*.

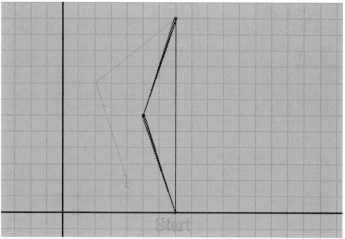

IK_FK_Blending_01.mb

2 Turn on Ik Fk Control

- Select the IK handle and open its Attribute Editor.

- In the **IK Solver Attributes** section of the **ikHandle1** tab, turn on **Ik Fk Control**.

▼	**IK Solver Attributes**		
Ik Blend	1.000	⎯⎯⎯⎯⎯⎯⎯⎯⎯	
	☑ Ik Fk Control		
IK Solver	ikRPsolver ▼		
Pole Vector	-0.300	0.000	0.000
Offset	0.000		
Roll	0.000		
Twist	0.000		
Twist Type	Linear ▼		

Ik Fk Control turned on

3 Animate the arm using IK

- Make sure that you're at frame **1** on the **Time Slider**.

- Select the IK handle and set a keyframe on it by hitting the **s** key.

- Advance to frame **10**.

- Move the IK handle to the first marked position.

- Set a keyframe.

- Advance to frame **20**.

- Move the IK handle to the second marked position and set a keyframe.

- Advance to frame **30**.

- Move the IK handle to the third marked position and set a keyframe.

Outliner tip

To see all the joints in a hierarchy in the Outliner, Select the first and last joints, then in the Outliner, select **Show → Selected**.

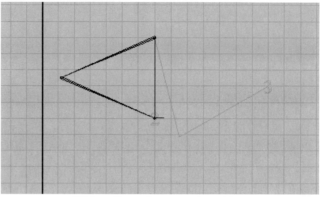

IK handle at the second position

4 Switch from IK to FK animation

You will now switch from IK to FK control of the arm between frames **30** and **40**. When blending from IK to FK animation, you must set keys for both the skeleton joints and the IK handle during the transition period.

- Make sure that you are still at frame **30**.

- Select the first and second joints in the arm and set keyframes for them.

  Setting keys for the joints at the same frame that you stopped using IK is necessary to define the transition range for the blend from IK to FK.

- Advance to frame **40**.

- Select the IK handle again.

- Find the **Ik Blend** attribute in the **Channel Box**.

- Set its value to **0**.

- Set a keyframe for the IK handle.

  By keying the IK Blend value at zero at frame 40, you are telling Maya that control of the arm has been switched from IK to FK between frames 30 and 40.

5 Animate the arm using FK

- While still at frame **40**, pose the arm in the fourth marked position by **rotating** the joints.

- Set a keyframe for both the shoulder and elbow joint.

- Advance to frame **50**.

- Pose the arm in the fifth marked position by **rotating** the joints.

- Set keys for both joints again.
- Advance to frame **60**.
- Pose the arm in the sixth marked position by **rotating** the joints.
- Set keys for both joints again.

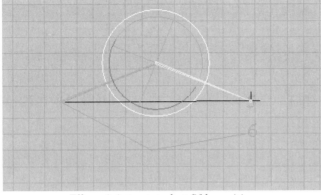

Elbow joint rotated at fifth position

6 Switch back from FK to IK animation

Now that you are finished animating the arm using FK animation, you will switch back to IK control.

- Select the IK handle. Note that it is still where you left it at frame **30**, and that its IK Blend value is still **0**.
- Set another key for the IK handle at the current frame (frame **60**, the last frame that you set keys directly on the joint rotations).
- Advance to frame **70**.
- Set the IK handle's **Ik Blend** value back to **1**. The arm is now controllable with the IK handle.
- Move the IK handle to the seventh marked position and set a keyframe for it.
- Deselect the IK handle and scrub through frames **60** and **70** in the timeline by click-dragging with your left mouse button.
- Advance to frame **80**.
- Move the IK handle back to the original start position and set a keyframe.
- Rewind and play the animation. The skeleton chain should achieve each position, animating seamlessly between IK and FK as it goes.

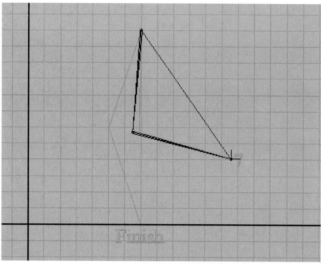

IK handle moved to seventh position

IK/FK Blending and the Graph Editor

When you switch between IK and FK and vice versa, the Graph Editor displays the animation curves of an IK handle and its joints partly as solid lines and partly as dotted lines.

When you display an animation curve for Translate X, Y, or Z of an IK handle, the curve is displayed as a solid line when IK Solver Enable is On. The curve is a dotted line when Solver Enable is Off. In other words, the solid line show where the IK handle controls the joint chains animation. The dotted line shows where FK (keyed joint rotations) controls the animation.

The reverse is true for a selected joint in the handle's joint chain. When you display an animation curve for Rotate X, Y, or Z of a joint, the curve is displayed as a solid line when IK Solver Enable is Off. The curve is a dotted line when Solver Enable is On. In other words, the solid line shows where FK controls the animation. The dotted line shows where IK has control.

1 Select the IK handle

- Select the IK handle and go to frame **10**.

2 Open the Graph Editor

- Display the IK handle's animation curves by selecting **Windows →
  Animation Editors → Graph Editor**.

- Select **View → Frame All**.

The Graph Editor shows that from frames **1** through **30**, the IK handle has keyframes recorded for it.

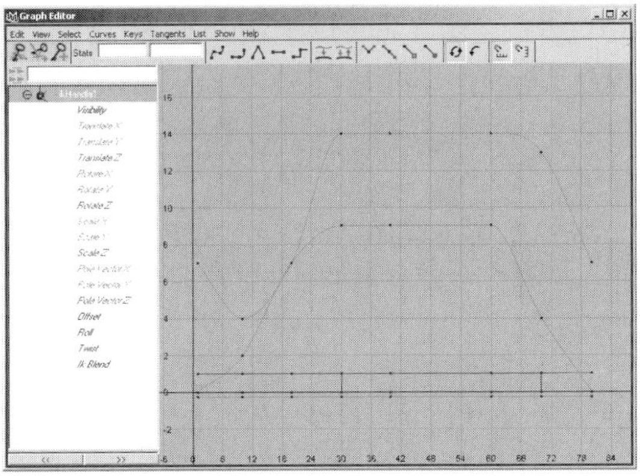

IK handle's animation curves

3 Adjust the Translate X curve

- Select the **Translate X** key at frame **10**.

- Hit the **w** key to invoke the **Move Tool**.

- Hold down the **Shift** key and **Click-drag** up in the Graph Editor to change the value of the key without changing its timing.

  As you adjust the key you should see the IK handle move along the X-axis.

4 Select joint2

- Select *joint2* and go to frame **40**.

5 Open the Graph Editor

- Display the joint's animation curves.

  The Graph Editor shows that from frames **30** through **70** the joint has keyframes recorded for it.

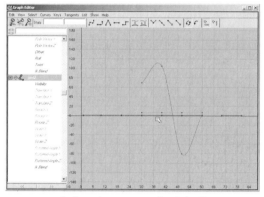

Animation curves for joint2

6   Adjust the Rotate Z curve

- Select the **Rotate Z** key at frame **40** and adjust its value.

   Once again you should see the joint update as you adjust its rotate
   Z value.

Note: Keys that are bordered by a solid curve on one side and a dotted curve on
the other, should be edited with caution since adjustments will likely
cause the skeleton chain to pop at that frame since the IK and FK will no
longer match.

MELVIN'S ARMS

You will now create Melvin's arms using skeleton joints and IK handles.
Again, you will use the character's pre-made geometry to aid in placing of
the joints. You will then define the control of the arms by setting the
preferred angle for the elbows, adding IK Rotate Plane solvers and then
constraining the solvers' Pole Vectors to control objects.

Creating the arm joints and setting preferred angle

In this exercise, you will explore an arm building technique that will set up
sophisticated skinning characteristics in the forearm. You will do this by
creating an extra joint between the elbow and the wrist. When you later skin
and add flexors to Melvin, this extra forearm joint will cause the forearm to
twist when the hand/wrist rotates.

It is important to ensure that joints between the elbow and wrist are created
in a straight line, making Melvin's arms as anatomically correct as possible.

You will build the arm joints with **Auto Joint Orient** set to **XYZ**. You will also manually set the preferred angle of the elbow joint after the joint has been created.

1 Open an existing scene file

- Open the scene file *Melvin_03_feet.mb*.

  This scene is identical to the scene that you created in the previous chapter.

Melvin skeleton without arms

2 Confirm that all of the pieces are in the right places

3 Create five joints for the left arm

In the front view, you will start next to the shoulder joint and create a series of five joints along the extended arm.

- Select the **Skeleton** → **Joint Tool** – ❑ and confirm that **Auto Joint Orient** is set to **XYZ** and set **World Axis Orient** to **-Z** .

- Place five joints along the extended arm as shown in the following figure.

- Press the **Shift** key as you place the successive joints to make sure that the elbow, forearm, and wrist joints form a straight line.

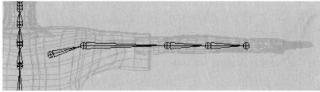

Arm joints

- Check top, side, and Perspective views for proper alignment. Rotate and scale as necessary. Do not translate any joints other than the root joint.

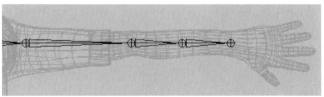

Arm joints aligned in top view

- Rename the joints *collarBone, shoulder, elbow, forearm,* and *wrist.*

4 Add prefix hierarchy names

- Add *left_* prefix hierarchy names to the arm.

5 Set the preferred angle of the elbow

- Select the *elbow* joint.

- Bend the elbow by rotating the *elbow* joint around the **Y-axis** until the wrist is pointed forward in the **Z** direction.

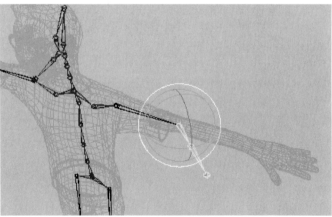

Setting the preferred angle for the elbow

- Select the *elbow* and with the **RMB**, select **Set Preferred Angle**.

- Return the *elbow* joint to its rest position by setting the value of all the **Rotation** channels in the **Channel Box** to **0**.

6 Parent the collarbone joint to the shoulder joint

- Select the *collarBone* joint, then **Shift-select** the *back_shoulderjoint* joint.

- Select **Edit** → **Parent**.

7 MIrror the arm joints

- Select the *collarBone* joint and mirror it by selecting **Skeleton** → **Mirror Joint** – □.

- Select the **YZ** as the plane to mirror across, **Behavior** as the **Mirror Function** and set **Replacement names for duplicated joints** to **Search For: left_** and **Replace With: right_**.

Maya should create another skeleton chain on the other side of Melvin's body with proper naming.

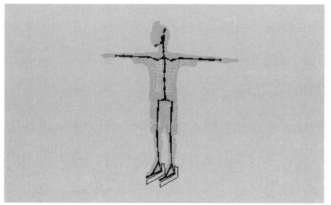

Completed arm joints

Tip: This process can be streamlined for the opposite arm. A mirror will not work properly because the local axes are not changed, however, the mirror can be used to line up the new arm. Mirror the arm and then draw a new skeleton chain by using the **v** key to snap to joints. Then delete the mirror copy.

---

8 Save your work

Setting up the IK Rotate Plane solver

You will now use the IK Rotate Plane solver for the arm. Rather than placing the IK handle on the wrist joint, you will use the forearm joint. You will then move the chain's end effector to the wrist. This will prepare Melvin's arm for rotating the forearm later.

1 Setup RP IK from the left shoulder to the left forearm

- Select the **Skeleton** → **IK Handle Tool** – □.

- Make sure that **ikRPsolver** is selected.
- Create an IK handle from the *left_shoulder* to the *left_forearm*.
- Rename the IK handle *Left_arm_IK* and the end effector *Left_armEffector*.

  The end effector is grouped under the forearm joint. You will need to open the Hypergraph or the Outliner to find this node.

Translating the end effector of the IK chain

The arm's IK handle was placed on the *forearm* joint. When you placed the IK handle you also created another node called the *end effector*. The end effector defines the end of an IK solver chain. Because you want to control Melvin's arms from his wrist, you will need to translate the end of the IK chain from the forearm to the wrist.

By default, the end effector is hidden and connected to a child joint of the last joint controlled in the IK chain, as if it were a sibling of that child joint of the last joint in the IK chain. So, when you move that child joint, the end effector will go along for the ride. IK is not invoked when an end effector is moved. This gives you the ability to reposition the IK chain/IK handle without invoking IK. As you will see, this is what you want to happen for Melvin's forearm. By changing the position of the effector, you are changing the end position of the IK handle down to the wrist without running IK through to the wrist.

Tip: If you move the end effector, it is advisable to save a new preferred angle.

---

1 Move the end effector to the left_wrist joint

- In the Hypergraph or Outliner, select the *L_armEffector*.
- Select the **Move Tool**, then press the **Insert** key to work with the pivot point of the chosen node.
- Move the end effector pivot along the **X-axis** to the center of the *left_wrist* joint.
- Press the **Insert** key to return to standard manipulator mode.

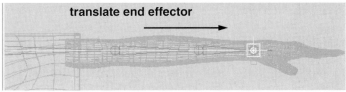

Translating the end effector

2 Move the IK handle along the X-axis

- Select the arm's IK handle.

- Move the IK handle along the **X-axis** to confirm that the forearm joint does not rotate.

  Now you can translate the IK handle from the wrist without the arm bending at the forearm. This is a necessary technique that enables you to rotate the hand while creating realistic movement and deformation of the arm joints and skin. Look at the way your wrist rotates or twists from the elbow. You will eventually drive the rotation of the forearm joint based on the wrist rotation.

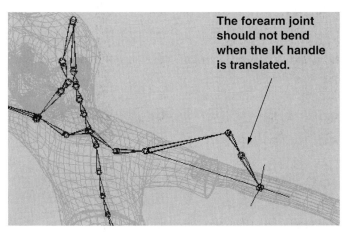

3 Save your work

WRIST AND ELBOW CONSTRAINTS

Constraints are objects that you assign to control specific aspects of other objects' transformations. You will use a point constraint on the wrist to control the movement of the arms. A point constraint is used to make one object move to another object. The IK handle at the wrist will be constrained to a cube shaped NURBS curve.

A Pole Vector constraint will control the rotation of the arms. The Pole Vector will always point to the Pole Vector constraint, providing a nice visual aid for positioning the elbows.

Adding Pole Vector constraints to the elbows

As mentioned earlier, it is sometimes easier to control the IK Rotate Plane solver's Pole Vectors by constraining it to an object. This will give you easy access to the control of Melvin's elbows.

The tricky part about using Pole Vector constraints on the elbows is deciding where to put them. Generally, a good place for the control object is directly behind the elbow. Determining whether or not to parent these control objects depends on how you want to control the elbows. In this lesson, you will parent them under the *backShoulderJoint* so they will move with Melvin.

1 Import the control objects and place them behind the elbows

- Select **File** → **Import** and navigate to the Imports folder within the scenes directory.
- Import the *transXform.mb* file.
- Rename the imported NURBS curve *left_elbow_PV*.
- **Group** *left_elbow_PV* to itself.
- Name the new group node *leftElbowBuffer*.
- Using point snapping, move *leftElbowBuffer* to the *left_elbow* joint.
- **Scale** *leftElbowBuffer* down to about **0.15**.
- **Move** *leftElbowBuffer* back along **Z**.

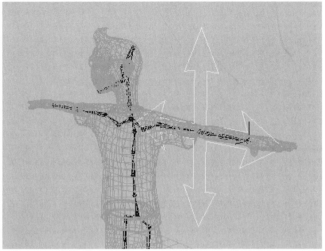

leftElbowbuffer before being scaled down

2 Add Pole Vector constraints to the elbows

- In the Work Area, select *left_elbow_PV*, then **Shift-select** the *left_arm_IK* handle.
- Select **Constrain** → **Pole Vector**.

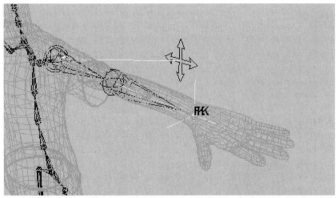

left_arm_IK Pole Vector constrained to left_elbow_PV

3 Parent leftElbowBuffer under backShoulderJoint

- Select *left_elbow_PV* and hit the **up arrow** key on the keyboard to pick walk up to the *leftElbowBuffer* node.
- **Shift-select** *backShoulderJoint*.
- Press the **p** key to parent *leftElbowBuffer* under *backShoulderJoint*.

Note that *left_elbow_PV* was grouped to itself to keep its translation and rotation values zeroed out. Select the *leftElbowBuffer* node and note its transformations. The transforms applied to *leftElbowBuffer* are the result of being parented under a joint node. The *leftElbowBuffer* node inherits the transformations from backShoulder joint, allowing the *left_elbow_PV* node's values to remain at zero.

4 Restrict Channels on left_elbow_PV

Since *left_elbow_PV* is one of Melvin's control objects, you should lock and make non-keyable any channels that should not be changed. This will prevent animators, including yourself, from manipulating Melvin in ways that he was not meant to be. Locking attributes, and removing them from the Channel Box is an important step in making Melvin behave like a predictable, digital puppet that anybody can use.

- Select *left_elbow_PV*.

- **LMB-select** all **Rotate, Scale,** and **Visibility** channels in the Channel Box and select **Lock and Hide Selected.**

  Now when *left_elbow_PV* is selected, it can only be ~~rotated~~ *translated*.

5 Restrict Channels on leftElbowBuffer

Since this node will never be directly manipulated by the animator, all of its channels can be locked and made non-keyable.

- Select *leftElbowBuffer* and lock and hide all of its channels.

6 Repeat for the right side

7 Save your work

Constraining the wrist to a control object

Just as you Point Constrained the Pole Vectors to a NURBS control object, you will do the same for the wrist IK handles. These control objects will provide an easy selection method for grabbing the arm and placing it for keyframing. They will also provide a convenient place to put extra attributes for hand controls.

1 Import the control object

- Import *cubeXform.mb* from the *scenes/Imports* directory.

- Place the cube at the *left_wrist* joint. Use the **v** key to snap the locator to the IK handle.

- Rename the cube *left_armControl*.

2 Scale and Freeze Transformations on the cube

- **Scale** *left_armControl* down to about **0.25**.

- Select **Modify** → **Freeze Transformations**.

3 Point constrain the locators to the wrist IK handles

- Select *left_armControl*, then **Shift-select** the *left_arm_IK* handle.

- Select **Constrain** → **Point**.

4 Orient constrain left_armControl to the left_wrist joint.

- Select the *left_wrist* joint, then **Shift-select** *left_armControl*.

- Select **Constrain** → **Orient.**

  Orient constraining the *left_armControl* to the *left_wrist* joint will keep the control object aligned with the wrist and hand as you pose the arm.

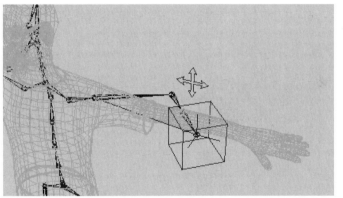

left_armControl driving arm

5 Restrict Channels on left_armControl

- Select *left_armControl*.

- **Lock and Hide Selected** its **Rotate**, **Scale** and **Visibility** channels.

6 Save your work

Controlling Melvin's shoulders

Now that you have setup an effective control system for Melvin's left arm, you will create a control to easily manipulate his left shoulder.

1 Import and place the control object above the left shoulder

- **Import** *arrowXform.mb* from the *scenes/Imports* directory.

- Rename it *left_clavicle_control*.
- **Group** it to itself.
- Name the new group node *leftClavicleBuffer*.
- Using point snapping, move *leftClavicleBuffer* to the *left_shoulder* joint.
- Scale *leftClavicleBuffer* down to about **0.15**.
- Move *leftClavicleBuffer* just above the shoulder geometry.

2   Move left_clavicle_control's pivot to the left_collarBone joint

- Select the *left_clavicle_control* node and invoke the **Rotate Tool**.
- Select the **Insert** key to switch to **Edit Pivot** mode.
- Snap the pivot to the *left_CollarBone* joint.
- Select the **Insert** key again to switch back to standard mode.

3   Parent Constrain left_collarBone to left_shoulder_control

- Select *left_clavicle_control* and then **Shift-select** the *left_CollarBone* joint.
- Select **Constrain** → **Parent**.

4   Restrict channels on left_shoulder_control

Since Parent constraints drive translation and rotation, you will now lock and make unkeyable all channels for *left_shoulder_control* except rotation.

- Select *left_clavicle_control*.
- **Lock and Hide Selected** all **Translate, Scale,** and **Visibility** channels.

5   Parent leftClavicleBuffer under backShoulderJoint

- Select *left_clavicle_control* and hit the **up arrow** key on the keyboard to pick walk up to the *leftClavicleBuffer* node.
- **Shift-select** *backShoulderJoint*.
- Press the **p** key to parent *leftClavicleBuffer* under *backShoulderJoint*.

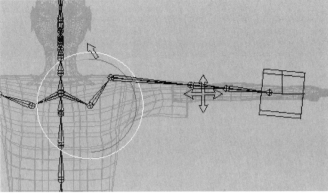

left_collarBone joint rotated by left_clavicle_control

6 Repeat for the right arm

Hiding the IK handles

Now that Melvin's controls are setup, the IK handles should be put away to prevent them from accidentally being manipulated.

1 Add the left and right_arm_IK handles to the untouchables layer

- Select the IK handles for both arms and add them to the *untouchables* layer.

  By adding them to this layer you are preventing them from being inappropriately manipulated, but at the same time they are easy to find just by making the untouchables layer visible again.

Testing the character

Melvin is starting to take shape, at least the underlying skeleton is forming. You now have the most basic control points for blocking out motion for Melvin:

- Left and right ankle selection handles;

- Left and right wrist locators;

- Skeletal root selection handle.

Work with the character and the handles you have created. Try placing the elbow Pole Vector constraints in different places to see how they aid in controlling the arm. Experiment with other setups like the following:

Pole Vector placement and parenting

In this chapter, you parented the Pole Vector control objects to the backShoulder joint. You may also want to explore leaving them unparented to see what happens.

Some prefer to use the twist attribute on the IK handle to control the rotation of the arm. An attribute could be added to the locator and then the two could be connected with the Connection Editor.

Summary

This section explored the use of the rigging techniques associated with setting up arms. The Rotate Plane solver or RP solver is well suited for working with two joint situations like arms and legs. It is a superset of the Single Chain solver or SC solver. The RP solver contains attributes that add a further level of control to the animator and help prevent inappropriate solutions such as those that result in flipping or illogical rotations. This section also demonstrated the use of animation constraints for building up a layer of control. In this case, a series of control objects were used to constrain the IK handle and its Pole Vector. Another object was used to control the rotation of the joint where the IK solution started to provide additional control in posing the character's arms and shoulders.

IK Spline solver

4

In this chapter, you will add an IK Spline solver to Melvin's back. This will control how his back sways and bends when he moves. It will also provide you with a realistic relationship between the pelvis and the spine.

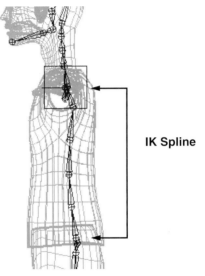

IK Spline

Melvin's spine

Once the solver is in place, you will cluster points on the spline to help create controls.

In this chapter, you will learn the following:

- How to set up a basic IK Spline solver;
- How to use clusters for added control over the spline curve;
- How to parent the clusters to control objects;
- How to associate Melvin's spine and pelvis motion;
- How to create global and local control mechanisms.

IK Spline in the back

When you use IK Spline, there are several things to keep in mind:

- Keep the curve as simple as possible for the IK Spline. For the most part, the default of 4 CV's works fine. Note that the curve created when setting up the IK Spline solver will attempt to stay as simple as possible.

- Do not let the IK Spline solver touch or cross any root joints. In the case of Melvin, you do not want the IK Spline solver to start or end at the *back_root* joint. You may recall that in Chapter 1, you added a joint just above the *back_root* joint. You want the IK Spline movement to be relative to that of the backbone joint and not the root joint.

  You do not want the solver to cross any root joints because this would cause the rotation of multiple skeleton chains. In the case of the back, it would not only rotate the back but both hips as well. While the hips and the back do rotate together in real life, this motion can be difficult to animate on a digital character. For this reason, you are separating the control of the pelvis from the control of the back using a small joint.

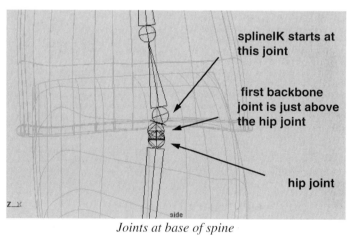

Joints at base of spine

- Create clusters for the CV's to make selecting and animating easier.

  Clusters have translate, rotate, and scale attributes while CV's only have position attributes. This means that CV's can't be keyframed as accurately as clusters can.

Adding the IK Spline solver

The IK Spline solver allows you to control a chain of joints, like Melvin's spine, with only a few control points. Animating a flexible back with forward kinematics requires you to keyframe the rotation of each joint individually. With IK Spline you will control all of the back joints with three control points.

1 Open an existing file

- Open the scene file *Melvin_04_arms.mb.*

2 Add an IK Spline handle to the backbone

- Select **Skeleton** → **IK Spline Handle Tool** – ❐.

- Click **Reset** to set it to the default settings.

IK Spline option window

- Turn **Off** the **Auto Parent Curve** option

- Select the joint above the *back_root* joint, *back_a*, to define the start joint of the chain.

- Select the *back_shoulder* joint to place the IK handle.

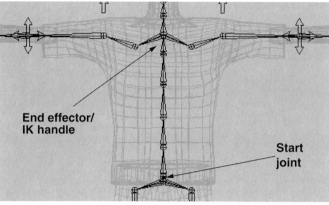

IK Spline joints

An IK system is created with a curve running through the selected joints. You can then control this joint system by selecting the control vertices of this curve and translating them.

3 Name the new nodes

- Rename the new IK chain *backSpline_IK* and label the curve *back_curve*.

4 Save your work

Test the IK Spline

There are two ways to operate the IK Spline. The Twist attribute will rotate each of the joints in the solution around the X-axis, causing a twisting action up Melvin's spine. Moving CV's in the *back_curve* will allow you to pose Melvin's back in a serpentine manner. You should try both methods.

1 Test the Twist Channel

- Select the *Back_spline_IK* handle.

Note: The feedback window will tell you that "some items cannot be moved in the 3D view". This warning simply means that Spline IK handles cannot (and are not meant to) be translated the way that SC or RP IK handles are.

- In the Channel Box, select the **Twist** attribute.
- **MMB-click+drag** in the Perspective view window to change the value with the virtual slider.
- Reset the **Twist** value back to **0** when you're done.

- With the *back_spline_IK* handle still selected press the **t** key to show the manipulator for the back. Select the manipulator ring around the *back_spline_IK* handle and use it to twist the back. This manipulator is another way to access the twist.

    You may want to experiment with the twist type as well. It can be accessed through the Attribute Editor.

2 Pose the spline IK by moving CVs

- Select the *back_curve* in the Outliner.
- Switch to component mode.
- Select the CV at the top of the curve and translate it.
- Select the next CV down and translate it.
- Undo until the *back_curve* is back to its original shape.

Clusters for the IK Spline CVs

The curve used by the IK Spline solver has four CV's. Currently, the only way to select these CV's is in component mode. To make selection easier and consistent with the rest of Melvin, you will add clusters to the back spline's CV's. The clusters will then be constrained to NURBS curve control objects.

Tip: Use the Pick Masks to select the curve in the work area. In object mode, select Everything Off, then toggle On the Curve icon.

---

1 In Component mode, select the top CV

- Select the *back_curve* that was created with the IK Spline handle.
- Change to component mode.
- Set the **Pick Masks** to **Display Hulls** to help in selection.

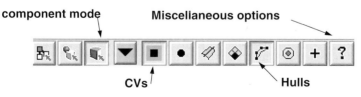

Selection masks buttons

- Select the top CV.

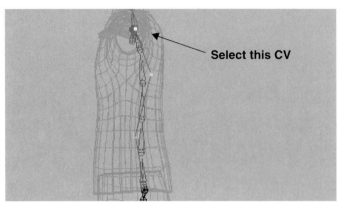

Select this CV

2 Create a cluster for this CV

- With the CV selected, select **Deform** → **Create Cluster** – ❑ and reset the option window.

- Press **Create**.

- Rename this cluster *back_cluster1*.

3 Cluster the next CV

- Create a cluster for the next CV. Label it *back_cluster2*.

4 Create a cluster for the next two CV's

- Now select the bottom two CV's and create a cluster out of them.

- Name the cluster *backCluster_hip*.

5 Move *backCluster_hip*'s pivot

- Select *backCluster_hip* and select the **Rotate Tool**.

- Hit the **Insert** key to invoke **Pivot Editing** and **snap** the pivot to the *back_root* joint.

6 Test the skeleton

- Move the top two clusters to test movement in the back.

- Rotate the *backCluster_hip* cluster.

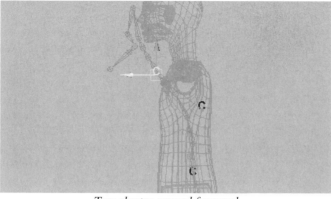

Top cluster moved forward

Note: Moving the *backCluster_hip* cluster will produce an undesirable effect.

Creating control objects for the clusters

In keeping with the control selection scheme for Melvin, you will now create NURBS curves to be used as control objects for the clusters.

1 Create the NURBS curves

- Select **Create** → **Text** – ❐, and in the **Create Curves** Options window type "**1 2 h**" in the text field.
- Make sure that **Curves** is selected in the **Type** section.
- Click on the **Create** button.

2 Rotate the text object

- **Rotate** the text object **90**-degrees on **Y**.

3 Unparent the individual curves

- Open the Hypergraph and find the text object.
- Select the lowest level of Transform nodes in the hierarchy.
- Select **Edit** → **Unparent**.
- Delete the original group node.

4 Rename the text curves

- Rename the curves *spineControl_1*, *spineControl_2*, and *hipControl*.

5 Position the text curves

- In the side view, move *spineControl_1* so that it is lined up with the *backCluster_1* cluster.

- Line *spineControl_2* up with *backCluster_2*.

- Line up *hipControl* with the *back_root* joint.

6 Scale the curves down

- Scale the text curves down so that they are still easy to see and select, but not so big that they get in the way of anything. A scale of **0.3** to **0.5** should be good.

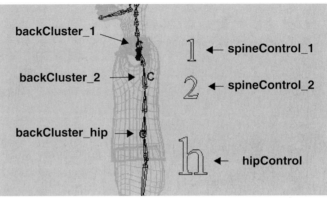

Text curves in position

7 Move the curves' pivots

- Snap *spineControl_1*'s pivot to *backCluster_1*, *spineControl_2*'s pivot to *backCluster_2*, and *hipControl*'s pivot to the *back_root* joint.

8 Freeze Transformations

- Freeze the transformations for all 3 text curves.

9 Constrain the clusters to the control objects.

Each of the clusters must now be constrained to its respective control object.

- **Point constrain** *backCluster_1* to the *spineControl_1* text curve.

- **Point constrain** *backCluster_2* to the *spineControl_2* text curve.

- **Parent constrain** *backCluster_hip* to the *hipControl* text curve.

10 Constrain the backRoot joint to the hipControl curve

As you may have noticed, translating the *backCluster_hip* causes part of Melvin's skeleton to tear away from the root joint. Translating the hipControl curve will have the same effect unless the *back_root* joint is constrained to the *hipControl* curve.

- Select *hipControl*, then **Shift-select** the *back_root* joint.
- **Parent constrain** the two.

11 Test the action

- Translate *spineControl_1* and *2* to test the action of Melvin's back.
- Translate and rotate *hipControl* to test this control object.
- When you're finished experimenting, set all three control objects' **translate** and **rotate** values back to **0**.

12 Restrict channels

Since *spineControl_1* and *2* are only meant to be translated, their rotate, scale, and visibility channels should be locked and hidden. The hipControl object only needs to rotate so lock and Hide, hipControl's translate, scale, and visibility channels.

13 Save your work

Create control objects for Melvin's whole body

When animating Melvin you will want a control object that represents Melvin's overall transformation. Having just setup an effective control system for Melvin's back, this is a good time to setup that control.

1 Create a NURBS circle

- Select **Create → NURBS Primitives → Circle – □**.
- In the **Options** window, set the **degree** to **linear**, and the **number of sections** to **6**.
- Click the **Create** button.
- Name the circle *localControl*.

2 Position localControl at Melvin's root joint

- Snap *localControl* to Melvin's *back_root* joint.

3 Scale localControl up

- Scale *localControl* up so that it's large enough to be easily pickable. A value of **4.5** should be good.

4 Set localControl's Rotation order

- Select *localControl* and open its Attribute Editor.

- Set its **Rotate Order** to **XZY**.

5 Freeze localControl's transformations

- **Freeze** *localControls*'s transformations and delete its history.

6 Parent the control objects to localControl

- **Parent** *spineControl_1*, *spineControl_2*, and *hipControl* under *localControl*.

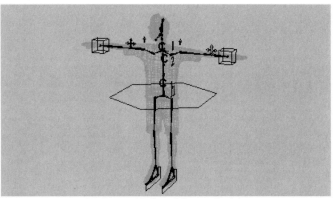

Melvin with localControl object

Driving Melvin's back twist from the localControl object

As part of animating Melvin, you are going to want to animate the twisting of his spine. As you saw earlier, the Twist attribute on the backSpline_IK handle controls this action. But since selecting the IK handle is impractical, you will add a custom attribute to the localControl curve, then connect that attribute to the IK handle's twist channel.

1 Add a twist attribute to the localControl node

- Select *localControl*.

- Select **Modify** → **Add Attribute...**

- In the Add Attribute window, set the following:

    Attribute Name to **Back Twist**;

    Data Type to **Float**.

- Press **OK**.

2 Connect the new twist attribute to IK spline's twist attribute

- Select **Window** → **General Editors** → **Connection Editor...**
- Select *localControl*.
- In the **Connection Editor**, click **Reload Left**.
- Select *Back_splineIK*.
- In the **Connection Editor**, click **Reload Right**.
- In the **Connection Editor**, select **Back Twist** as the *Output* and **Twist** as the *Input*.
- Close the Connection Editor.

  These two nodes are now connected. The *localControl* node's *Back Twist* attribute will now drive the IK spline's *Twist*.

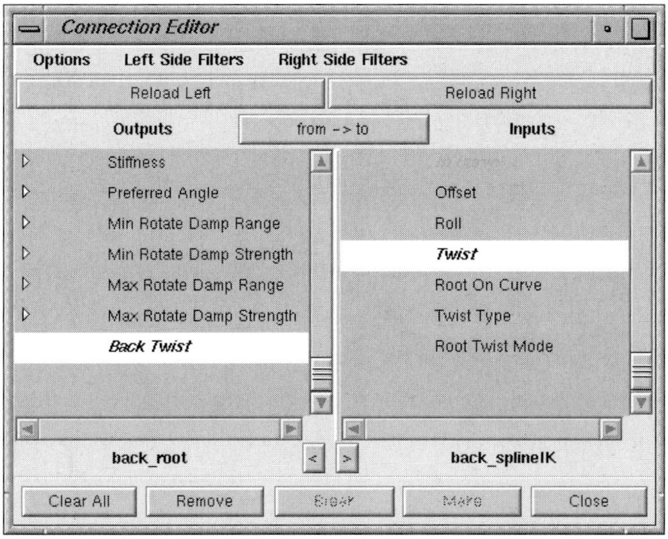

Connection Editor

Note: The custom twist attribute should be added to whatever control object the animator thinks is convenient and logical. In this case, the Back Twist attribute is being added to the localControl object, but it could also have been added to the *hipControl* object.

---

3 Restrict channels

- **Lock and Hide** *localControl*'s scale and visibility channels.

4 Test the action

- Use the virtual slider to test the *Back Twist* channel.
- **Translate** and **rotate** *localControl* to test Melvin's action.

5 Save your work

Adding an additional level of control

You will now add an additional level of control to Melvin by creating a globalControl object, and parenting localControl under it. This hierarchy will allow you to separate actions whose values tend to increase or decrease, like Melvin walking across a room, and values that tend to oscillate, like Melvin's pelvis rotating as he walks.

This approach to animation will be discussed in the next chapter.

1 Create the globalControl object

- Create another NURBS circle. This time, set the **curve degree** to **cubic**.
- Name the circle *globalControl*.

2 Position globalControl at the back_root joint

- Like *localControl*, snap *globalControl* to the *back_root* joint.

3 Scale globalControl up

- **Scale** *globalControl* up so that it is easy to identify and pick. A value of **5.5** should be good.

4 Set globalControl's Rotation order

- Set *globalControl*'s **Rotate Order** to **XZY**.

5 Freeze transformations

- **Freeze** *globalControl*'s transformations and delete its history.

6 Restrict channels

- **Lock and Hide** *globalControl's* scale and visibility channels.

7 Parent localControl to globalControl

- Select *localControl,* then **Shift-select** *globalControl* and press the **p** key to setup the hierarchy.

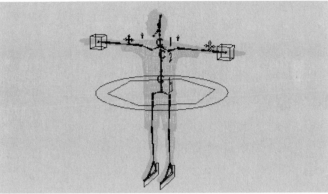
Melvin with globalControl object

8 Save your work

Finishing touches

While you have been conscientious and restricted the channels for Melvin's control objects as you created them, it's a good idea to double-check that each of the control objects don't have any unwanted channels appearing in the Channel Box. Also, the *backSpline_IK* handle and the *back_curve* should be placed on the untouchables layer.

1 Place secondary controllers on the untouchables layer

- In the Outliner, select the three back clusters, *backSpline_IK* and *back_curve.*
- Place them all on the *untouchables* layer.

2 Save your work

Summary

The Spline IK solver is ideal for controlling a long chain of joints such as those found in a snake or animal back. It is based on the use of a NURBS curve and therefore is a powerful link to other parts of Maya. A NURBS curve, for example, can be deformed using non-linear deformers or animated as a soft body which utilizes Maya's dynamics. The Spline IK does require special attention to joint orientation and alignment. The Spline IK solver also requires a method for animating the NURBS curve CV's. In our character, we chose to use the cluster deformer which allows you to, in a sense, move the individual NURBS CV's up into a world space transformable object that can be keyframed with translation, rotation, and even scaled motion.

5 Animating a walk

Now that you have Melvin's controls setup, it is time to start animating him. You will start with a walk cycle where you animate Melvin walking forward. This involves planting his feet and animating the pelvis so that it follows accordingly.

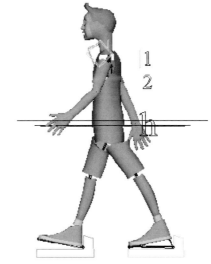

Melvin walking

In this chapter, you will learn the following:

- How to set up low resolution geometry;

- How to organize your keyable attributes into Character Sets;

- How to set Breakdown keys;

- How to edit animations in the Graph Editor with buffer curves.

ANIMATING MELVIN

In this chapter, you will animate Melvin walking. This is where you begin to test out the controls you have worked on over the last few chapters.

There are several approaches to animating a character. This chapter is by no means meant to be an exhaustive examination of character animation, but it will go through a basic animation workflow which can easily be adapted to your own personal workflow requirements.

Working with low resolution geometry

When animating a character, it is essential that the character be nimble and responsive. Having to wait for a character to update after making some change to the pose will unacceptably impair the animation workflow.

While it is beneficial to see how the character's geometry will look as it is animated, it's generally not necessary to see the character's final deforming geometry to pose the character. When animating, interactive performance is much more important than visual refinement, and bound geometry will have a serious impact on your character's interactivity.

To improve Melvin's performance during animation, low resolution geometry will be parented to Melvin's joints. This will keep Melvin quick and easy to work with.

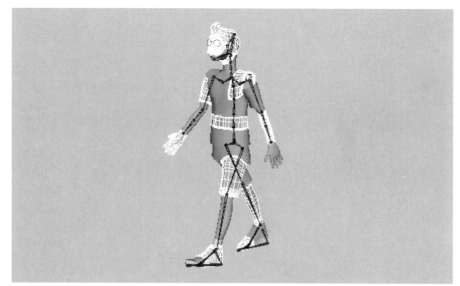

Low res geometry parented to joints

1 Open an existing file

- Open the file called *Melvin_05_spline.mb*.

2 Make geometry invisible

Most of the geometry in this scene will eventually be bound to Melvin's joints, but for now it's not needed so it should be made invisible.

- Make the *melvinDeform* and *melvinNonDeform* layers invisible.

3 Import low resolution geometry

To speed up Melvin's performance during animation, while still allowing you to see what he looks like as you animate him, low resolution geometry will be parented to his joints.

- **Import** *melvin_lowResGeometry.mb* from the *imports* folder.

4 Parent the geometry to the neighboring joints

To make the imported geometry move with Melvin, each piece needs to be parented to the appropriate joint.

- Select *left_hand*.

- **Shift-Select** the *left_wrist* joint.

- Press **p** to **parent** the surface to the skeleton.

- Repeat for all the other surfaces.

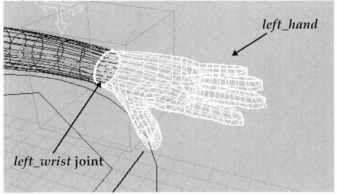

Parent the left_hand to the left_wrist

5 Save your work

Note: If you would like to move on to making Melvin walk, a file named *Melvin_05_lowRes.mb* has been prepared that already has the low resolution geometry parented to Melvin's skeleton.

MAKING MELVIN WALK

It is now time to begin animating Melvin. You are going to use the skeleton setup you created and animate a simple walk cycle. Before you start, you will use the Character Sets to simplify the selection and keyframing process.

Character Sets

A Character Set in Maya is a collection of attributes organized in a central place from the same or separate objects that are intended to be animated together. Character Sets don't have to be actual physical characters like Melvin, they only need to be a collection of attributes that you want to animate.

The benefit of working with Character Sets is that you don't have to worry about keyframing each individual attribute in the set. Once the Character Set is active, simply pose your selections and set a keyframe to key each attribute in the Character Set.

You have created Melvin so that he is easily controlled by only a few control objects. Now you are going to organize those objects into a central collection, further simplifying the animation process.

Note: The attributes of a Character Set are aliased to the original attributes. They are intermediate attributes that are directly connected to the attributes you are animating.

Selecting Character Sets or nodes and setting the current character

You can select Character Sets from either the Outliner or Hypergraph or you can use the menu **Character → Select Character Set Nodes**.

You can set the current Character Set from the menu **Character → Set Current Character Set** or from the pull-down menu in the lower right-hand corner of the Maya timeline at the right-hand side of the **Range Slider**.

Pull-down menu at the right-hand side of the Range Slider

Creating characters

1 Open the scene

- Open the scene file named *Melvin_05_lowRes.mb*.

2 Adjust the Pick Masks

The first step to creating a Character Set is to select all of the objects that are going to be included in that set. To do this, adjust your Pick Masks and make the selections through the interface.

- Turn everything **Off** in your **Pick Masks**.

- Turn **On NURBS Curves.**

  The main reason you are adjusting your Pick Masks is because you don't want unnecessary objects to be included in your Character Sets.

Pick Masks with only NURBS pickable

3 Make the selections and Create the Character Set

- Select all of the control objects:

  left_armControl, left_elbow_PV, left_clavicle_control, right_armControl, right_elbow_PV, right_clavicle_control, spineControl_1, spineControl_2, hipControl, localControl, globalControl, left_footControl, and *right_footControl.*

- Select **Character → Create Character Set – □.**

  In the Create Character Options, select **Edit → Reset Settings** to apply the default settings which include the omission of Scale and Visibility attributes.

- In the **Name** field type *Melvin*.

- Press **Create Character Set.**

Each of the channels included in the Character Set should now appear yellow in the Channel Box.

4 Editing the Character Set

As each of Melvin's control objects were created, you restricted unnecessary channels by locking them and making them non-keyable. Because of this, Melvin's Character Set doesn't contain any extraneous channels. Unnecessary channels in a Character Set create Static Channels (animation curves which represent no change in value) which increase file size and reduce interactive performance.

Although you have taken care to prevent unwanted channels in the Character Set, it is a good idea to check the Character Set in the Relationship Editor to make sure that there is nothing there that you don't want.

- Select **Window → Relationship Editors → Character Sets...**

- Click on the plus sign beside the Melvin Character Set.

  All of the channels in this Character Set should be listed.

- Check to make sure that there are no unwanted channels.

Relationship Editor

5 Removing channels from the Character Set

- If you find an attribute that you don't think belongs, select it, then select **Edit** → **Remove Highlighted Attributes** from the left side of the Relationship Editor.

Note: You can also add and remove attributes from selected Character Sets by using the menus **Character** → **Add to Character Set** and **Character** → **Remove from Character Set**.

Setting up for keyframing

Before you begin to set keys for the walk cycle, it is a good idea to change your **Move** and **Rotate Tools** from their default settings, to settings that will be more beneficial to character animation.

1 Switch your transformation modes for Translation and Rotation

- Select **Modify** → **Transformation Tools** → **Move Tool** – ❒.

- Select **Local** from the Option window.

- Set **Retain Component Spacing** to **Off**.

  Using the **Move Tool** in the Local option will allow you to move objects according to their local space, rather than world space, which is generally preferable when animating a character.

- Select **Modify** → **Transformation Tools** → **Rotate Tool** – ❒.

- Select the **Gimbal** option.

  Simply using the Gimbal option will not prevent your nodes from experiencing Gimbal Lock, but it will give you a clear indication of when you are in danger of Gimbal Lock occurring. It also allows you to manipulate a single rotation channel at a time, as opposed to the cumulative rotations that occur when using the Rotate Tool in the default Local mode.

Note: While using the Local and Gimbal options for the Move and Rotate Tools will make many tasks easier during animation, you will occasionally find it necessary to switch back to the default modes when setting up your character.

---

2 Change Set key options

- Click on the **Animation Preferences** button to open the Animation Preferences window.

- In the **Categories** column, select **Keys**.
- In the **Tangents** section of the Animation Key Preferences window, turn **Weighted Tangents** on.

  Weighted Tangents provide more control over the shape of a curve between keys in the Graph Editor.

- Set the Default **In** and **Out Tangent** types to **Clamped**.

  Clamped keys are a good starting point for character animation because they prevent value "overshoot" between keys of similar value, while providing Spline like smoothness between keys of different values.

- Click on the **Save** button.

3 Set the animation range

- Set the **Start Time** to **1** and the **End Time** to **120**.
- Set the **Playback Start Time** to **1**, and the **End Time** to **30**.

  Setting the Start/End, and Playback times differently will allow you to focus on the animated cycle range of 1 to 30 while setting up the animation, then easily view the cycled animation from frames 1 to 120.

Time Slider ranges

4 Save your work

ANIMATING THE WALK

Artistically speaking, a good walk cycle should not only get the character from point A to point B, it should express the character's personality. Technically speaking, a good walk cycle should start with a generic walking "template" that can easily be modified to reflect the character's mood.

Creating a walk cycle involves animating a character in several key positions. You want to start with both feet on the ground, then animate one leg lifting as it shifts forward. The first part of this process is the animation of the feet sliding on the ground. The lifting of the feet will be added afterwards.

Keying the first two steps

1 Go to frame 1

2 Set the IK Blend for Melvin's arms to zero

While Melvin's arms could be animated with IK, FK is generally more appropriate for this type of action.

- Make the *untouchables* layer **Visible** and **Non-referenced**.
- Include IK Handles in your Pick Mask.
- Select the *left* and *right_arm_IK* handles.
- Set the **IK Blend** values to **0**.
- Make the *untouchables* layer **Invisible** and **Referenced** again.

3 Confirm that Melvin is the current Character Set

- Make sure that the name *Melvin* is displayed in the **Current Character Set** window.

- If *Melvin* is not listed, click on the **Select Current Character Set** button and select *Melvin*.

  Now when you set a key, a key will be set for all attributes that are included in the set.

4 Pose Melvin

The first step in animating Melvin's walk cycle is posing him.

- Turn IK Handles **Off**, and NURBS curves **On** in your Pick Masks.
- Select *left_footControl* and **move** it to **-2** along Z.
- Select *right_footControl* and **move** it to **1.5** along Z.

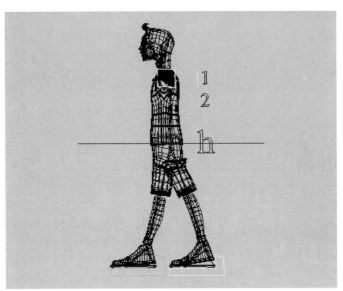

Melvin posed at frame 1

Note: At this point, Melvin's feet will lift away from the control objects a little bit. This will be corrected later by animating Melvin's vertical motion with the localControl object.

---

5 Set a key

- Hit the **s** key to set a key.

6 Determine Melvin's stride length

For a cycled walk to behave properly, it is important that the feet and body be coordinated in their movements.

- Draw an **Edit Point** curve between the *left* and *right_invHeel* joints.

  This EP curve will regulate Melvin's stride length.

Note: It may be easier to draw this curve by temporarily making the **melvinJoints** layer invisible.

---

7   Move the EP curve's pivot to the front of the curve

- Using curve snapping, move the curve's pivot all the way to the front of the curve.

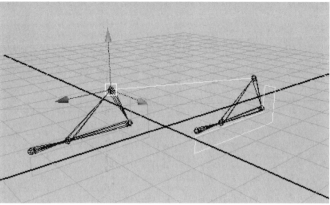

The EP curve's pivot

8 Scale the curve on Z

- Change the curve's **Z Scale** value to **-1**.

9 Duplicate the curve

Now that you know how far to move Melvin's foot forward, you will duplicate the curve to determine how far to move the globalControl object.

- Duplicate the curve at the default settings.

- Snap the duplicated curve to Melvin's *rootJoint*.

10 Flatten the curve

Currently, the duplicated curve is on a diagonal. To make it easier to work with for the globalControl, you will flatten it out along X.

- With the duplicated curve selected, switch to component mode.

- Select all of the CV's that are not at **0** along X.

- Invoke the **Move Tool**.

Note: It will be necessary to change the Move Tool options from Local to World for this operation.

- Click on the X-axis handle of the manipulator to constrain movement along the X-axis.

- Hold down the **x** key to invoke **Grid snapping**.

- In the top window, click on the X-axis Manipulator again and drag the selected CV's until they are aligned at **0** along **X**.

Manipulator tip

In the Perspective view, you may want to be able to restrict interactive movement of Melvin's arms or legs along either the XY, YZ, or XZ planes.

By default the move manipulator works either along a single axis using the axis handles or along the view plane using the center of the manipulator.

Manipulate along YZ
- Select the **Move Tool**.

- Press the **Ctrl** key and click on the **X-axis** handle. The center of the manipulator changes to show that it is aligned with the YZ plane.

- Click drag on the middle of the manipulator to work along the chosen plane.

Icon changes

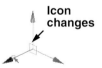

To choose a plane, press the **Ctrl** key and click on the axis handle that is perpendicular to the desired plane. To return to the default mode, press the **Ctrl** key and click on the center of the manipulator.

- Switch back to object mode.

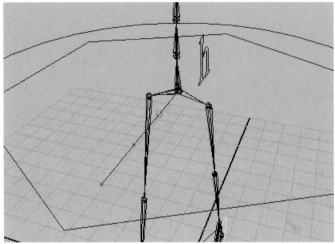

The duplicated EP curve after being flattened

11 Advance to frame 15

12 Move the left foot forward

- Select the *left_footControl* and snap it to the end of the first EP curve.

13 Move the globalControl forward

- Select the *globalControl* and snap it to the end of the second EP curve.

14 Set a key

15 Test the animation

- **Click-drag** between frames **1** and **15** in the **Time Slider** with your **LMB** to test the animation.

16 Advance to frame 30

17 Adjust the EP curves

- Select the first EP curve.
- Move its pivot to the front of the curve.
- Set its **Scale Z** value to **1**.
- Snap the duplicated EP curve back to the *backRoot* joint.

18 Move the right_footControl and globalControl objects again

- **Snap** the *right_footControl* to the end of the first curve.

- **Snap** the *globalControl* to the end of the duplicated curve.

19 Set another key

20 Test the animation

- Play the animation.

21 Delete the EP curves

22 Save your work

Cycling the animation

Now that the first step has been animated, you will cycle the curves to keep Melvin walking.

1 Open the Graph Editor

- Select **Window → Animation Editors → Graph Editor**.

- Select the *Melvin* Character Set in the left-hand column of the Graph Editor.

- Select **View → Frame All** to display all of the *Melvin* Character Set's animation curves.

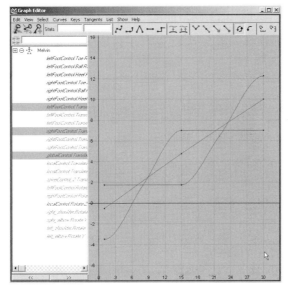

Animation curves in Graph Editor

2 Select the animation curves in the Graph Editor

- **Click-drag** a selection marquee over all of the curves.

- To display the values of the animation curves outside of the recorded keyframe range, select **View** → **Infinity**.

3 Cycle the curves

- Select **Curves** → **Post Infinity** → **Cycle**.

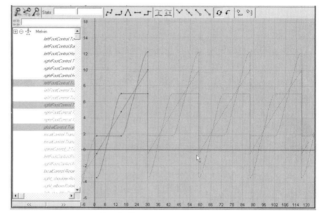

Cycled animation curves

Auto Key

Auto Key is a useful way of quickly animating in Maya. To use **Auto Key**, you must first set an initial key on the channels that you want animated. Auto key has the following conditions:

- **Auto Key** will only work on channels that have already been keyed.

- If a Character is selected, a key will be set on each attribute in the **Character Set** at each pose on the timeline.

4 Increase the Playback range to 1 to 120

- **Click-drag** on the box beside the **30** in the **Current Range** slider and drag it until the current **playback range** is **1** to **120**.

5 Play the animation

Note: Instead of moving forward, Melvin keeps covering the same ground every 30 frames. This is because the Cycle option was used. For Melvin to move forward in the cycle, the Cycle With Offset option must be used.

6 Cycle the curves with Offset

- With the curves still selected, select **Curves** → **Post Infinity** → **Cycle With Offset**.

- With the curves still selected, select **Curves** → **Pre Infinity** → **Cycle With Offset**.

  Cycling before the recorded keys is not essential, but can be helpful once you start editing curves.

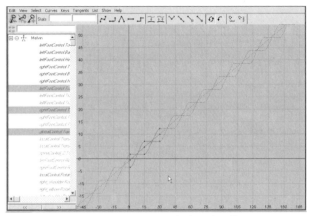

Animation curves cycled with offset

7 Play the animation

Melvin should now continue to move forward as he walks.

8 Turn off the Melvin Character Set

For the time being, the Melvin Character Set should be turned off so
that individual attributes can be edited.

- Select **None** in the **Current Character Set** window.

9 Improve the timing by adjusting the animation curve's tangency

Right now, when you play the animation, there is some jerkiness to the
motion of Melvin's feet. This is because the animation curves aren't
interpolating well between the frames at the beginning and the end of
the cycle.

- Select the *globalControl* object and both foot controls.

- Open the Graph Editor.

- Select **Translate Z** in the column on the left for each of the
  control objects.

  Selecting curves this way displays only the selected curves.

- The curve for *globalControl*'s Z translate is fine so it can be left
  alone, but there is a clear break in tangency for the *footControl*'s Z
  translate curves.

- Select the Z translate curves for the two foot controls.

- In the Graph Editor, select **Tangents → Flat**.

- Play the animation. The motion of the feet still starts and stops,
  but the action is not so sharp.

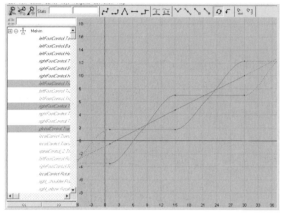

Translation Z curves with Flat tangency

Note: It is important when working with cycled animation that the curves interpolate appropriately from the last frame in the cycle to the first frame in the cycle. In this case, Flat tangency was used to ensure a smooth interpolation between the frames.

---

10 Save your work

Raising the feet

Currently, Melvin's feet drag along the ground as he walks. Now you will animate the raising of his feet using Breakdown keys. Breakdown keys are different from standard keys in that they maintain their relative position between regular keyframes. This is useful for actions that, by their nature, tend to have relative timing. In the case of Melvin's walk, the timing of the raising of the foot is relative to the foot hitting the ground, so it is beneficial for the timing of the feet raising to adjust themselves according to changes made in the timing of the foot falls.

1   Go back to frame

- Go back to frame **1** and set the **playback range** to **1 to 30**.

2   Select leftFootControl

3   Find the "passing" frame

- Switch to the side view and **Click-drag** in the **Time Slider** until the left foot lines up with the right foot.

4 Lift the left foot

- **Translate** *left_footControl* **1** unit on **Y**, and **rotate** it **15** degrees on **X**.

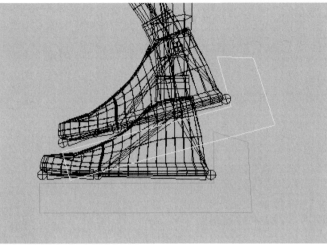

Left foot raised and rotated

5 Set a Breakdown key

- From the Animate menu, select **Animate** → **Set Breakdown**.

- A blue tick will appear in the timeline denoting a Breakdown key.

6 Advance to the next passing frame and repeat for the right foot

- Advance to the frame where the right foot lines up with the left foot.

Note: You may find that the feet don't perfectly line up as they pass. Select the frame where they are the closest.

- Lift and rotate the right foot to match the left foot.

7 **Set another Breakdown key**

8 **Set the playback range to 1 to 120**

9 **Play the animation**

10 **Change the In and Out of the tangency of the curves**
- In the Graph Editor, display the Translate Y curve for the *left_footControl.*
- Select the key at frame **15**.
- Select **Tangent** → **In Tangent** → **Linear**.

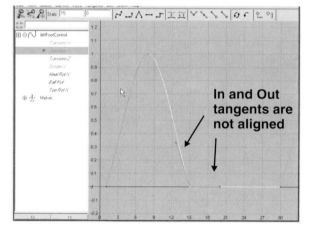

In and Out tangents are not aligned

Frame 15 with In Tangent set to Linear

Before changing the In Tangent of this key, the curve decelerated as it interpolated into the key, causing the foot to decelerate as it approached the ground. Now, the curve interpolates into the key at more of a constant speed, causing the foot to hit the ground at a constant speed.
- Select the Translate Y curve for *right_footControl.*
- Select the key at **frame 15** and change its **Out Tangent** to **Linear**.

11 **Play the animation**

12 **Save your work**

Animating the rolling heel action

Now you will animate the motion of Melvin's heels as they hit and peel off of the ground.

1 Animate rightFootControl's heel rotation

- Go to frame **1**.
- Set *rightFootControl's Heel Rot X* value to **-10**.
- Set a key for that channel by **LMB-clicking** on the channel to select it, then **RMB-clicking** on the channel and selecting **Key Selected**.
- Go to frame **4**.
- Set *Heel Rot X* to **0**.
- Set a key.
- Go to frame **30**.
- Set *Heel Rot X* to **-10**.
- Set a key.

2 Animate leftFootControl's heel rotation

- Go to frame **15**.
- Set *leftFootControl's Heel Rot X* value to **-10**.
- Set a key.
- Go to frame **18**.
- Set *Heel Rot X* to **0**.
- Set a key.

3 Adjust the Heel Rot X curves

The heel action is close, but the curves can be improved.

- Display the curves for both *left* and *rightFootControl* in the Graph Editor.
- Select both *Heel Rot X* curves and change their tangency to **Flat**.
- Select the *Heel Rot X* channel for the *rightFootControl*.
- Select the key at frame **4**.

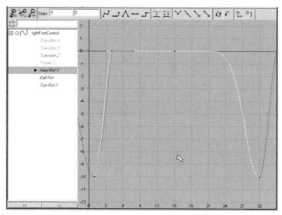

Key at frame 4 with unified tangency

- Select **Keys → Break Tangents** or click on the **Break Tangents** button in the Graph Editor.

  With its tangency broken, the In and Out Tangent handles on the key can be independently edited.

- Select the tangent handle on the left side of the key and invoke the **Move Tool**.

- **MMB-click+drag** so that the tangent handle points toward the key at frame **1**.

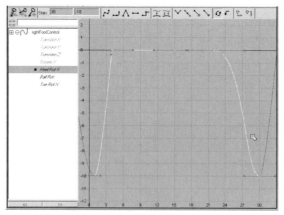

Key at frame 4 with broken tangency

- Select the key at frame **22**.

- Select **Keys → Free Tangent weights**, or click on the **Free Tangents button** in the Graph Editor.

- Select the tangent handle on the right side of the key.

- Hold down the **Shift** key, then **MMB-click+drag** to adjust the shape of the curve.

  Changing the Tangent weight adjusts the timing of the curve. In this case, the timing out of the key is made slower.

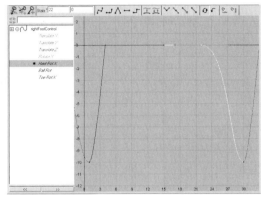

Key at frame 22 with tangent weight adjusted

4 Adjust Heel Rot X for the left foot

- Select the key at frame **18**, break its tangency, and point the left tangent handle at the key at frame **15**.

- Select the key at frame **8**, free its tangent weight, then adjust the shape.

5 Compare the curves

- Display *Heel Rot X* for both feet in the Graph Editor.

- Make sure that they are basically the same shape. If necessary, adjust the curves so that they match each other.

6 Save your work

Animating the foot peeling off the ground

Now that you have animated the heel action, you will animate the foot peeling off of the ground.

1 Animate leftFootControl's ball rotation

- Go to frame **1**.

- Set *leftFootControl's Ball Rot* value to **0**, and *Toe Rot X* to **10**.

- Set a key for those channels.

- **MMB** to frame **30**.

- Set another key for the *Ball Rot* and *Toe Rot X* channels.
- Go to frame **27**.
- Set *leftFootControl's Ball Rot* value to **10**, and *Toe Rot X* to **0**.
- Set a key for those channels.

2 Animate rightFootControl's ball rotation

- Go to frame **15**.
- Set *rightFootControl's Ball Rot* value to **0**, and *Toe Rot X* to **10**.
- Set a key for those channels.
- Go to frame **12**.
- Set *rightFootControl's Ball Rot* value to **10**, and *Toe Rot X* to **0**.
- Set a key for those channels.

3 Play the animation

4 Flatten the Ball Rot and Toe Rot X curves for both feet

5 Save your work

Animating Melvin's pelvis motion

Now that Melvin's basic forward motion has been established, you will animate the up and down motion as he walks.

1 Go to frame 1

2 Move localControl down on Y

- **S**elect *localControl* and translate it down along Y until there is a slight bend in Melvin's knees.

A value of **-0.2** on Y is a good starting point.

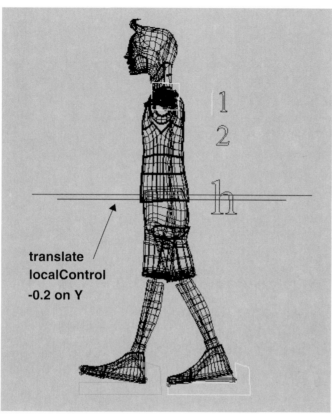

localControl translated -0.2 on Y

3 Set a key

- Set a key for the Y translate channel.

4 Go to frame 15

- **MMB-click+drag** to frame **15** in the Time Slider. Dragging with the **MMB** allows you to change where you are in time without animation updating.

5 Set a key

6 MMB to frame 30 and set another key

7 Play the animation

Melvin's walk should seem a little more natural now.

8 Advance to the first passing frame

- Advance to the frame where the left foot passed the right foot, probably around frame **8**.

9 Switch to the front view

10 Translate localControl

Now animate Melvin's vertical and side-to-side motion at the passing positions.

- Select *localControl* and transform it to:

   Translate X to **-0.4;**

   Translate Y to **-0.07;**

   Rotate Z to **-1.5.** Set a key.

11 Test the animation

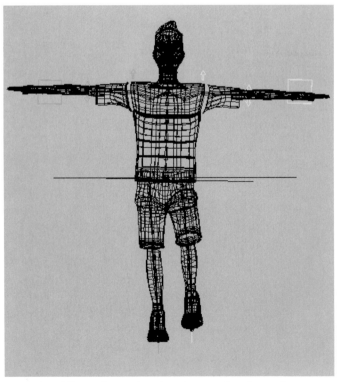

localControl translated and rotated at frame 8

12 Advance to the next passing frame

- Advance to the frame where the right foot passed the left foot, approximately frame **22**.

13 Translate localControl again

- Select *localControl* and **transform** it to:

  Translate X to **0.4;**

  Translate Y to **-0.07;**

  Rotate Z to **1.5.**

14 Set a key

15 Play the animation

- Increase the **playback range** to **1** to **120** and play the animation.

16 Check the animation curves for localControl

- Translate X's tangency may need some minor adjustments at frames **1**, **15**, and **30**.

- Change Rotate Z's **Tangency type** to **Spline** and adjust the tangency, if necessary.

- Play the animation in the front view.

- Make any additional changes to Translate X, Y, or Rotate Z's tangency to improve the smoothness of Melvin's walk.

  For the time being, don't adjust the actual values of the curve's keys.

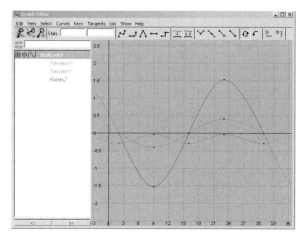

Checking the animation curves

17 Save your work

Compensating for Melvin's center of gravity

Now that you have animated Melvin's side to side action, it's a good time to adjust the movement of his feet and body to compensate for his shifting center of gravity. First you will adjust his feet.

1 Adjust leftFootControl at the passing frame

- Select *leftFootControl* and advance to the first passing frame.

- Set its **Translate X** value to **-0.2**.

- Set a Breakdown key for this channel.

    You are using a Breakdown key because the other keys you set for this object at frame 8 were Breakdown keys.

2 Adjust rightFootControl at the next passing frame

- Select *rightFootControl* and advance to the next passing frame.

- Set its **Translate X** value to **0.2**.

- Set a Breakdown key for this channel.

3 Play the animation

4 Adjust Melvin's spine

- Select *spineControl_2*.

- Go to the first passing frame.

- Set *spineControls_2*'s X Translate value to **0.07**.

- Set a key for this channel.

- Advance to the next passing frame.

- Set *spineControls_2*'s X Translate value to **-0.07**.

5 Adjust the curves as necessary

6 Save your work

Offset localControl's timing

Melvin's basic body motion is complete. Now is a good time to refine it a little by offsetting the timing of some of his actions.

1 Offset localControl's curves

- Select *localControl* and open the Graph Editor.

- Select all of the curves.

- In the Selected Key's Time field type:

  +=1

  +=# is a very useful tool for adjusting the values of a curve as a whole. In this case, typing +=1 will push each key in the selected curves back one frame in time. This function also works with subtraction, multiplication, and division.

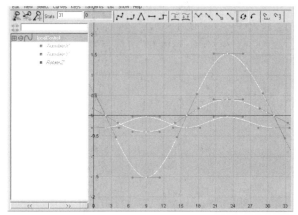

+=1 operation in Selected Key field

2 Play the animation

- Set the **playback range** to **1** to **120**.
- Play the animation.

3 Save your work

Animating Melvin's arms

In this scene, Melvin's arms only need to swing at his side, so FK will be used rather than IK. Since Melvin's arm joints weren't included in the Melvin Character Set when it was created, they should be added before they are animated.

1 Go to frame 1

2 Select the elbow and shoulder joints for both arms

- Make sure that the *melvinJoints* layer is visible.
- Turn on the **Select Skeleton Joints** Pick Mask.
- Select the *left_* and *right_shoulder*, and *left_* and *right_elbow* joints.

3 **Add the arm joints to the Melvin Character Set**

- Select **Windows** → **Relationship Editors** → **Character Sets...**

- Select the *Melvin* Character Set in the left-hand column.

- Select **Edit** → **Add Objects To Character Set**.

4 **Remove unnecessary attributes from the Melvin Character Set**

- Click on the plus sign beside the *Melvin* Character Set to display all of its attributes.

- Scroll down in the Character Sets column until you find the attributes for the arm joints.

- Select all attributes for the arm joints EXCEPT rotation.

- Select **Edit** → **Remove Highlighted Attributes**.

Unwanted attributes selected in the Relationship Editor

The rotation channels for the arm joints are now included in the Melvin Character Set. This will make it easier to keep track of things in the future if you start working with the Melvin Character Set again.

5 Select the left and right_shoulder joints

6 Rotate them 85 degrees on Z

7 Animate the Y rotation of both shoulders

- **Rotate** *left_shoulder* **20 degrees** on **Y**.

- **Rotate** *right_shoulder* **-25 degrees** on **Y**.

- Key the rotation for both joints by holding down the **Shift** key and pressing the **e** key.

- Use the **MMB** to advance to frame **30**.

- Set another key for rotation only.

- Go to frame **15**.

- **Rotate** *left_shoulder* **-25 degrees** on **Y**.

- **Rotate** *right_shoulder* **20 degrees** on **Y**.

- Key the rotation for both joints.

8 Animate the rotation of the elbows

- Go to frame **1**.

- Set the **Y rotate** for *left_elbow* to **-20**.

- Set a key for that channel.

- **MMB** advance to frame **30**.

- Set a key for Y rotation.

- Go to frame **15**.

- Set a key for **Y rotate** at **0 degrees**.

- Go to frame **1**.

- Set the **Y rotate** for *right_elbow* to **0** and set a key.

- **MMB** advance to frame **30**.

- Set a key for Y rotation.

- Go to frame **15**.

- Set a key for Y rotate at **-20** degrees.

9 Cycle the animation

- Select both left and right shoulder and elbow joints.

- Cycle the Rotate Y curves in the Graph Editor and correct the tangency as is necessary.

10 Offset the animation

- Select both shoulder joints and offset their timing by using +=1.
- Select both elbow joints and offset their animation using +=3.

11 Save your work

Using Buffer Curves to edit animation

When animating, you will often find it helpful to compare the results of a change made to an animation curve with the original curve. Buffer Curves allow you to easily switch back and forth between two version of the same channel.

1 Select both elbow joints

2 Open the Graph Editor

3 Select the curves for Y Rotation

4 Create Buffer Curve Snapshots

- Select **Curves → Buffer Curve Snapshot**.

  Maya has created a duplicate of the two rotation curves.

- Select **View → Show Buffer Curves**.

5 Scale the curves

- Select **Edit → Scale – ☐**.
- **Reset** the **Scale Keys** Options window.
- Set the **Value Scale/Pivot values** to **2.0** and **0**.

Method	⦿ Scale/Pivot		○ Start/End	
Only Scale Specified Keys	☑			
Time Scale/Pivot	1.0000		0.0000	
Value Scale/Pivot	2.0000		0.0000	
New Start/End Times	1.0000		10.0000	

Options for Scale keys window

This will scale the values of the keys by a factor of 2, using zero as the scale pivot.

- Click the **Scale Keys** button.

The Y rotation values for both elbows have now been doubled and the Buffer curves show the original values.

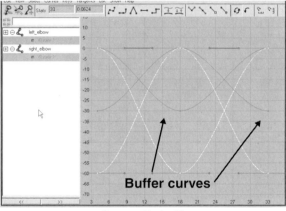

Rotate Y's buffer curves

6 Play the animation

7 Swap the Buffer curves

The motion of the elbows is different, but it's hard to say whether or not it's better. You will now swap these curves with the Buffer curves which currently store the original rotation values.

- In the Graph Editor, select **Curves** → **Swap Buffer Curves**.

The Graph Editor now uses curves with the original rotation values.

8 Play the animation

The original curves provide too little rotation, while the new curves provide too much. You will now scale the curves again to split the difference.

9 Scale the keys again

- Select the curves for Y rotation.

- Invoke the **Scale Tool** by pressing the **r** key.

- Hold down the **Shift** key, then click with the **MMB** near **0** in the Graph Editor and drag up to scale the keys.

- Stop when the keys are about halfway between the old and new values.

10 Play the animation

11 Save your work

Adjusting Melvin's overall animation

The principle advantage of this approach to animating a walk cycle is that once it is setup, it is easy to edit and modify the walk. You will now make adjustments to the curves to change how Melvin walks.

1 Scale globalControl and the two feet to make Melvin walk faster and farther

- Select *globalControl* and both foot controls.

- Select the **Translate Z** curves for all three nodes in the Graph Editor.

- Select **Edit → Scale**.

- **Reset** the **Scale Keys Options** window.

- Set the **Value Scale/Pivot** values to **1.5** and **1**.

  This will scale the values of the keys by a factor of 1.5, using 1 as the scale pivot.

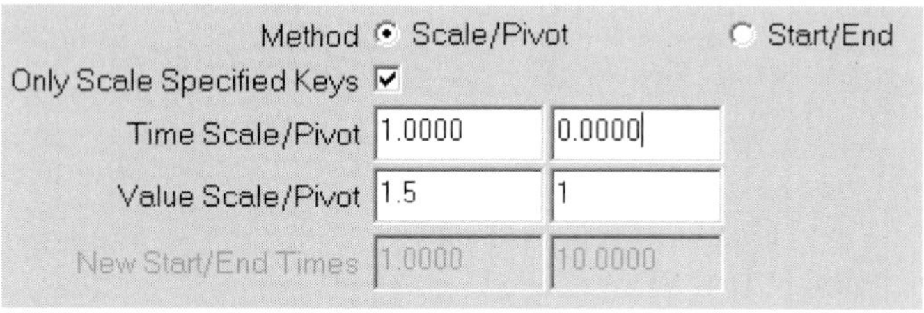

Method	⦿ Scale/Pivot	○ Start/End
Only Scale Specified Keys	☑	
Time Scale/Pivot	1.0000	0.0000
Value Scale/Pivot	1.5	1
New Start/End Times	1.0000	10.0000

Scale Keys options

- Click the **Scale Keys** button.

2 Play the animation

Melvin now covers fifty percent more ground in the same time.

3 Use Move Tool to adjust Melvin's vertical motion

- Select *localControl*'s Y Translate curve in the Graph Editor.

- Select the keys at the top of the curve.

- Invoke the **Move Tool**.

- Hold down the **Shift** key and **Click-drag** the keys up.

- Stop when you think Melvin is at a good height.

Be careful not to straighten Melvin's legs all the way, or his knees will pop as he walks.

4 Play the animation and adjust the keys

- Continue adjusting the values of the Translate Y keys while the animation is playing.

- Experiment with both upper and lower keys until you are satisfied with Melvin's movement.

5 Experiment with localControl's Z Rotation

- Select *localControl*'s Rotate Z curve in the Graph Editor.

- Select **Modify → Transformation Tools → Scale Tool – ❑**.

- Click on the Graph Editor's title bar. A new set of options should appear in the Scale Tool's Options window.

- Select Manipulator.

- A box will appear around the selected curve.

- Play the animation and scale the curve by adjusting the manipulator.

  Be careful to only scale the keys up or down and not side to side, or the timing will be thrown off.

- Experiment with the scale values while the animation plays until you are happy with the motion.

6 Save your work

Cleaning up the scene

Although Melvin was set up carefully, and his Character Set contains no unnecessary attributes, Static Channels (animation curves that represent no change in value) have been generated. Any attribute that is included in the Character Set but has not been manipulated thus far, such as the *spineControl_1*'s attributes, will have Static Channels.

Now that Melvin's walk is basically done, it's a good time to delete these channels. Deleting the channels will have no effect on Melvin's walk, but it will reduce the size of the scene file.

1 Delete the Static Channels

- Select **Edit → Delete By Type → Static Channels**.

- Play the animation.

  Melvin's walk should be exactly the same.

2 Save your work

Summary

Animation is a key part of character rigging because a rig must be tested and qualified as it is being put together. You will want to have a high degree of confidence in a rig before you have gone too far down the path of skinning and building higher orders of control. Animation at this stage can be done in a rudimentary fashion and using stand-in or low res geometry is a good method of streamlining the performance.

Understanding the animator's needs is also an important function of the character rigger. Building easy to understand and easy to operate controls is an important part of rigging. Giving an animator a simple collection of keyframing points is imperative. The animator should not have to search for every attribute that will receive animation. The animator should be able to select one object and then apply a keyframe to this object which then applies keyframes on all of the required attributes. This is what a Character Set is used for. Creating higher orders of operation or automated functionality is another important aspect of rigging. In this manner, an animator can animate a certain object and then the other logical entities can be carried along "for free". Using the Connection Editor and Set Driven Key (SDK) for this are very common approaches to automating secondary or dynamic motion, for example.

6 The Hand Joints

In this chapter, you will build the skeletal structure for Melvin's left hand. You will design the hand to have sophisticated articulation while still being simple to animate. You will verify the local rotation axis of each joint, since the hand will be animated using Forward Kinematics. The correct orientation of the axes will be crucial to your success when you use Set Driven Key to control the fingers.

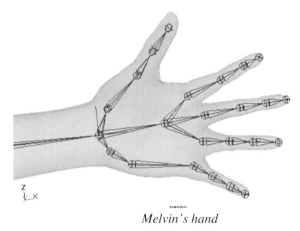

Melvin's hand

In this chapter, you will learn the following:

- How to verify and correct a joint's local rotation axis;

- How to build a hand skeleton;

- How to place the hand joints for proper skinning and motion;

- How to test the motion using Forward Kinematics.

**Editing joints:
Rotating and Scaling**

After you create joints, you can reshape the skeleton by using a combination of rotating and scaling:

Rotate method
- **Select** the joint.
- Select **Rotate Tool.**
- Rotate the joint to affect the selected joint and all the lower joints.

Scale method
- **Select** the joint.
- Select **Scale Tool.**
- Scale the joint to stretch the joint's bone and reposition all the lower joints.

Using these two editing techniques, you can reposition your joints without affecting the joint orientations in the chain.

JOINT ORIENTATION

Each joint has a Local Rotation Axis that defines how the joint will react to transformations. For most parts of a character, the default orientation will be fine. When setting up more complex situations, like Melvin's hands, it is important to make sure that all the joints' axes of rotation are aimed in a consistent manner.

Why should you use Auto Joint Orient?

By using Auto Joint Orient, you make sure that the Local Rotation Axes of the joints are all aligned with the bones that follow. This will help control the joints transformations if you choose to use Forward Kinematics. It can also have an effect on how your clusters work later when you skin your character.

1 Draw joints with Auto Joint Orient turned off

- Select **Skeleton → Joint Tool – ❑** and set the following:

    Auto Joint Orient to **None**;

    World Axis Orient to **None**.

- In the front window, draw several joints in an **S** pattern.

    You will see that the round joint icons are all aligned with the X and Y axes, not with the bone that follows the joint.

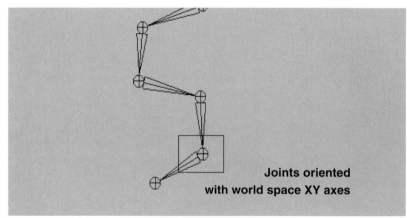

S pattern joints

2 Draw joints with Auto Joint Orient turned On

- Select **Skeleton** → **Joint Tool** – ❐ and set the following:

    Auto Joint Orient to **XYZ**;

    World Axis Orient to **None**.

- In the front window, draw several joints in an **S** pattern.

    The round joint icons are all aligned with the bone that follows it. Because there is no bone to align to, only the last joint is aligned with the world space.

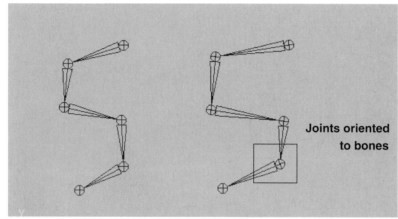

Auto oriented joints

Joints oriented to bones

3 Draw joints with World Axis Orient turned on

- Select **Skeleton** → **Joint Tool** – ❐ and set the following:

    Auto Joint Orient to **XYZ**;

    World Axis Orient to **+Z**.

- In the front window, draw several joints in an **S** pattern.

    As with the last skeleton, the round joint icons are all aligned with the bone that follows it. The Y-axis has been aligned to the world +Z-axis.

4 Display the joint axes

- Select the fourth joint in all three of the hierarchies.

- Press **F8** to go into component mode.

- Check the **?** box in the Status Line. This should display the local rotation axes of the selected hierarchies.

Editing joints

You can edit your joints with the Move tool or by moving the joint pivot:

Move method
- **Select** the joint.
- Select **Move Tool.**
- Move the joint to position the selected joint and all the lower joints.

Pivot method
- **Select** the joint.
- Select a transform tool, then the **Insert** key.
- **Move** the pivot to position only the selected joint.

If you use this method then the orientation of the joint above the edited joint will be broken. You can correct this using the following script:

```
joint -e -oj xyz
```

This will re-orient the selected joints as if they were created with the **Auto Orient** option.

The first skeleton has its axes aligned with world space while the second skeleton has its axes pointing down the bone. The third skeleton has its first axes pointing down the bone and it's second axes pointing in the world +Z direction.

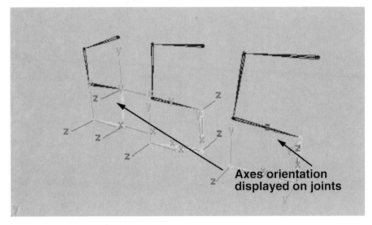

Local rotation axes displayed

5 Rotate joints around the X-axis

- In the Channel Box, click on the **Rotate X** channel.

- **MMB-click+drag** in the front view. This lets you edit the **Rotate X** channel value interactively.

The second and third skeletons rotates nicely around the bone while the first skeleton is rotating in world space with no relation to the bone at all.

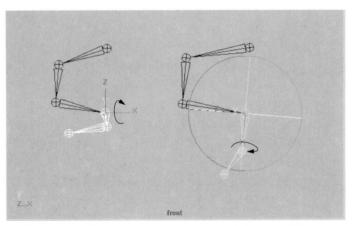

First two skeletons joints rotated around their local X axes

- When you are finished, press the **z** key to undo the rotations.

How editing joints affects joint orientation

In the side bars on the two last pages, you can see that there are four ways of repositioning joints. The first two; scaling and rotating, will always maintain your chosen joint orientation while moving, and pivot location will prevent your local rotation axes from being aligned properly with the bones.

You can use all four methods for editing joints but move and pivot will require that you re-orient your joints as outlined in the side bar.

How to correct flipped axes

In addition to making sure that one axis always points down the bone, you also want to make sure that the other axes relate to the skeleton in the same way.

1 Display the joint axes as a selectable component

You will now learn how to correct the orientation of a joint's axes by rotating it into the proper position. You must first display the local axes as components.

- Select the root joint of the second **S** shaped skeleton.

- Press **F8** to go into component mode, then click on the **?** selection mask button.

   You can see the local axes for all the joints. The first two axes are pointing to the right side of the skeleton while the next two are pointing towards the left. You can now select and edit the two flipped axes.

Note: Don't worry about the last joint. Its local axis isn't oriented towards anything and doesn't affect how the skeleton works.

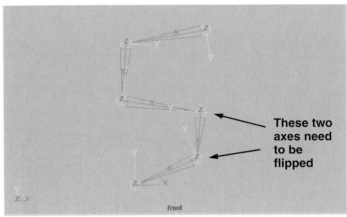

Joints rotated around X-axis.

2 Rotate the joint axes interactively

One way of rotating the local axes is to select them and rotate them interactively.

- Select the local rotation axis on the fourth joint down.

- **Rotate** the axes to flip it around **180 degrees**.

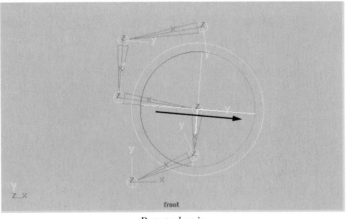

Rotated axis

3 Rotating the joint axes using a script

You can also rotate the axes more accurately by entering a simple line script in the command line. Because the joints were created with **Auto Orient** set to **XYZ**, the flipped axis only needs to be rotated 180 degrees.

- Select the local rotation axis on the fifth joint down.

- In the Command Line, enter the following command:

```
rotate -r -os 180 0 0
```

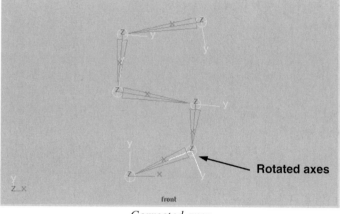

Corrected axes

The World Axis Orient option which is available at the time of joint creation will eliminate the need to worry about flipped secondary axis in most cases.

When do you worry about the local rotation axis?

To determine the proper axis for your joints, you need to understand what you are going to do with the joints. Read the following text to explore some of the possibilities. This topic is discussed throughout the book in more detail. You may want to return to this list when you are more familiar with the options available:

- **Forward Kinematics** - For Forward Kinematics, it is important that joints which are not aligned with the world axis be able to rotate correctly, local to their direction. This is very apparent in the fingers and you will be looking at this in much more detail later in this chapter. How a finger joint rotates is directly linked to the orientation of its local rotation axis. The finger joints should only rotate around one axis, so it is important that the axis be aligned directly down the bone.

- **Expressions** - If you write an expression to rotate all the joints of the back around the Z-axis, you would want them to rotate in a consistent direction. If one of the axes was flipped, the task of writing an expression would be much more difficult.

- **Set Driven Key** - The reasons for having consistent orientation are similar to the reasons outlined for expressions.

- **Inverse Kinematics** - The differences are not as apparent when IK goes through the joints, but in many cases, joints will only need to rotate around the axis, and having the local rotation axis set before adding IK will help with this - especially in the areas of hinge joints such as knees and elbows.

- **Skinning and flexors** - The orientation of the local rotation axis will affect the default flexor attributes as well as the skinning behavior in certain cases. This will be discussed later in the book.

- **Constraints** - With orient constraints, the result will depend on whether the two objects involved in the constraint have similar, or the same orientation.

You may recall that you created the joints with Auto Orient set to XYZ. This forces the X-axis to point down the bone toward the child joint. If the joints are translated when adjusting their placement, you will need to adjust their orientation so they still point down the bone. Note that if their positions are adjusted by rotating and/or scaling, the joint orientation will still point down the bone.

Changing joint orientation

When moving joints after they are created, it is possible that the move will change the orientation of the local rotation axis. It is important to note that if a joint is either rotated or scaled, the local rotation axis will be transformed with it and the X-axis will still point down the bone.

Notice though, what happens if a joint is translated - either with the Translate Tool or the Translate-Insert Tool. The joint orientation stays the same and no longer points down the bone. **Skeleton → Orient Joint** can be used to fix any problems related to the translation.

It is important to note what is happening when the joint orientation is changed with the Orient Joint Tool and/or by rotating the axis directly in the interface. Open the Attribute Editor and notice what changes and what doesn't change:

Rotate - doesn't change - you want this value to stay the same.

Joint Orient - changes so that the Rotate attributes don't have to change.

BUILDING MELVIN'S HAND

There are a number of ways to create a skeletal system for a hand. Your goal is to set up a hand that is both simple to animate and articulate in how the joints can be positioned.

The following is a diagram of the hand that shows you the joints that you will be creating in this chapter:

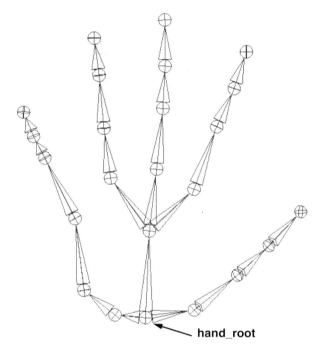

Image of hand joints

These bones do not look exactly like the bones in an anatomy book, but they will give you good control over the surfaces that make up Melvin's hand. You will even control the two bones coming off to the left and right of the *hand_root* joint, so that they rotate inwards to a semi-cupped shape.

You are going to build the hand skeleton as an integrated part of the whole skeletal structure. This means that you will continue building joints off of the existing skeleton hierarchy.

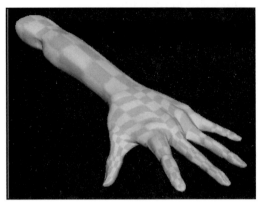

The arm and hand

Joint orientation

To setup the hand for Forward Kinematic motion, you will draw all the joints with **Auto Joint Orient** set to **XYZ** and **World Axis Orient set** to **-Z**. Once this is complete, you will then confirm that all the rotation orientations for the hand joints are set properly. You should note that some of the thumb joints will need to rotate in slightly different directions compared to the other fingers, therefore you will set up their local axes differently.

With the joint orientations set correctly, you will be able to bend the fingers by rotating them around their local axis instead of in world space.

Creating the middle finger

You will begin building the hand based on both the templated Melvin geometry, and the placement of the current wrist joint. The first joint you create (*hand_root*) will start just to the right of the *left_wrist* joint.

Most of the other fingers will stem from the middle finger, so you will create it first. When creating the joints for the hand, you won't need to use Grid Snap because the joints will not always be in a straight line.

1 Open an existing scene file

- Open the scene file called *Melvin_06_readyForHands.mb*.

- Template the *melvinDeform* and *melvinNonDeform* layers to avoid picking the skin. Make sure that you can select joints since you'll need to parent the hand joints to the arm joints.

- Make the leftControls and rightControls layers invisible to temporarily remove visual clutter around the hands.

2 Create new joints for the middle finger

In a top view, starting near the wrist joint, create a skeletal chain consisting of **6** joints: **2** joints will serve as the wrist and palm, and **4** as the middle finger. Make sure Auto orient the joints to **XYZ** and **World Axis Orient** to **-Z** .

- Click just to the right of the *left_wrist* joint to start a new hierarchy.

- Place joints as shown in the following figure.

  The first joint created will become the root joint and eventually be the joint that the hand rotates on.

- Label the joints:

  hand_root, middle_palm, middle1, middle2, middle3, middle4.

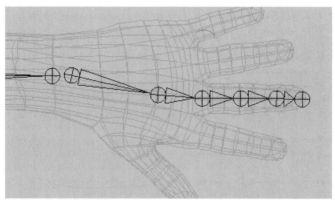

Wrist joints with middle finger

3 Line the new chain up with the arm

While the new chain looks well positioned in the top view, switching to the front view will show that the new hand chain needs to be moved up so that it is aligned with the existing arm joints.

- Select the *hand_root* joint and invoke the **Move Tool**.

- Click on the Y-axis handle to constrain movement along **Y**.

- Hold down the **v** key to temporarily invoke point snapping, then **click+drag** near the arm joints with your **MMB** until the *hand_root* joint snaps into position.

In the Perspective view, you may want to be able to restrict interactive movement of Melvin's arms or legs along either the XY, YZ, or XZ planes.

By default the move manipulator works either along a single axis using the axis handles or along the view plane using the center of the manipulator.

Manipulate along YZ

- Select the **Move** tool.

- Press the **Ctrl** key and click on the **X-axis** handle. The center of the manipulator changes to show that it is aligned with the YZ plane.

- Click drag on the middle of the manipulator to work along the chosen plane.

Icon changes

To choose a plane to work with, press the **Ctrl** key and click on the axis handle that is perpendicular to the desired plane. To return to the default mode, press the **Ctrl** key and click on the center of the manipulator.

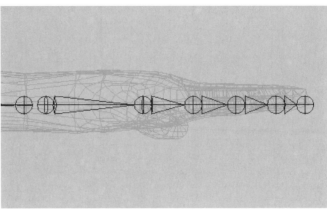

hand_root moved into position

4   Verify the joint alignment in the hand

From side and perspective views, make sure the joints line up in the middle of the hand and are scaled appropriately.

- Select the *middle_palm* joint and move it up so that the finger joints line up with the top of the finger geometry.

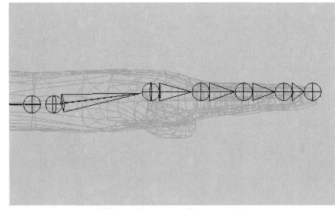

middle_palm moved into position

Knuckle Placement

Proper knuckle placement is important for defining good deformations later on. The knuckles should be closer to the top of the finger. The first knuckle should be set back in the hand. Look at your own hand for reference and notice where the knuckles are.

Tip: In the perspective view, select **View → Frame Selection** to center the camera around the selected finger joints, or press the **f** hotkey.

- If necessary, **Rotate** and **Scale** the finger joints so that they line up properly with the finger geometry.

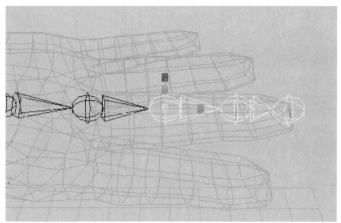

middle2 joint before being scaled

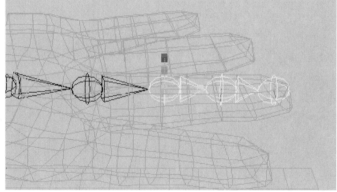

middle2 joint scaled to improve knuckle position of middle3

Tip: Make sure the **Rotation** manipulator is working in **Gimbal Mode**.
Check this in the Tool Settings window, accessed by double-clicking the
Rotate manipulator icon in the Tool shelf.

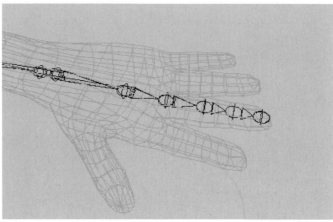

Aligned joints

Creating index and ring fingers

The index and ring fingers will stem from the *middle_palm* joint.

1 Create the index finger joints

You will now create the index finger by continuing the chain from the *middle_palm* joint.

- In a top view, click on the *middle_palm* joint to continue the skeleton chain from here.

- Place the next 4 joints according to the finger geometry.

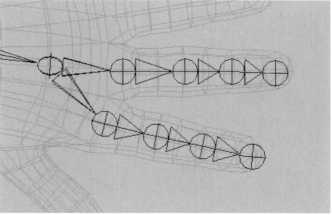

Index finger joints

2 Verify the joint alignment

From side and perspective views, make sure the joints line up properly in the index finger.

- **Rotate** and **Scale** the joints so that they line up as in the figure below.
- Label the joints *index1, index2, index3, index4.*

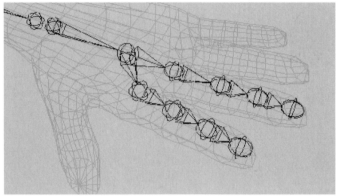

Aligned index finger joints

3 Create the ring finger

- Repeat these steps to create the ring finger.
- Name the ring finger joints: *ring1, ring2, ring3,* and *ring4.*

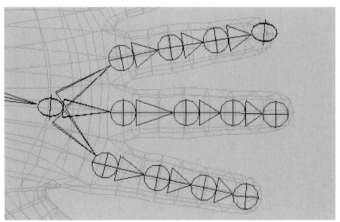

Ring finger joints

Creating the pinky finger

The pinky finger will be a little different than the index and ring fingers in that it will start down near the base of the hand. You are not stemming the pinky finger from the *middle_palm* because you want it to work independently of the three middle fingers, allowing you to pose the hand into a cupped position.

1 Create the pinky finger joints

- In a Top view, create **6** joints for the pinky side of the palm as well as the pinky finger.

- Name the joints *pinkyPalm1, pinkyPalm2, pinky1, pinky2, pinky3, pinky4*.

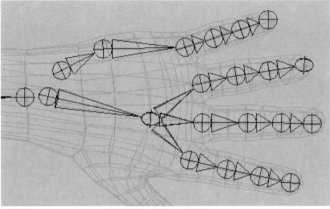

Pinky finger joints

2 Align the pinky finger joints

Since this chain was drawn in the top window, like the original *hand_root* chain, it will need to be moved up on Y to align it with the rest of the hand joints.

- From the front, side and perspective views, make sure the joints line up with the *hand_root* joint.

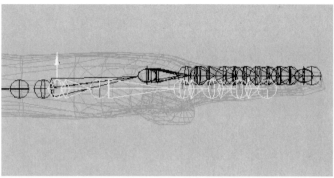

pinkyPalm1 aligned with hand_root joint

3 Move pinkyPalm2

- Move *pinkyPalm2* along Y about halfway between its current position and the rest of the fingers.

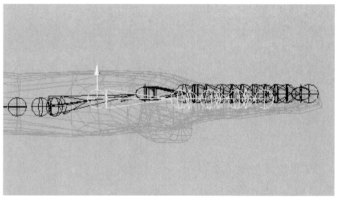

pinkyPalm2 partially lined up with the rest of the fingers

4 Move pinky1

- Move *pinky1* so that the rest of the pinky joints line up with the other finger joints.

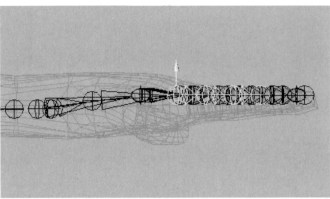

pinky1 aligned with the other finger joints

5 Verify position and rotation of joints

- **Rotate** and **Scale** the pinky joints as necessary to correct their position in the hand geometry.

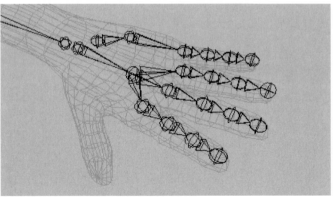

Alignment of joints

6 Make final adjustments

- Make Melvin's geometry fully visible by setting the *melvinDeform* layer to Reference mode and turning Hardware Shading on.

- **Move, Rotate**, and **Scale** the finger joints to make any necessary final adjustments.

- Template the *melvinDeform* layer once you're done.

7 Parent the pinkyPalm1 joint to the hand_root joint

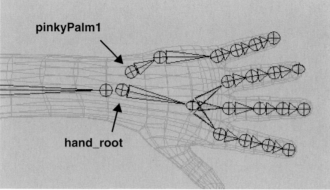

Pinky finger

Creating the thumb

The thumb will be created similarly to the pinky, but the way it articulates will be different. The first couple of joints stemming from *hand_root* will be ball joints (they can pivot around more than one axis). Later, when checking the rotation axes, you'll need to decide how these first few joints rotate to create realistic articulation of the thumb.

1 Create the thumb joints

- In a top view, create **4** joints for the thumb.

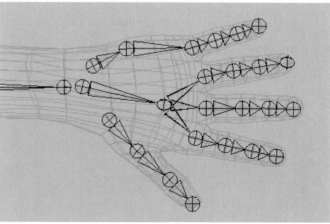

Thumb joints

- From side and perspective views, make sure the joints line up in the middle of the hand.

- **Rotate** the parent joint so all of the joints line up along the thumb.

- **Scale** some of the joints so they extend the length of the thumb.

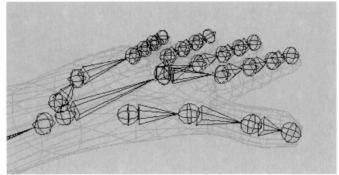

Alignment of thumb joints

- Rename the joints: *thumbPalm, thumb1, thumb2, thumb3*.

- Parent *thumbPalm* to the *hand_root* joint.

Parenting the joint chains

Currently, there are 3 separate joint chains making up Melvin's hand. They must now be parented into the arm hierarchy.

1 Parent the thumb and pinky to the hand_root

- Select the *pinkyPalm1* and *thumbPalm* joints and parent them to the *hand_root* joint.

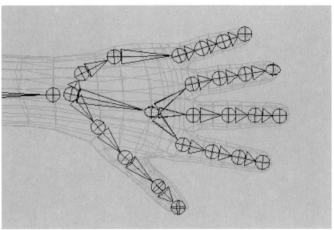

pinky and thumb parented to hand_root

2 Parent the hand_root joint to the arm

- Select the *hand_root* joint and parent it to the *left_wrist* joint.

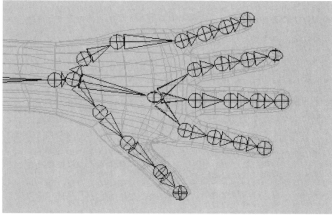

hand_root parented to left_wrist joint

Joint names

You should now have a hand constructed and labelled as follows:

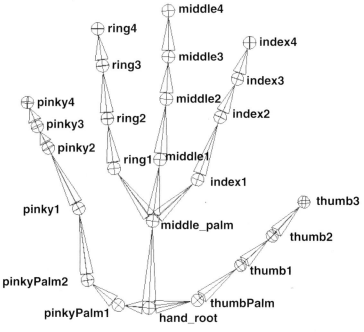

Hand joints named correctly

JOINT ORIENTATION

At the beginning of this chapter, you explored the concept of orienting your joints properly using the joints local axes. The joints for the hand were created with **Auto Joint Orient** set to **XYZ** and **World Axis Orient** set to **-Z**. By default, the X-axis will point down the bone and the Y-axis will point in the world -Z axis.

Orienting joints

If you use the Translate Tool while you are editing the locations of the hand joint positions, the orientation axis of the translated joint stays at the orientation in which it was created. This means that it will no longer be aligned with the bone. You must therefore re-orient the joints.

1 Re-orient the joints

- **Select** the *hand_root* joint and then select **Skeleton → Orient Joint–**
  ❐. In the options box set the following:

    Orientation to **XYZ**;

    Second Axis World Orientation to **-Z**;

    Hierarchy check **On** the **Orient child joints**.

  This will re-orient the joint(s) as if they were created with auto orient set to XYZ and World Axis Orient set to -Z.

- Verify their orientation by displaying the local rotation axis in Component mode.

Looking at the palm of the hand from the arm, the joint orientations should be as follows:

- X pointing down the joint;

- Y pointing towards the pinky;

- Z pointing up.

Command flags

To view the flags for a command, you can type `help command_name` in the Script Editor.

Tip: There are times when joints are not affected by the above command. If the joints won't re-orient with the given command, a common trick is to select **Modify → Freeze Transformations** to reset the local rotation axes to the world space axis before trying to reorient the axes.

Note: If the joint positions were changed by rotating or scaling, their orientations will be OK. Only when they are translated (the joint moved or the joint pivot moved), should the above workflow be considered.

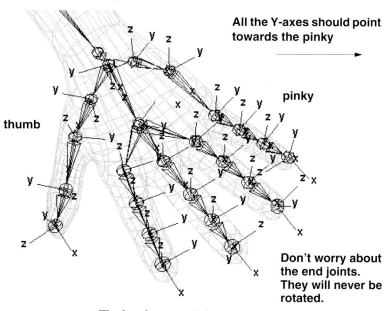

The local axes on joints

Thumb orientation

The rotate axis of the thumb joints will differ from the other fingers. You will need to adjust each of these individually. One of the best references is to look at how your thumb articulates. Notice the *thumb1* and *thumb2* joints are hinge joints.

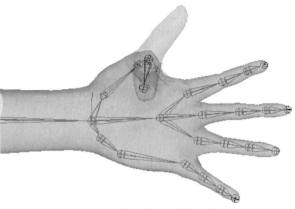

Rotation of thumb

1 Set up the thumb1 and thumb2 orientation

The *thumb1* and *thumb2* joint's Y rotation will control the curling of the thumb, so their Y-axis should be aligned accordingly. Using the geometry as your reference, rotate the axis until Y is pointing directly out the side of the thumb. Both joints will have similarly aligned rotate pivots.

- In Component mode, use the Rotate manipulator to adjust the rotate pivots as shown in the following two figures:

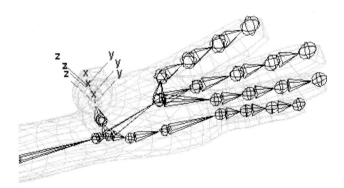

Thumb joint orientations

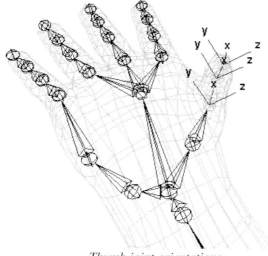

Thumb joint orientations

2 Thumb palm and Pinky palm orientation

To later facilitate the cupping of the hand, the *palm1* and *pinkyPalm* joints need to have their axes aligned with the middle finger. This way, the two outside fingers can be easily rotated around the X-axis to bring the fingers in.

- Align the X-axis of the *thumb_palm* joint with the direction of the middle finger.

- Display the geometry to see how the thumb will be oriented at bind pose.

- The *pinky_palm1* joint orientation needs to be aligned similarly to the *thumb_palm* joint (aligned in the direction of the middle finger).

Tip: You can go back after the skin has been bound and fine-tune these orientations.

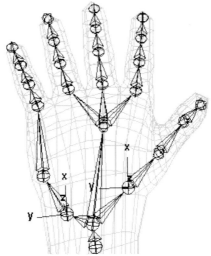

pinkyPalm1 and thumbPalm orientation

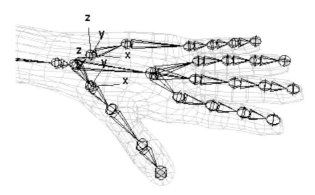

pinkyPalm1 and thumbPalm1 orientation

Note:	Some people like to set the local axis of the *pinky_palm1* joint and the *thumb_palm* joint to both point into the center of the hand. This means a positive rotation will point them in and a negative rotation will point them out.

Setting the preferred angle

Now you have created all the joints for the hand. Assuming everything positioned correctly, you need to tell Maya what all the joints' preferred angles are. This will allow you to return to the preferred position later in the chapter when you start changing the joint rotations.

1 Set the preferred angle for the hand joints

- Select the *hand_root* joint.

- Select **Skeleton** → **Set Preferred Angle** – ❑ and set the following:

  Recursive to **On**.

  This will set the preferred angle for all the joints below the *hand_root* joint.

Tip: Confirm the preferred angle by rotating some of the joints, then selecting the hand_root and **Skeleton** → **Assume Preferred Angle**.

Creating the right hand

To create the right-hand, you will now duplicate the left hand and then mirror it.

1 Duplicate hand_root

- Select the *hand_root* joint.

- Duplicate it at the default settings.

2 Unparent the duplicated hand

- With the duplicated hand still selected, unparent it.

3 Mirror the duplicated hand

- Select **Skeleton** → **Mirror Joint** – ❑ to mirror the duplicated hand.

- Set **Mirror Across** to **YZ** and **Mirror Function** to **Behavior**.

- Click the **Mirror** button.

4 Delete the duplicated hand

Currently, there are two left hands on top of each other so you will now delete the duplicated hand.

- **LMB-click** on the bone between *hand_root* and *left_middle_palm*.

- Check the Channel Box. If *hand_root* is selected, drag a selection marquee over the same bone to toggle the selection to *hand_root1*.

- Delete *hand_root1*.

5 Parent the duplicated hand to the right_wrist joint

6 Add prefix hierarchy names

- Add *right_* and *left_* prefix hierarchy names to all of the joints in each hand.

7 Save your work

Summary

Creating joints and orienting them quickly and reliably is the trademark of a good rigger. There are many tricks to setting up joints quickly including snapping, parenting, and duplicating. Often, once the joints have been created and positioned, they will have improper orientation. This can be quickly remedied by using a MEL command to re-orient a batch of joints at once. Understanding why Maya assigns orientation based on child joint orientation can help you predict where a problem "flip" of local rotation orientation may occur. This is the main problem that can occur when using the Auto Orient option for joint creation. The thumb is a complex finger and requires special attention for orientation and control.

The Hand Controls

In the previous chapter, you set up all the joints for Melvin's left hand. At this stage, the hand could be animated by rotating each finger joint using Forward Kinematics. Because this could be a tedious task, this chapter will focus on developing a set of controls that will drive the rotations of all the hand joints. You will use Set Driven Key to control the fingers and movement of the hand.

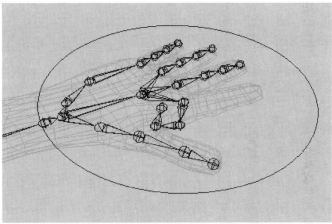

Hand controls

In this chapter, you will learn the following:

- How to use Set Driven Key to control the finger joints;

- How to make connections with the Connection Editor.

Set Driven Key Basics

It is important to understand that Set Driven Key is a curve relationship between two attributes in Maya. In the Graph Editor, the horizontal axis represents the driver attribute values and the vertical axis represents the driven attribute values. The curve represents the relationship between these two attributes.

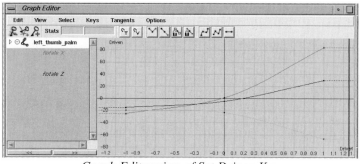

Graph Editor view of Set Driven Key

Because Set Driven Key is a curve relationship, it is possible to adjust the tangents of this curve and add additional keys. This will allow for some interesting behavior. For example, if the rotate attribute of an elbow is driving the size of a bicep muscle, the curve could be edited so that when the elbow reached its maximum bend, the bicep shakes a little as it flexed.

CONTROLLING THE WRIST AND FINGERS

You can now add a NURBS circle to the hand to use as a manipulator for the wrist and a control center for articulating the fingers. It is necessary to create a control object for the fingers in addition to the existing control object for the arm because the arm's control object will be left behind when the arm is manipulated with FK.

Creating the hand control

You'll start by creating a NURBS circle for the hand control. You will add attributes to it so you can keyframe and control all the hand motion by selecting this curve.

1 Open an existing file

- Open the file *Melvin_07_hands.mb.*

2 Create a NURBS circle

- Create a default NURBS circle and name it *left_handControl.*

- Using point snapping, move the circle to the *left_middle1* joint.

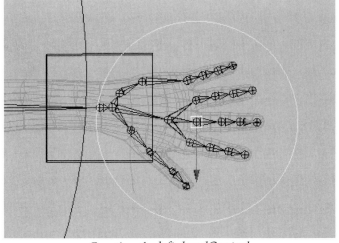

Creating the left_handControl

3 Move the left_handControl's pivot
- Snap the circle's pivot to the *left_hand_root* joint.
- Freeze its transformations and delete its history.

4 Parent constrain the left_handControl to the left_hand_root joint

5 Restrict left_handControl's channels
- **LMB-select** all Translate, Rotate, Scale, and Visibility channels in the Channel Box for *left_HandControl* and **RMB-select Lock and Hide Selected.**

6 Add attributes to the left_handControl
You will add attributes to *left_handControl* to control the fingers.
- Select *left_handControl*.

- Select **Modify** → **Add Attribute**. Set the following:

  Attribute Name to *indexCurl*;

  Make Attribute Keyable to **On**;

  Data Type to **Float**;

  Attribute Type to **Scalar**;

  Minimum Value to **0**;

  Maximum Value to **10**;

  Default Value to **0**.

- Click the **Add** button.
- Repeat the steps outlined above to add the following attributes:

  middleCurl, ringCurl, pinkyCurl, pinkyCup, thumbCurl.

- Add the following attributes to *left_handControl*:

  thumbRotX, and *thumbRotZ*, and *fingerSpread* and set the **Min**, **Max**, and **Default values** to **-10**, **10**, and **0**, respectively.

  These are the attributes that you will control with Set Driven Key. They now show up in the Channel Box for the *L_wristLocator*.

Tip: You can also edit the added attribute's name, its keyable state, and its min/max values after you've created it by selecting **Modify** → **Edit Attribute.**

---

7 Save your work

SET DRIVEN KEY TO CONTROL THE FINGERS

Now that you have all the attributes to eventually control the articulation of the fingers, you need a tool to connect the two. Set Driven Key is perfect for this task because it sets up an editable relationship between two attributes based on a curve in the Graph Editor.

Bending fingers with Set Driven Key

In the case of bending the index finger, you can have its joints rotate when you change the value for the *indexCurl* attribute. When *indexCurl* is set to **0**, none of the index finger joints will be rotated, but when you change *indexCurl* to **10**, the joints will rotate. For motions like spreading the fingers, the **Min** and **Max** should range from **-10** to **10**, where **-10** moves the fingers closer together and **10** moves them further apart.

When setting up the Set Driven Key, you can do all the selecting and manipulating in the work area or use the Outliner or Hypergraph if selecting becomes tedious. The objects can be selected from inside the Set Driven Key Editor as well.

Driving the index curl

The techniques you use to set up the index curl are the same for all the Set Driven Key setups. You will set the controls so you can curl the finger by changing the value of the indexCurl attribute.

1 Open the Set Driven Key window

- Select the **Animate** → **Set Driven Key** → **Set** – ❒.

  The Set Driven Key window appears. It is divided in two parts, Driver and Driven. The attributes you just created will be the Drivers and the joint rotations on the hand will be the Driven objects.

2 Select the Driver node and attribute

- Select *left_handControl*.

- Click **Load Driver**.

  Notice that *left_handControl* appears in the list of Drivers. You should only see one driver object.

- Select *indexCurl* from the list of keyable attributes.

3 Select the Driven node and attribute

In the Set Driven Key Editor, you will use the **rotateY** attribute of the index joints as the driven attribute. To rotate the joint around one axis, you only need to drive that rotation attribute.

- **Shift-select** the 3 index joints (*left_index1, left_index2, left_index3*).

- Click **Load Driven**.

  Notice that the selected objects appear in the Driven Objects list.

- Select the driven objects, then select *rotateY* from the list of attributes (refer to the following figure). Note that the local rotation attributes are set up so that the fingers (which are hinge joints) only need to rotate around one axis.

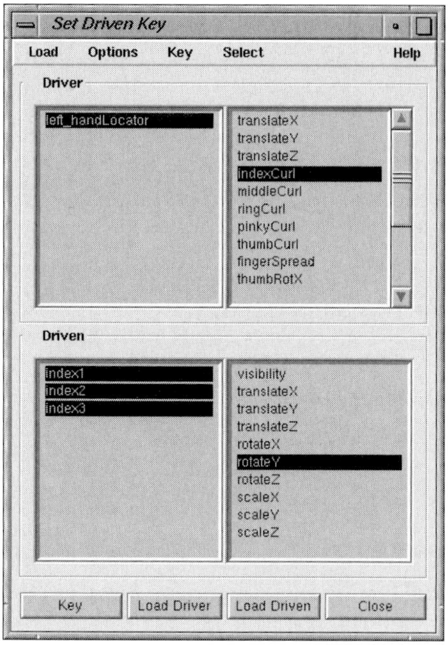

Set Driven Key window

4 Set an initial key position

- Select the *left_handContriol* in the Set Driven Key window to verify that *indexCurl* is set to **0** in the Channel Box.

- Click **Key** in the Set Driven Key window.

5 Set a second key position

- In the Set Driven Key window select *left_handControl* by clicking on its name and in the Channel Box, set *indexCurl* to **10**.

- Curl all the joints so that they rotate about 90 - 100 degrees. Check the limits of the rotation of your own finger for reference.

Note: When rotating the joints into position, it's important that they only rotate on the Y axis. Either set the Rotate manipulator to Gimbal mode, or rotate the joints by adjusting their values in the Channel Box.

- Press **Key**.

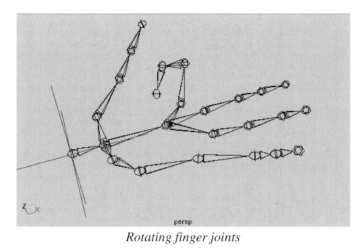

Rotating finger joints

Tip: It is better to "over-rotate" the joints. If you don't rotate the joints enough, you may have to edit them later. If you over-rotate the position, however, you don't have to move the attribute to its full range.

---

6 Test the values

Select *left_handControl* and test different values for *indexCurl* between 0 and 10.

- In the Channel Box, click on the name of the attribute (it should highlight to designate that it is selected).

- In the perspective viewport, **MMB-drag** to change the value of the selected attribute in the Channel Box.

7 Use Set Driven Key for the other fingers

- Repeat steps 1 to 6 for the *middle*, *ring*, *pinky*, and *thumb* joints.

Note: The thumb has 2 joints to curl and the fingers have 3.

Driving the finger spread

You also want the hand to be able to spread its fingers. Use Set Driven Key again to control the action. This time you'll use attributes that have a range between -10 and 10, with 0 being the rest position, or preferred angle.

1 Use Set Driven Key to drive the finger spreading

- Load the *left_handControl fingerSpread* as the **Driver** attribute.

- **Shift-select** *left_index1, left_middle1, left_ring1, left_pinky1*.

- Click **Load Driven**.

- Select the joints and their rotateZ channels.

- Set a key with **fingerSpread** at **0** and the selected finger joints in their rest position.

- Set a key with **fingerSpread** at **10** and the selected finger joints spread to their widest position.

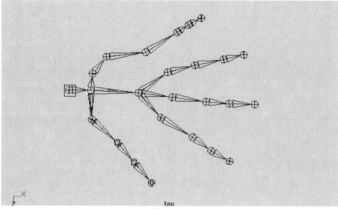

Open finger spread

- Set a key with **fingerSpread** at **-10** and the selected finger joints in a closed position.

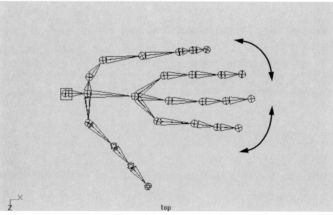

Closed finger spread

2 **Test the results**

- Test the range of motion between **-10** and **10** by changing the **fingerSpread** attribute.

3 **Save you work**

Driving the pinky cup

Another function of a real hand is the ability of the palm to form a cup. This is achieved by rotating the bones of the pinky side of the hand. You'll again control this action using Set Driven Key to rotate the *pinky_palm* joint around the axis that is parallel to the direction of the middle finger.

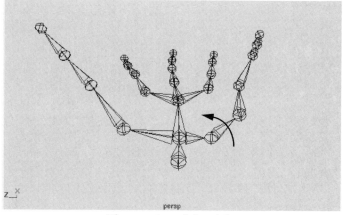

The cupping of the pinky

1 **Use Set Driven Key**

- Load the *left_handControl pinkyCup* as the **Driver**.
- Load the *left_pinkyPalm1* rotateX as the **Driven** objects.
- Set a key with *pinkyCup* set to **0** and all the joints at their preferred angle.
- Set a key with *pinkyCup* set to **10** and the *pinkyPalm* joint rotated up.

2 **Test the results**

- Select the *left_handControl* and test different values for *pinkyCup* between **0** and **10**.

You now have the ability to cup one side of the palm. The other side will get its motion from the movements of the thumb.

THE THUMB

The thumb is different from the other fingers in that its base pivots on a saddle joint and has much more freedom of movement than the finger joints. Where the fingers rotate around one hinge joint, the saddle joint will rotate around 2 axes.

When you set up the thumb motion, you need to allow for flexible articulation that mimics the orbiting provided by a saddle type joint. This is broken down into RotateX and RotateZ. It also requires you to change the rotation axis so that it is not aligned with the direction of the joint, but with the direction of the hand, as shown in the following figure:

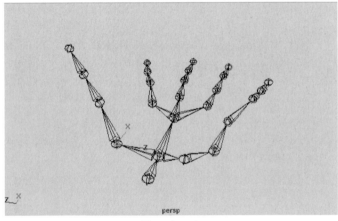

Thumb axis

Driving rotation of the thumb

The following exercise is the same as all the Set Driven Keys for the other fingers. Because this thumb joint articulates differently, it is important to make sure that the local rotation axes are set correctly before creating any Set Driven Keys.

- **X-axis** is parallel to the direction of the middle finger.

- **Z-axis** is normal to the palm.

1 Drive the rotation of the thumb
- Select **Animate → Set Driven Key → Set – ❑**.
- Select *left_handControl* and click **Load Driver**.
- Select *left_thumbPalm* and click **Load Driven**.

- Select *thumbRotX* as the Driver attribute and **rotateX** as the **Driven** attribute.

- Set a key with *thumbRotX* at **0** and the **thumbPalm** joint at its rest position/orientation.

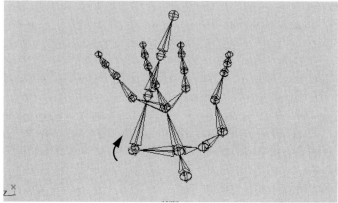

Thumb rotation

- Set *thumbRotX* to **10**.

- **Rotate** the *thumbPalm* in the **X-axis**, to the point where the thumb crosses the palm towards the pinky.

- Click **Key**.

2 Set the second key position

Set a key with *thumbRotX* at **-10** with the *thumbPalm* joint x-rotated out towards the back of the hand.

- Set *thumbRotX* to **-10**.

- Rotate the *thumbPalm* in the X-axis, so that the thumb is rotated to where the hand is in a flat pose.

- Click **Key**.

3 Test the operation of the thumb in this direction

Driving thumbPalm joint with thumbRotZ

Combined with the motion above, setting up this motion will allow the thumb to touch the base of the index finger.

1 Load the Driver and the Driven attributes

In the Set Driven Key window, load the *left_handControl* as the driver and the *thumbPalm* joint as the driven object.

- Select **Animate** → **Set Driven Key** → **Set** – ❑.
- Select *left_handControl* and click **Load Driver**.
- Select *left_thumbPalm* and click **Load Driven**.
- Select *thumbRotZ* as the Driver attribute and **rotateZ** as the Driven attribute.

2 Set Keys for these attributes

- Set a key with *thumbRotZ* at **0** and the *left_thumbPalm* joint at its rest position.
- Set a key with *thumbRotz* at **10** and the *left_thumbPalm* joint rotated in **z** towards the index finger.

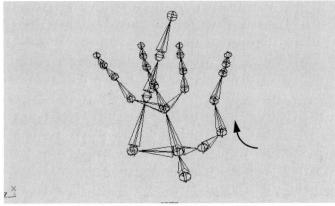

Rotations of thumb

- Set *thumbRotZ* to **10**.
- **Rotate** the thumbPalm in the Z-axis, where the thumb crosses the palm towards the base of the index finger.
- Click **Key**.

3 Set another key

Set a key with *thumbRotZ* at **-10** with the *left_thumbPalm* joint Z-rotated out towards the wrist.

- Set *thumbRotZ* to **-10**.
- Rotate the *left_thumbPalm* in the Z-axis, where the thumb is rotated in the direction of the wrist. The thumb should be almost perpendicular to the palm.
- Click **Key**.

4 **Test the operation of the thumb in this direction**

5 **Save you work**

Test the controls

One of the true tests of articulating the hand is to form the fingers into a cupped shape. Here are a couple of poses to try out by adjusting all the finger attributes:

- Try to make the pinky and the thumb touch.

- Shape the fingers into a cup.

- Create a sphere and place it in the palm of the hand, then wrap the fingers around the ball.

Controlling the wrist action

The *left_handControl* will be used to orient the hand.

By adding three new attributes to left_handControl, you can drive the rotation of the wrist. Two of these attributes, *wristUpDown* and *wristSide*, will drive the y and z rotation of the *left_hand_root* joint. For the *wristTwist* attribute, the motion should not be driven from the wrist, but from the forearm joint. Assuming all the local rotation axes are set correctly (X-axis points down the bone), the wristTwist can drive the x rotate attribute of the forearm joint.

1 **Create new attributes for the wrist locator**

On the *left_handControl*, create 3 new attributes: *wristTwist*, *wristSide*, and *wristUpDown*.

2 **Make a connection**

In the Connection Editor you will set up the connection:
L_wristLocator.wristTwist → *left_forearm.rotateX*

- Select **Window** → **General Editors** → **Connection Editor...**

- Select *left_handControl* and **Reload Left.**

- Select *left_forearm* and **Reload Right.**

- Select *left_handControl.wristTwist* and then select *left_forearm.rotateX*.

  This will make the *L_wristLocator.wristTwist* attribute control the *left_forearm.rotateX*.

Connection Editor

The Connection Editor sets up direct relationships between channels. The input channel will have the same value as the output channel.

More complex relationships can be created by adding one of the utility nodes to the stream.

3 Make two more connections

- Repeat the previous step to make the following connections:

left_handControl.wristSide → *left_hand_root.rotateZ*

left_handControl.wristUpDown → *left_hand_root.rotateY*

4 Save your work

5 Add the left_handControl to the leftControls layer

6 Repeat for the right hand

Summary

In this section, you have worked further with joints and their attributes. You should have a good understanding of joint orientation and the importance of maintaining control of your character from central, easy to select, locations. The animator must be able to quickly access and manipulate the character controls from logical points of operation. For example, if the animator is positioning the hand, it is logical to assume that the animator will also want to work with the fingers from this same object or point of selection. Set Driven Key is also the workhorse of controlling many objects from a single attribute. The fingers in this case are given a good range of motion from just a few attributes that have been centrally located, thanks to SDK rigging.

Smooth Skinning

In this chapter, you will explore Maya's Smooth Skinning function. Smooth Skinning provides smooth deformations around joints by allowing multiple joints to have influence on the same CV.

In later chapters, you will examine other methods of skinning geometry to skeletons such as Rigid Binding and indirect binding with lattices and wrap deformers.

In this chapter, you will learn the following:

- How to Smooth Bind surfaces to bones;
- Editing weights with the Paint Skin Weights Tool;
- Importing/exporting different weight maps;
- Tips and t ricks for weighting Smooth Skinned surfaces.

CHAPTER 8

SMOOTH SKINNING MELVIN

Bind Skin is the most common technique of attaching geometry to skeletal joints. With Smooth Bind, the bound skin points are weighted across many different joints, with each joint having a different weight of influence depending on the joint's hierarchy and/or distance from the particular skin point.

The bound geometry point (CV's, poly vertices, lattice points) can be thought of as a "skin point". These are put into a skin cluster node after they are bound. These points all have weight of 1.0, but the weights can be shared between many different joints and influences.

The weight or participation of the skin point can be locked or held to a specific value. This will inhibit the weight from changing as adjacent skin weights are adjusted and a total value of 1.0 is maintained. When you hold the weight of an influence object, you are locking that value.

1 Open an existing file

- Open the scene file *Melvin_08_handControls.mb*.

2 Add ribs to the skeleton

When smooth binding a skeleton, it is a good idea to add a few more joints in areas that might need more influence when you deform the character. These extra joints help smooth out deformations and help to set up the character for less weighting later on. They also help the geometry maintain volume under extreme deformations. For Melvin, you are going to give him some rib bones. These new rib bones will help smooth out deformations around the shoulder and the upper torso area.

- Select the **Skeleton → Joint Tool**.
- One at a time, place 3 joints along the left side of Melvin's shirt.

   Try to place the joints so that they are aligned vertically with the joints in the spine. Make sure that you are in the front view when you are adding the joints.

- Name the joints *left_rib1*, *left_rib2* and *left_rib3*.

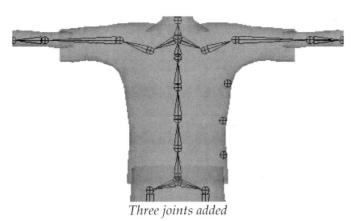

Three joints added

- Mirror the joints across the YZ plane.

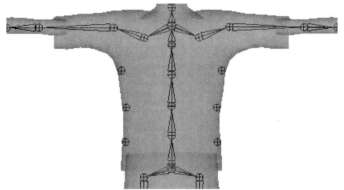

Joints mirrored across the YZ plane

- Parent the joints to the spine.

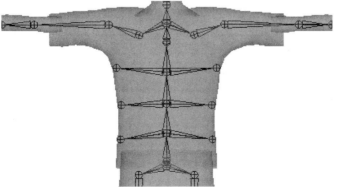

Ribs created by parenting joints to the spine

3   Hide all of the surfaces that don't need to be bound

Some of the surfaces in the scene don't need to be bound right now.

- Make the *melvinNonDeform* layer invisible.

4   Assign Melvin's head to the melvinNonDeform layer

Melvin's head will be bound later, so for now it can be placed on the melvinNonDeform layer.

- Select Melvin's head.

- **RMB-click** on the melvinNonDeform layer and select **Add Selected Objects**.

The head will be discussed in a later chapter.

5   Select the surfaces to be bound

- **RMB-click** on the melvinDeform layer and select **Select Objects**.

6   Select root skeleton

- **Control-select** the *back_root* joint in the Outliner.

7   Smooth Bind Melvin

- Select **Skin** → **Bind Skin** → **Smooth Bind** – ❏ and set the following:

    Bind to **Complete Skeleton**;

    Bind Method to **Closest Joint**;

    Max Influences to **5**;

    Dropoff Rate to **4.0**.

- Press **Bind** to attach (bind) the skin to the skeleton and establish weighting.

The Smooth Bind Skin Options window

Binding by **Closest Distance** specifies that joint influence will be based *only* on the distance between the skin points and the joints. This method ignores the hierarchy of the skeleton.

Max Influences are the number of joints that will have influence on a individual skin point. Setting the **Max Influences** to **5** means that each skin point will not have more than **5** joints affecting it.

Setting the **Dropoff Rate** is another way to determine how each skin point will be influenced by different joints. The Dropoff Rate controls how rapidly the influence of each joint on individual skin points are going to decrease with the distance between the two. The greater the dropoff, the more rapid the decrease in influence with distance.

Tip: The Dropoff Rate can be adjusted on individual joints after the character is skinned. The Max Influences can also be adjusted after the character has been skinned, except the new setting takes effect only on the selected surfaces instead of the entire character.

---

8 Test the results

- Test the results of the Smooth Bind by moving Melvin's arms and legs. Pay particular attention to the shoulder, elbow, and pelvis areas.

- Remember to return Melvin to his original pose by setting the transform values of his control objects back to 0.

9 Save your work

EDITING WEIGHTS

Weighting a character has traditionally been a long and tedious task. Maya's Smooth Bind function eases the burden of this process by setting up good deformations with the default bind.

When Melvin was bound with the Smooth Bind function, a skin cluster node was created for each of the surfaces that was bound to the skeleton. Each of those bound skin points' weights are shared between multiple joints, and those are weighted according to the distance between the joints. When you weight a character, you are actually reassigning those weights to different joints to achieve better deformations.

After moving Melvin around a little bit, you may notice that the settings you used for the Smooth Bind give very good deformations, but it does leave some problem areas such as the pelvis and shoulder. These areas can be improved by editing the weighting of the skin points for the different joints that they are influenced by.

Smooth the hips

The first area that you are going to smooth out is the hips. You will put Melvin in a pose that illustrates problem areas and smooth out the deformations using the **Paint Skin Weights Tool**.

1 Disable IK

When posing a character for the purpose of evaluating and weightings the bind, it's generally a good idea to disable IK. This way the joints can be rotated directly, which tends to make it easier to evaluate the deformations around a joint.

- Select **Modify** → **Evaluate Nodes** – ❑ and toggle **IK Solvers** and **Constraints** off.

2 Hide the NURBS control objects

- In the front and Perspective views, select **Show** → **NURBS Curves** to toggle their display **Off**.

3 Switch display layers

To increase interactive performance, you can switch between the high and low res versions of Melvin. Display the lowResGeometry layer to position Melvin and the melvinDeform layer to examine the quality of the skinning.

4 Pose Melvin to show problem areas

Positioning Melvin in somewhat of an extreme position makes it easier to determine which areas of the skinning need to be adjusted.

- **Rotate** the shoulders so the left arm is oriented vertically.

- Bend the hips and knees.

5 Display in shaded view

- Press **5** to display the shaded view.

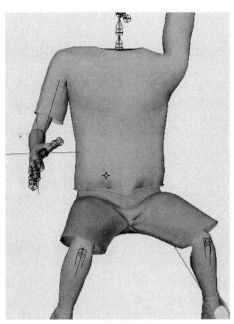

Melvin posed with default weighting

6 Show the high resolution geometry

After Melvin is in a pose that you like, display the high resolution geometry to see details in the skinning.

- Turn the visibility **Off** for the *lowResGeometry* layer.
- Turn the visibility **On** for the *melvinDeform* layer.

  This pose allows you to see a few problem areas when the arms and legs are rotated. The hips, shoulders, and trunk are the most obvious areas that need to be re-weighted and smoothed out.

7 Hide the shirt, arms, legs, and shoes

To avoid painting weights on other surfaces, hide the parts of Melvin that you are not going to work on.

- **Select** the *shorts* and **Shift-select** *back_root*.
- Select **Display** → **Hide** → **Hide Unselected objects**.

8 Adjust the pose

To make it easier to judge the distribution of influence in the shorts surface, it's a good idea to pose the joints symmetrically.

- Select *left_hip* and rotate it to **-65** on **X**, and **40** on **Y**.

- Select *right_hip* and rotate it to **-65** on **X**, and **-40** on **Y**.

9 Select the shorts

- Select the shorts.

- Select **Skin** → **Edit Smooth Skin** → **Paint Skin Weights Tool** – ❑.

The Paint Skin Weights window

- Within the **Stroke** tab, turn **Screen Projection** to **On**.

- Within the **Display** tab, set the following:

   Color Feedback to **On**.

   This allows you to see a greyscale representation of the weighting values associated to the bound surface being painted. White corresponds to a value of **1**, black a value of **0**. The shades of grey represent a value between **0** and **1**.

10 Correct the center seam

Chances are that Melvin's shorts are deforming unevenly in the center. You will correct this by adjusting the influence between the two hips and the *back_root* joint.

- Select *right_hip* in the **Influence** section.

- Set the **Paint Weights** operation to **Add**.

- In the **Brush** section, set **Opacity** to **0.1**.

- In the **Paint Weights** section, set **Value** to **1.0**.

  Adding weight to the *right_hip* will allow you to even out some of the influence.

- Paint the crotch and bum area of the left leg until the deformation evens out. Make sure you don't go too far, and end up with the deformation favoring the right side.

Note: Since the Opacity setting is low, the influence shouldn't change too abruptly as you paint.

- Select the *left_hip* in the **Influence** section.

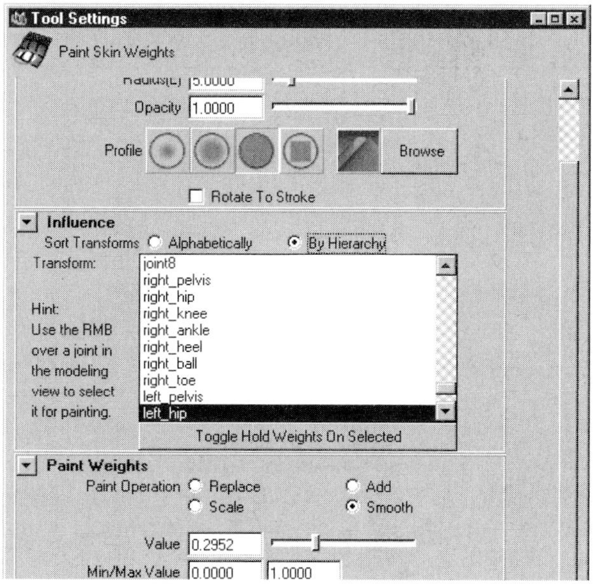

Selecting left_hip as the Influence to be painted

You can display the **influences** of the surface in the Paint Smooth Skin Weights window alphabetically or by sorting through its hierarchy.

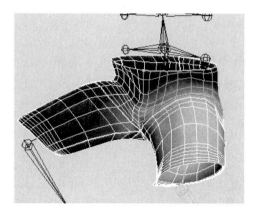

Weighting of the left hip with color feedback enabled

- Paint the crotch and bum area of the left leg to further even out the deformation.
- Switch back and forth between the left and right_hips to even out the deformation as much as you can.

Note: Painting weights on a character is an iterative process, so there will generally be a fair amount of going back and forth between your influences.

---

11 Smooth the hips

Once the deformation at the center of the shorts is fairly even, you should start smoothing the influence.

- Select *right_hip* as the influence.
- Switch the **Paint Weight** operation to **Smooth**.
- Turn **Opacity** up to **1.0**.
- Paint in the crotch and bum area.

  Smoothing at this point should help to further even out the deformation.

- Paint influence for the *left_hip*.
- Switch back and forth as necessary to even things out as much as you can.

  At this point, the deformation at the center of the shorts should be getting pretty even.

12 Add influence to the back_root joint

While adding influence to the two hips in the last step helped to balance the deformation, it has also removed influence from the *back_root* joint. You will now add some back.

- Select the *back_root* joint as an influence.

- Once again, set the operation to **Add** with an **Opacity** value of **0.1**.

- Paint the center of the shorts from front to back.

Note: Care should be taken not to worsen the deformation by adding too much influence to the back_root joint.

13 Flood smooth the back_root

At this point, the *back_root*'s influence throughout the shorts can probably use some smoothing. You will smooth the *back_root's* influence over the entire shorts surface by using the Flood Tool.

- Select the *back_root* joint.

- Set the **Paint Operation** to **Smooth**.

- Make sure that the **Opacity** is still at a low value like **0.1**.

- Click on the **Flood** button. There should be a minor adjustment of influence over the shorts.

  Since the Opacity value is so low, the amount of smoothing applied each time you click the Flood button is very minor. This allows you to Smooth the influence in gradual steps, stopping when you like the effect.

- Continue clicking on the **Flood** button until you are happy with the deformation.

Using the Flood button to set all weights to a common value

14 Smooth the hips in the pocket area

By now, the deformation in the crotch and bum areas should be pretty good. You will now start refining the upper hip areas where Melvin's pockets would be.

- Select the *right_hip* as an influence.
- Increase the **Opacity** to **1.0**.
- Paint in the pocket area of the shorts to improve the deformation.

Note: You may find it necessary to increase the Opacity value at this point.

- Switch to the *left_hip* and smooth its deformation.
- Smooth the influence for each hip in the back pocket area as well.

15 Flood smooth the back_root again

- Select the *back_root* joint and try flood-smoothing the influence at an **Opacity** value of about **0.2**.
- Continue flooding until you are satisfied with the deformation.

16 Remove influence from the back_c joint

The deformation in the shorts should be looking pretty good. Now is a good time to tidy up the influence that joints other than the hips and *back_root* are exerting over the surface. Because Melvin was smooth bound with a Max Influence value of 5, each point in the surface is being influenced by 5 joints. Chances are that joints in Melvin's spine have some influence over the shorts. You will now remove that influence by flood replacing the values.

- Select *back_c*.

  Note that it looks like the joint has no influence over the shorts.

- Open the **Display** section.
- Set the **Max Color** value to **0.1**.

Note: Changing the Max Color value doesn't change the amount of influence that a joint has, it simply adjusts how prominently that influence is displayed. Reducing the Max Color is particularly useful in situations where you are dealing with small values that don't normally show up.

- Set the **Paint Weights** operation to **Replace**.
- Set **Opacity** to **1.0** and **Value** of **0.0**.

- Click the **Flood** button.

17 Hold the weighting for back_c

With the *back_c* joint influence flooded to a value of 0, you will now want to keep that joint from getting weight added back to it while you edit other influence objects.

- Click the **Toggle Hold Weights On Selected** button.

  This will maintain the current value for skin points associated with the selected influence object, in this case the *back_c* joint.

18 Repeat for back_b

- Flood the influence value for *back_b* to **0**, then **Hold** its weighting.

19 Set Max Color back to 1.0

- Set the **Max Color** value back to **1.0** to return the display of influence back to normal.

20 Check the weighting for back_a

- In the Influences section, select *back_a*.

  You could remove the influence that *back_a* has on the shorts, but then the posing of the spine would have no effect on the shorts. As it is, a little influence is probably a good thing.

21 Scale the weighting on the knees

- **RMB-click** on the *right_knee* joint, and select paint weights from the radial menu.

- Set the **Paint Weights Opacity** to **0.2**, the **Operation** to **Scale**, and the **Value** to **0.2**.

- Click the **Flood** button until you're happy with the deformation at the knee.

- Repeat for the *left_knee* joint.

22 Save your work

Tip: Don't overwork a pose. It is easy to spend lots of time trying to get a pose into a perfectly weighted state while forgetting to test the skeleton in different poses. It's also important to consider that tiny imperfections may not be visible when a texture map is applied or if the camera is far from the problematic region.

Smooth the upper torso (optional)

After you've had some practice with the hips, it's time to move on to the upper torso area. The shoulders have traditionally been one of the hardest areas to skin correctly, but Maya's Smooth Bind function makes the process easier and quicker.

In this chapter, don't worry too much about smoothing the actual shoulder bone. You will be learning methods in the next chapter to correct the deformations around the shoulder.

1 Open file

- Open *Melvin_08_hipsDone.mb*.

2 Hide non-essential surfaces

When you were weighting the shorts, every surface was hidden except for the shorts. Now, you are going to do the same thing except you will be working on the shirt.

- Select the *shorts, arms,* and *legs*.
- Select **Display → Hide → Hide Selection**.

3 Disable IK

- Select **Modify → Evaluate Nodes – ❏** and make sure that **IK Solvers** and **Constraints** are toggled **Off**.

4 Repose Melvin

Pose Melvin so one shoulder is up and one shoulder is down so you can see the differences in the two arms.

- Select *left_collarBone* and rotate it **-30** degrees on **Z**.
- Select *left_shoulder* and rotate it to **-45** degrees on **Z**.

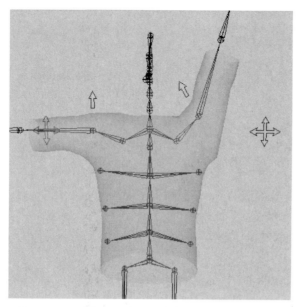

One arm up illustrating weighting to be adjusted

5 Adjust weights around the sleeve using Paint Weights

When Melvin lifts his arm, it would be nice if his whole shirt lifted up a bit, instead of just the very top of the shirt. To do this, you are going to smooth the weighting from the sleeve, through the armpit, and down the side of the shirt.

- Select the *shirt* surface.
- Select **Skin** → **Edit Smooth Skin** → **Paint Weights Tool** – ❏.
- Set **Opacity** to **1.0**, the **Paint Operation** to **Smooth**, and the **Value** to **1.0**.
- Select *left_shoulder* as the influence.
- Smooth the deformation in Melvin's armpit by painting down from the sleeve, through the armpit, and down the side of the shirt.

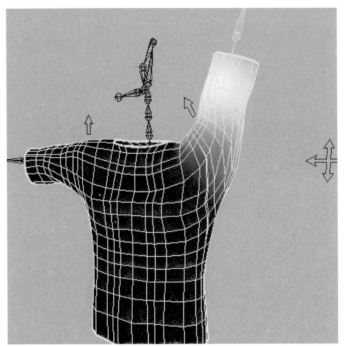

Melvin's shirt sleeve weighted

6 Repose Melvin and test

Put Melvin in a different pose to test the results of the weighting. Adjust the weighting with Maya Artisan™ as you see necessary. Paint weights as needed if problems come up with different poses.

7 Return to the Bind Pose

- Select Melvin's *left_shoulder* joint.

- Select **Skin → Go to Bind Pose**.

  Melvin should return to the pose at which he was bound.

8 Weight the hips

The weighting throughout Melvin's body is probably pretty good, but there may be problems with how much influence the hips have over the shirt.

- Rotate the *right_hip* joint up.

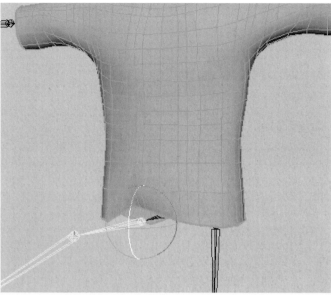

right_hip joint's influence over the shirt

9 Flood the weighting of the hips

- Select the *shirt* and open the **Paint Weights Tool** window.
- Flood replace both hips with a value of **0**.

10 Return Melvin to the Bind Pose

11 Smooth the other side

You will now use the Mirror Skin Weights Tool to mirror the weighting from the left side of Melvin's body to the right side.

- Select *shirt*.
- **Skin → Edit Smooth Skin → Mirror Skin Weights Tool – ❐**.
- Set **Mirror Across** to **YZ**, and make sure that **Positive to Negative** is toggled **On**.
- Click the **Mirror** button.

12 Test the deformation

- Pose Melvin both symmetrically and asymmetrically to test the mirroring of his skin weights.
- If necessary, paint weights in any areas that need work.

13 Return Melvin to the Bind Pose

14 Pose Melvin's spine joints

- **Shift-select** joints *back_a* through *back_e*.

- Rotate them on **Y** to pose Melvin leaning to the side.

- Smooth the weights for each of the rib joints.

15 Save your Work

PAINT WEIGHT TIPS

Although the **Smooth Bind** function and the **Paint Skin Point Weights Tool** simplify the process used for weighting a character, you may still encounter some pitfalls depending on the character you are working with. The following section provides some general tips and guidelines for making the Smooth Skinning process more efficient and also summarizes some of the key points of the workflow you've just completed.

Check for weighting from other influences

Each skin point has a total weight value of **1.0**, but that weight can be spread across many influences. If a group of skin points aren't behaving the way you want them to, it is possible that they are getting weights from different (and perhaps unwanted) influences.

To check or modify the assignments of weights of each skin point, pick a CV, then select **Window → General Editors → Component Editor**.

Component Editor			
List			
Weighted Deformers \ Joint Clusters \ SkinClusters \ Springs \ Particles \ Polygons \ AdvPolygons			
	back_e	back_neckJoin	back_root	back_shoulderJoin
hiresClothes_Mel				
cv [8] [4]	0.028	0.000	0.000	0.000
detachedSurfaceS				
cv [3] [3]	0.064	0.000	0.000	0.008
cv [4] [2]	0.031	0.000	0.000	0.006
cv [4] [3]	0.007	0.000	0.000	0.002

Adjusting weighting using the Component Editor

Adjust the Dropoff Rate

When you originally smooth bound the skin, you set the **Dropoff Rate** for each of the influences. The Dropoff Rate determines how much the weighting decreases as the distance between the influence and the skin point increases. Increasing the Dropoff Rate helps localize the weighting for the selected joint. To adjust the Dropoff Rate after skinning, select the *Transform* node of the desired joint, and adjust **Dropoff** in the **Smooth Skin** section of the Attribute Editor.

Adjusting the weighting Dropoff Rate

Adjust the Max Influences

You have an option to set the number of **Max Influences** on each surface that was bound. For Melvin, you set the **Max Influences** to **5**, which means that a total of five influences can participate in the weighting on a given skin point. This adds up to a lot of weighting and re-weighting since changing the weighting of one skin point has a "rippling" effect on the weights of the other skin points. As the number of max influences increases, so does this complexity of interdependent weighting.

In many cases, it is easier to lower the **Max Influences** of each surface than trying to track down which influence controls which skin point. Lower Max Influence settings will help to localize the control of the weighting. Note that a Max Influence setting of **1** causes the surface skinning to behave like a rigid skinned setup.

To change the Max Influence setting, pick the surface(s) to adjust and select **Skin** → **Edit Smooth Skin** → **Set Max Influences...**

Adjusting Max Influences

Equalize weighting between multiple surfaces

If the tangency between two patches is giving you problems, it is often easiest to set the same weighting value on the two surfaces to get a uniform weight across the seam, then smooth out the weighting between the two surfaces. This technique is helpful because all of the values are set to a uniform state before the smoothing process begins.

Toggle hold weighting values

There are times when you can feel like you are chasing your tail when weighting complex surfaces and influence objects. You can toggle on and off a hold flag for each influence object. This will hold or lock the value and prevent the act of weighting to change this setting.

When you add an influence object to a skinned object, it is a good idea to lock this influence object to a value of 0 when it is created. This will help prevent the new influence object from disrupting your existing weighting.

Flood values across surfaces

As you have seen, depending on the number of **Max Influences** set when the original **Smooth Bind** function is applied, there can be many joints affecting the same skin point. At times, it is easiest to select the surfaces and an influence and **Replace** all of those weighting values with a common value using the **Flood** button.

This is particularly useful for removing unwanted weighting applied to the root joint, or other joints that should not have any influence on the surface.

Prune small weights

After spending time weighting a character, you might notice that after smoothing a surface a few times, a small amount of weight might be added to many different influences. Generally, the amount of weight is very small and hard to detect but it does affect where weight is distributed when weights are adjusted on a particular influence. When you take weight away from a surface, the weight gets distributed to every surface that has an influence on it, even if it is only a small weight.This also might have a significant influence on speed, performance, and the size of the file.

Pruning weights is the process of removing weight from all of the influences below a specified threshold. To prune weights, select all of the surfaces that you would like to edit and select **Skin** → **Edit Smooth Skin** → **Prune Small Weights.** Enter the amount of weight that you would like to prune below:

Prune Weights options window

Summary

Smooth Skinning and Rigid Skinning are the two types of skinning available in Maya. Smooth Skinning allows for more control over the skinned surface using only joints as the driving objects. Rigid Skinning relies on other deforming structures to be layered on top such as flexors and lattices. Smooth Skinning uses an influence approach. Joints and other objects can be designated as influence objects that affect the skinned surface. The amount of influence and the portion of the surface to be influenced is determined through assigning a weighting relationship between the influence objects and the surface components. Maya Artisan painting is often the most efficient method of editing this relationship. Understanding the Maya Artisan Paint Weights Tool is critical to properly skinning and weighting your skinned surfaces.

9 Influence Objects

In this chapter, influence objects will be examined to aid the deformations of the smooth bound geometry. Their transforms can be used to manipulate the position of skin points to either smooth out deformations or to add effects to the skin. For this chapter, you are going to add influence objects to replicate an elbow, a bicep, and to correct deformations around the shoulder.

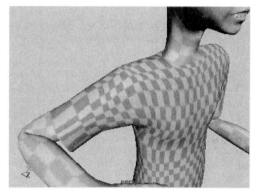

Lattice bound to the bones

In this chapter, you will learn the following:

- How to create influence objects;

- How to automate deformations with influence objects and SDK;

- How to weight influence objects and the surrounding skin to provide realistic deformations.

CHAPTER 9

INFLUENCE OBJECTS

Influence objects deform smooth bound skin by manipulating the transformations of the skin points. These objects can be animated to move as a muscle would deform, or they can be parented to a joint to act like a rigid bone. Influence objects can also be placed within the geometry to smooth out deformations and to maintain volume throughout the character.

Adding an elbow

The default smooth bind gives very good deformations in parts of the character. However, it doesn't do a good job with replicating bones such as knees and elbows. For this exercise, you are going to add an influence object to create an elbow for Melvin.

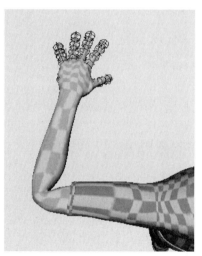

Default elbow bend without any influence objects

1 Open file

- Open the *Melvin_09_smoothed.mb.*

2 Return to Bind Pose

A skeleton must be at bind pose for the influence objects to work. If a character is not in the bind pose, Maya will not create the influence object.

- Select **Modify → Evaluate Nodes → Ignore All**.
- Select any one of Melvin's joints.
- Select **Skin → Go to Bind Pose**.

Tip:	If you made a Bind Pose button with the Record Pose script, it will be easier to use that instead of disabling the nodes and returning to bind pose through the menus.

3 Use a polygonal sphere as elbow influence object

For Melvin's elbow, you are going to create an underlying object that will be deformed with the rest of the arm. This elbow will be created from a polygonal sphere. You are going to use polygons instead of NURBS to make it easier to differentiate between skinned surfaces and influence objects.

- Select **Create** → **Polygon Primitives** → **Sphere**.

- Rename the sphere *elbow_Influence*.

4 Move the sphere into position

- **Translate** the *elbow_Influence* so it is in the same location as the *left_elbow* joint.

5 Deform the sphere so it resembles a bone

- **Scale** the *elbow_Influence* so it resembles the shape of a bone.

- You may need to tweak individual vertices to get the look you are after. Try to shape and position the object so it fits between the *left_elbow* joint and the back edge of the *left_arm* geometry.

Disabling Nodes

Whenever IK or joints are driven by constraints or expressions, the **Go To Bind Pose** button will not immediately work. To make it work, you can select **Modify** → **Disable All Nodes**. This toggles off the control of any nodes that may prevent you from reaching the *Bind Pose*. Don't forget to **Enable All Nodes** to animate with the controls you've created.

Elbow_Influence positioned and deformed

6 Select appropriate geometries and create influence

In order to create influence objects, you must select your objects in the proper order. The first selected object will be what is going to be influenced and the last selected object will be the influence object itself.

- Select the *leftArm* geometry.

- **Shift-select** *elbow_Influence*.
- Select **Skin** → **Edit Smooth Skin** → **Add Influence**.

7 Parent elbow influence to appropriate joint

You are going to parent the influence object to a joint so the influence object moves with the rest of the skeleton.

- Select *elbow_Influence* and **Shift-select** the *left_shoulder* joint in the Perspective window.

- Select **Edit** → **Parent**.

When you created the influence object, Maya created a **base** object and hid it from view. You will also parent this base object to the shoulder bone. The **base** object stores the component information of the influence object. Without the base object, you would not be able to manipulate the components of the influence object.

- Select *elbow_InfluenceBase* from the Outliner or the Hypergraph.

- **Shift-select** the *left_shoulder*.

- Select **Edit** → **Parent**.

8 Test the results

- Rotate the elbow to see the deformations around the elbow.

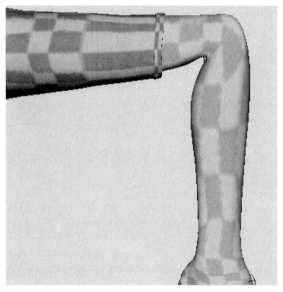

Improved elbow deformation after applying influence object

Note:	Don't worry if the influence object is sticking through your geometry. When you create an influence object, Maya automatically turns **Off** the **Primary Visibility** in the object's Render Stats. The influence object will not render unless you manually turn **On** the **Primary Visibility** in the Attribute Editor.

9 Save your work

- Select **File** → **Save Scene**.

Add a bicep muscle bulge

Melvin was bound with the Smooth Bind function and, although it creates good deformations around most of the body, it won't allow you to create flexors the way that a rigid bound skeleton will. To create the bulge in the bicep when Melvin bends his elbow, you are going to create an influence object and animate it with Set Driven Key.

Because there are many steps that are the same when you create influence objects, many of these steps will be familiar to you.

1 Open file

- Open *Melvin_09_elbowInfluence.mb.*

2 Return to Bind Pose

Just like when you added the elbow influence object, you need to be in bind pose to add an influence object.

- Select **Modify** → **Evaluate Nodes** → **Ignore All**.

- Select **Skin** → **Go to Bind Pose**.

3 Create polygonal sphere to act as an Influence

- Select **Create** → **Polygon Primitives** → **Sphere**.

- Rename the sphere *bicep_Influence*.

4 Position and deform the sphere

- **Translate** the *bicep_Influence* to where the bicep muscle would be on the arm. Make sure that it is close to the front of the *left_Arm* surface.

- **Scale** the sphere so it looks roughly like a bicep muscle. You might need to adjust some vertices in component mode.

- **Rotate** the sphere to help align it.

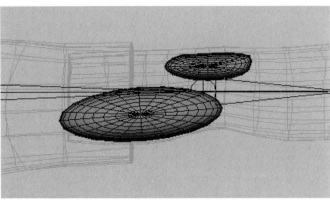

Bicep_Influence translated, rotated, and scaled into position

5 Select the surfaces and create Influence

For the deformation of the bicep to look correct, it should affect the arm surface and the shirt sleeve. *bicep_Influence* will be added to both surfaces, but to prevent *bicep_Influence* from affecting the weighting that was done to the shirt surface, it will be added later.

- Select the *left_Arm* geometry and **Shift-select** *bicep_Influence*.
- Select **Skin** → **Edit Smooth Skin** → **Add Influence** – ❑.
- **Reset** the window.
- Press **Add**.

Tip: If you have weighted Melvin and are happy with the results, you might want to add the influence object with **zero** weight. Adding the influence object with zero weight will not affect the weighting that you already did, but you will have to paint in weight before you see the influence object working.

---

6 Parent bicep_Influence to left_shoulder

You will now parent the influence object to a joint so it moves with the rest of the arm joints.

- Select *bicep_Influence*, then **Shift-select** *left_Shoulder* joint.
- Select **Edit** → **Parent**.

Also parent the influence object's **base** to the shoulder.

- Select *elbow_InfluenceBase* from the Outliner or the Hypergraph.
- **Shift-select** the *left_shoulder*.

■ Select **Edit** → **Parent**.

7 Rotate the elbow to test deformation

To check out the effect of the influence object, rotate the elbow joint. Most likely the effect is not obviously noticeable, but if you look in the area where the bicep meets the forearm, you should be able to see that the "spaghetti" elbow effect is now gone. You will now refine the effect by setting up a Set Driven Key relationship between the influence object and the rotation of the elbow joint.

The elbow joint

8 Straighten the elbow rotation

Because you are going to set up a **Set Driven Key** relationship, it is easiest to start with the elbow straightened out.

■ Select the *left_elbow* joint.

■ Select **Go to Bind Pose**.

9 Select the vertices

There is an attribute in each influence object's Channel Box that allows you to select between using the object's Transform node or its components as the driving force to create the deformations. You are going to be using its component information to get the desired deformations from the bicep.

■ Select the influence object.

■ Press **F8** to switch to component mode.

■ Select all of the vertices on the influence object.

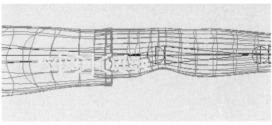

Selecting all the bicep vertices

10 Turn on Use Components

In the Channel Box of the influence object, a list of **Outputs** are connected to the influence object. Each one of those skinCluster outputs has an attribute called **Use Components** that needs to be switched to **On** for Maya to evaluate the influence's vertices rather than its transform.

- Select the *skinCluster* Output.

- Switch the **Use Components** attribute to **On**.

Channels Object	
bicep_InfluenceShape	
CVs (click to show)	
INPUTS	
polySphere2	
OUTPUTS	
skinCluster1	
Envelope	1
Use Components	on
Use Components	on
Normalize Weigh	on

Enabling Use Components in the Channel Box

11 Prepare Set Driven Key

- Select **Animate → Set Driven Key → Set – ❑**.

- Load the selected vertices as the **Driven**.

- Load the *left_elbow* as the **Driver**.

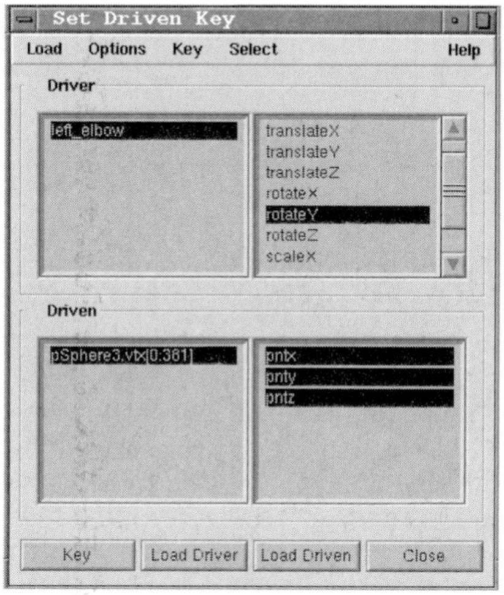

Set Driven Key window

12 Set a Driven Key for initial position

In order to set a driven key, you will need to set the desired attributes on the **Driver** and the **Driven**.

- Select the *left_elbow.rotateY* as the **Driver** attribute.
- Select the *vertex.pntx*, *vertex.pnty*, and *vertex.pntz* as the **Driven** attributes.
- Press **Key**.

Note: Depending on how you selected the vertices, you may see a list of every vertex on the influence object. If you see this, just select them all and then select all of the attributes on the right side of the window.

---

13 Rotate the elbow

The best way to see the deformations of the influence object is to rotate the elbow so it is bent.

- Rotate the *elbow* joint to about **-100** on **Y**.

14 Deform the influence object

- Scale the vertices until you see a bicep deformation that you are happy with. The arm surface should update each time you move a vertex.

Note: You may find it helpful while scaling the vertices to move their temporary pivot to the upper left corner of the sphere's bounding box, as seen from the top window.

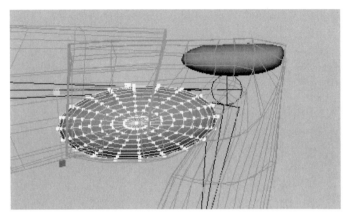

Rotating the elbow and positioning the bulge

15 Add a Set Driven Key for the rotated position

- Press **Key** in the **Set Driven Key** window to complete the relationship between the joint rotation and the influence object.

16 Test the results

Rotate the elbow and test the deformations of the bicep. The bicep should now grow as the elbow rotates.

17 Save your work

Add bicep_Influence to the shirt

You will now add *bicep_Influence* as an influence object to the shirt. You could have added *bicep_Influence* to the arm and shirt geometry at the same time, but since that addition was done at the default settings, it would have undone the weighting that was done to the shirt. You will now add *bicep_Influence* while locking the current weight values of the shirt.

1 Add bicep_Influence to the shirt

For the deformation to appear natural, the bicep_Influence should also affect the shirt surface.

- Select the *shirt* surface, then **Shift-select** *bicep_Influence*.

- Select **Skin** → **Edit Smooth Skin** → **Add Influence** – ❑.
- Toggle **Lock Weights** on and set the **Default Weight** to **0.0**.

  This will prevent the addition of the *bicep_Influence* from undoing all the weighting that has already been done for the arm and shirt. The influence for *bicep_Influence* will need to be painted afterwards.

- Press **Add**.

2 Rotate the elbow to test the deformation

- Rotate the elbow joint to **-100** on **Y**.

  Note that *bicep_Influence* is currently exerting no influence over the deformation of the shirt sleeve.

3 Turn on Use Components for bicep_Influence

- Select *bicep_Influence*.
- In the Channel Box, select the skinCluster output for the shirt.
- Turn on **Use Components**.

4 Display just the shirt and arm

- Select the arm and shirt geometry.
- Hide all unselected geometry.
- Deselect the arm geometry.

5 Add influence to bicep_Influence

- With the shirt surface selected, open the **Paint Skin Weights Tool** window.
- Toggle off **Hold Weights On Selected**.
- Set **Opacity** to **0.1**, the **Paint Operation** to **Add**, and **Value** to **1.0**.
- Paint the shirt sleeve to add influence to *bicep_Influence*.

Note: Make sure that Max Color in the Display section is set to 1.0.

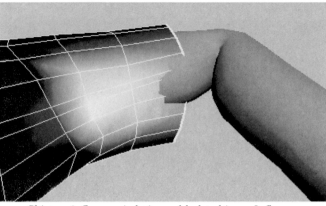

Shirt as influence is being added to bicep_Influence

6 Smooth weighting

- Once the shirt sleeve is no longer penetrating the bicep, start smoothing the weighting.

   Experiment with Flood smoothing and smoothing by brush strokes to see which one works best for you.

7 Rotate the elbow to test the deformation

- Rotate the elbow joint and make any adjustments necessary to refine the deformation of either the shirt or the arm geometry.

8 Save your work

Add an influence object for the shoulder

You probably could have just painted the weights of the shoulder to get the deformation that you wanted. However, adding influence objects to the shoulder will help maintain the volume in the shoulder area and is a quicker solution to getting good shoulder deformation.

1 Return to bind pose

- Select the *back_root* joint and select **Skin → Go to Bind Pose**.

2 Create an influence geometry for the shoulder

- Model a shoulder from a polygon sphere.

- **Rename** the sphere *left_Shoulder_Influence*.

- **Move** the *left_Shoulder_Influence* so it rests just where you want Melvin's shoulder to be.

- **Parent** the *left_Shoulder_Influence* to the *left_collarBone* joint.

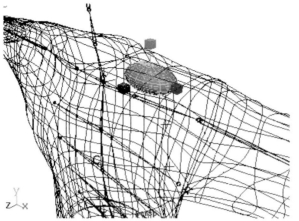

Positioning a modified sphere as a shoulder influence object

3 Create an influence object

- Select the shirt surface.

- **Shift-select** the *left_Shoulder_Influence*.

- Select **Skin** → **Edit Smooth Skin** → **Add Influence** – ❒.

- Make sure that Lock Weights is toggled on with a default value of **0.0**.

- Click the **Add** button.

4 Paint the weights

Just like you did for the *bicep_Influence*, *left_Shoulder_Influence's* weighting must be added to and smoothed for the shirt surface.

- **Rotate** *left_Shoulder* joint up to **-90** degrees on **Z**.

- Select the shirt surface.

- Hide all unselected objects.

- Open the **Paint Skin Weights Tool**.

- Select *left_Shoulder_Influence* as the influence to be painted on.

- Add and smooth the weighting of *leftShoulder_Influence*.

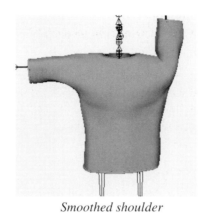

Smoothed shoulder

5 Test the results

Place Melvin in different poses to test the deformations around the shoulder. You might need to repaint the weights again if the shoulder does not deform properly in other positions.

6 Save your work

Mirror the influence

You could repeat everything that you have done for the other side of Melvin's body, but, fortunately, you don't have to do everything. The influence objects can be duplicated and the weighting of their influence can be mirrored from the left side of Melvin's body to the right.

1 Select the three influence objects

■ **Shift-select** all three of the influence objects.

Be careful not to select the arm or shirt surfaces.

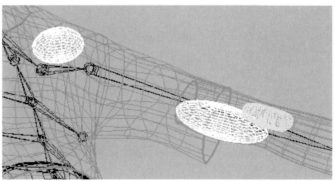

The three influence objects selected

2 Duplicate the influence objects

- Open the **Option** window for **Duplicate** and reset it.
- Set the **Group Under** option to **World**.

  This is necessary because the influence objects are currently parented to Melvin's skeleton. If they were duplicated at the default settings, then the duplicates would also be parented under the same joints as the originals.

- Click the **Duplicate** button.

3 Group the duplicates

- Group the three duplicates together.

4 Scale the duplicate's group node

The duplicates must now be transformed over to the other side of Melvin's body. Applying a **-1** scale to the group node will do this.

- Set the **Scale X** value for the new group node to **-1**.

5 Unparent the duplicates

- Select each of the duplicated objects.
- Select **Edit → Unparent**.

6 Rename the duplicated influence objects

- Rename each of the duplicates to reflect the fact that they are now on the right side of Melvin's body.

7 Assign the duplicates as influence objects with no weight

The three duplicated objects will now be assigned as influence objects to the shirt and arm. It's important that they be added with zero weighting so that they don't undo the weighting that's been done so far.

- Select the *shirt*, then **Shift-select** the *right_shoulder_Influence* object.
- Select **Skin → Edit Smooth Skin → Add Influence – ❐**.
- Toggle **Lock Weights** on and set the **Default Weight** to **0.0**.
- Click the **Add** button.
- Now assign the other objects as influence objects.

  Remember to assign *right_bicep_Influence* to the *shirt* and the *arm* surfaces.

8 **Parent the new influence objects and their bases to the skeleton**

- Parent *right_shoulder_Influence* and *right_shoulder_InfluenceBase* to the *right_collarBone* joint.

- Parent *right_bicep_Influence, right_elbow_Influence, right_bicep_InfluenceBase, right_bicep_InfluenceBase1,* and *right_elbow_Influence* to the *right_shoulder* joint.

9 **Unlock the weighting for the influence objects**

You are about to mirror the weighting from the left side of Melvin's body to the right side, but before you can do that, the new influence objects must have their weights freed so that they can receive the new weighting values.

- Select the *shirt* surface.

- Open the **Paint Skin Weights Tool** window.

- Toggle **Hold Weights On Selected** off for *right_shoulder_Influence* and *right_bicep_Influence.*

- Select the *arm* surface.

- Open the **Paint Skin Weights Tool** window.

- Toggle **Hold Weights On Selected** off for *right_elbow_Influence.*

  The weighting for *right_bicep_Influence* should already be toggled off.

10 **Mirror the shirt's weighting**

Now that the duplicates have been added as influence objects, and their influence weights have been freed, you will mirror the weighting from the left side of Melvin's body to the right side.

- Select the shirt surface.

- Select **Skin → Edit Smooth Skin → Mirror Skin Weights – □**.

- Make sure that **Mirror Across** is set to **YZ**, and that **Direction Positive to Negative** is toggled **On**.

- Click the **Apply** button.

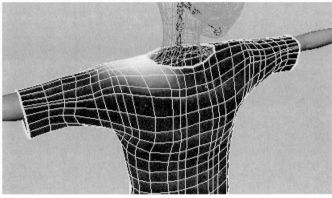

Shirt's weighting mirrored

11 Mirror the arm's weighting

You just mirrored the weighting from the left side of the shirt surface to the right side. Melvin's arms are a single piece of geometry, but since they are symmetrical, you can still mirror their weights.

- Select *left_arm*.

- **Shift-select** *right_arm*.

- Click the **Mirror** button in the **Mirror Skin Weights** window.

12 Test the weighting

The weighting on each side of Melvin's body should be the same. Pose Melvin's arms and shoulders to check the weighting. When you're done, return Melvin to the Bind Pose.

Note: You can also check the symmetry of the weighting by using the Paint Skin Weights Tool window, and comparing left and right side influence objects. If you find that some influence objects have failed to receive any weighting, simply perform the Mirror Skin Weights again.

---

13 Save your work

Summary

Influence objects can be joints or objects that are carried along with the joint hierarchy. Very interesting rigs can be established using influence objects that are being driven by joint rotation or other character movements. Influence objects can even be driven by dynamics as soft bodies or using the Jiggle Deformer to establish secondary or reactive movements under the skin. Influence objects can also be used to "correct" problem areas such as those encountered at the shoulders or hips.

10 Kick the Can

In this chapter, Melvin will walk up to a discarded tin can and kick it. This exercise makes use of several tools and techniques that are common to character animation such as walking, interaction with another object, anticipation, and follow through.

Footage of kicking the can

In this chapter, you will learn the following:

- How to use a motion study as a guideline for the animation;

- How to use Image Planes;

- Creating and editing clips using Trax;

- How to work with the Graph Editor;

- How to Playblast your animation.

Animation controls

You will begin by looking at how your character has been built up to this point. You have completed binding Melvin's skin and have several controls for animating him:

- Left and right arm controls (arm position using IK);
- Left and right hand controls (rotate hand and forearm, finger controls);
- Left and right foot controls (leg control position and foot manipulation);
- Global control (ascending/descending translation and rotation of Melvin);
- Local control (cycling/oscillating translation and rotation of Melvin);
- Spine controls (posing the upper section of the spine);
- Hip control (rotating the pelvis/lower spine);
- Pole Vector constraints for elbows.

Animation workflow and tools

With this chapter, you will experiment with several techniques. Try using the following suggestions that could be used when animating.

This is an outline of a suggested animation workflow that you can follow - or you can take this any direction you choose. Whichever workflow you use, there are several helpful animation tools and techniques that you might want to keep in mind.

Storyboarding

The storyboard is where you hope to find as many problem areas and special requirements as necessary. Here is where you note and plan for timing issues that may occur.

Motion study

Once you have completed the storyboard to assess the basic timing and actions of the character, you need to see how a person kicks a can.

"When in doubt, go to the motion study," has been said by many of the professionals at leading production companies. There is no substitute for learning character animation from real live examples. Included is a motion study of a person approaching, then kicking a can.

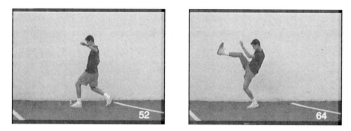

Motion study footage

IMAGE PLANES

You can use the digitized video as flipbooks and also bring them into
Maya as image planes. Fcheck serves as a great method for quickly
viewing the reference motion. While not as fast, image planes work really
well as a frame-by-frame placement guide.

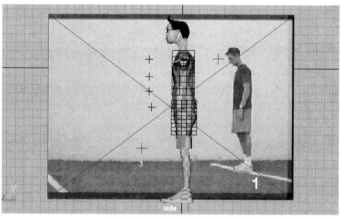

Image plane added to the side window

Because the motion tests are filmed from the side, you must set up the
image plane for the side camera. This is the basic workflow for getting the
image planes to work:

1 Open an existing file

- Open the file *Melvin_10_noImagePlane.mb.*

2 Add an image plane to the side camera

- Select side camera.

- In the Attribute Editor, click the **sideShape** tab.

The sideShape tab

- Under **Environment**, click **Create**. This will create an image plane.

The Environment folder

- Under the **Image Plane** attributes, click **Browse** to read in the digitized video sequence from the *motionTests* folder into **Image Name**.

Note: If the image has no alpha, you should change the **Display Mode** to **RGB**.

- Toggle **Use Frame Extension** on.
- Go to frame **1**.
- Make sure the **Frame Extension** value is set to **1**.
- Set a keyframe for the **Frame Extension** value by **RMB-clicking** on it, and selecting **Key Selected**.
- Go to frame **120**.
- Set the Frame Extension value to **120**.
- Set another key.

  The image plane will now display the sequence of images from **1** through **120** when you play the animation.

- Toggle **Fixed** for Image Plane. If you zoom or pan the side view, the image plane will still be the same size relative to your scene.

- Under **Placement Extras**, adjust the following:

  Width and **Height** to scale the image plane to the size of the current scene.

  Center XYZ to position the image plane.

Image plane attributes

BLOCKING

Before setting keys for the detailed motion, you'll block the shot. Blocking a shot consists of setting key poses every 5-10 frames to rough out the animation. Working with Character Sets is a good way to set general keyframes on all of the attributes in your Character Set.

For scenes where the motion is not repetitive, it is important to study the extreme positions the character gets into. For the kick, look for the back swing, the plant, and the follow through of the kick. These are the poses that really define the feel of the animation.

After blocking, you'll review this generalized motion asking the following questions:

- Does the motion and timing work in this scene?
- Is the motion too fast/slow?
- Is there continuity with other shots?

You don't want to worry about the details of the motion until you are comfortable with the generalized motion.

Main Keyframes

- Frame 10 - Just starts to move from passive position.
- Frame 35 - First step.
- Frame 52 - Plants feet for kick; notice arm position.
- Frame 56 - Contact with the can; note weight distribution.
- Frame 64 - Follow through; notice the extension.
- Frame 88 - Landing after the kick; hips rotate.

Note: This is only a guide of where the extreme poses could be. Take a look at the motion tests and setup a list of the poses you wish to block.

IN-BETWEENS AND BREAKDOWNS

Once you have finalized the blocked motion, it's time to start rounding out the motions. The in-between is responsible for creating the interpolations from one blocked key to the next. It shapes the motion away from the linear point to point motion you have established.

In-betweens can occur every 3 to 5 frames or as needed. When your character is moving really fast (during the kick), the in-betweens could occur on every frame. At this stage, you are not concerned with perfect motion. The resulting motion will look better than the blocked motion, but it will still need some fine-tuning. Study the video; you may be surprised where and when these keys occur.

Consider using Breakdown keys for your in-between keyframes. Breakdown keys are designed to be placed between blocked poses so they can later be moved in the timeline to maintain the relationship between the standard keyframes. Although adjusting overall timing may not be used as much if you are working straight from a motion test, it is still a good idea to get in the habit of using Breakdown keys. It will also be useful if you decide to change the timing of your animation later on.

Also, consider using sub-characters for your in-between poses so you don't key all of the attributes in the entire Character Set. A main Character Set can be created to block out the animation, while sub-characters can be used to key specific parts of the character. For example, each leg can be its own sub-character that controls all of the motion for that leg and foot.

Try to avoid keying all of the attributes on an object like you did when you blocked out the motion for the animation. In some places, you may still want to set a key on all the keyable attributes. However, in other more focused places, you will want to key only the selected locator or selected joint/cluster via the selection handle. Use the **RMB** in the Channel Box to key individual attributes by selecting **Key Selected** or **Breakdown Selected**. This will result in liner curves in the Graph Editor. The fewer keys you set in this phase, the easier it is to make major changes later.

After you have completed a cursory in-between, save this file as your rough in-between. If you need to make major changes to the animation, this is where you will most likely start.

After the in-betweens are finished you will go back through and address the rough edges and start working on the details that make the animation interesting.

Adding in-betweens

The motion study is the chief guide for adding in-betweens. Some of the main movements that may escape the casual observer have been pointed out. This is a largely self-guided exercise based on motion study and your creative interpretation. Decide for yourself whether to use standard keyframes or Breakdown keys.

Working with this character

For this chapter, the character has had some adjustments made to his setup.

- An extra control object for Melvin's neck joints has been added to the Character Set.

Many times when you are animating while closely following a motion test, you will want more control over the posing of your character.

Kick the can

1 Set a key at the bind pose

While this step is not strictly necessary, it is often convenient to have recorded a keyframe for the character you're working with in the bind pose. That way, you can always go back to your character's default position regardless of the pose you're currently in.

- Adjust the **Range Slider** to include frame **0**.
- Set the current time to frame **0**.
- Make sure that the Melvin Character Set is active.
- Set a keyframe of Melvin in his current pose (the bind pose).

2 Key the character in the rest position at frame 1

Confirm he is posed correctly on top of the image plane.

- Go to frame **1**.
- Pose Melvin to match the actor in the image plane.
- Set a **key** for the Character Set.

3 Create Melvin's first step

The character takes his initial step by first falling forward and then bringing his foot forward to catch himself. Determine the mid-stride position and keyframe that pose. Use the motion study to determine the frame. Work in the following sequence:

- Translate *globalControl* to move Melvin forward.
- Translate *localControl* to move Melvin up and down as he walks.
- Rotate *localControl* as necessary to help position Melvin.
- Move the feet.
- Move the hands.

- Adjust the neck.
- Set a key.

4 Key the next step

- Using the image plane as your guide, continue animating Melvin.
- Go through each major body position.
- Note twist and turning of upper and lower body.

5 Kick the can

The kick's main movement besides the leg motion is the rotation that takes place in the upper and lower body. The mechanics of the rotation and balance influence the arm swing which is also pronounced.

- Note how quickly the key poses occur during the kick.
- When leaning Melvin back during the kick, do not rotate the *globalControl* object, use the *localControl* instead.

6 Create a Playblast of the animation

- Position the Perspective camera in an advantageous position to see all the action.
- Select **Window → Playblast... – □**.

  View the playback, scrub through, and note areas that need work.

Playblast

Window → Playblast... is a way to evaluate your animation quickly. It is a very fast screen grab of your animation. It will capture the animation as it is currently displayed, so you can see it in wire mode or shaded mode (which may take a little longer to calculate). The purpose of this tool is to get realtime playback by using a compressed file.

At each stage of creating the animation, you should use Maya's Playblast function to create motion tests to evaluate your animation in real time.

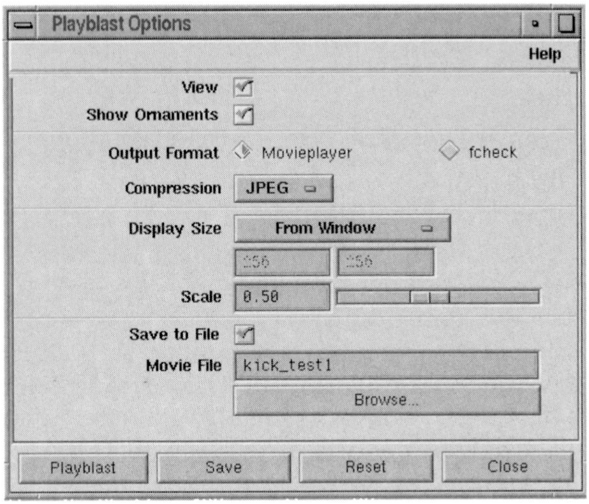

Playblast Option window

FINE-TUNING THE MOTION

Once you are comfortable with the in-betweens, you can start to finetune the motion. This is the stage that never ends. This is where you can find yourself tweaking and adding keys on every frame. You want to avoid doing that as much as possible. Here are some things to keep in mind that will hopefully keep you on target.

Work on major keys and in-betweens first, then secondary and tertiary keys next, working in layers of refinement.

Get your main keyframes looking as good as possible first, then break down into the next layer of in-betweens. Once this layer looks good, go to the next layer. You will find you have intimate knowledge of these milestone keys instead of having keys scattered all over the timeline.

Adjust the animation curves in the Graph Editor

In the Graph Editor, you can get a lot of mileage out of a key by working with the tangency or method of interpolation. Keeping keys on whole frames makes for much cleaner curve management and editing.

Remove superfluous keys

Remove keys that don't seem to be contributing or were made ineffective. This is best done in the Graph Editor where you can see the direct result on the curve by removing the key. If you make a mistake, simply undo the removal.

Test to Playblast

Test in the Work Area and in Playblast. It is often a good idea to take a break while you build a movie. Come back to the computer a little fresher to view the movie and plan the changes you will make.

Add subtle motions to major and minor joints and control points

You will often find that after the basic in-betweens are completed, it is time to look at parts of the character you have not keyed at all. The hands and head are very important, as are the shoulders and hip joints that will contribute to the motion of the attached joints. Rotations and translations in all dimensions are what make the subtleties of realistic movement.

Offset the motion of joints to achieve secondary motion

Offsetting is the act of delaying a joint's motion in relation to the surrounding joints. This is often seen as a breaking movement. When an arm, for example, moves toward an object that it wants to pick up, it does not move in unison at once toward its target. Rather, it will break at the main joint (elbow) first, then at the wrist, then the fingers.

Consider another example - the hand. When you make a fist, all of your fingers do not close at once. Some fingers may begin to close ahead of others while some may start late but finish first. These subtle movements and accelerations are at the heart of realistic motion.

Create a Trax Clip of your kick

After you have created your motion, you may find that alternate versions are required and/or alternate timings are being asked for. Trax is the method to use for editing your curves for duration and timing as well as blending into and out of alternate performances.

1 Create a bindPose pose

At frame 0, the character is posed in the bind pose. You may want to create a pose from this keyed position for later recall.

Make sure Melvin is the **Current Character**.

- Adjust the **Range Slider** to include frame **0**.
- Set the current time to frame **0**.
- Select **Create** → **Pose** – ❐ from the Trax Editor and name the pose *bindPose* in the Option window.
- Select **Create Pose**.
- Reset the **Range Slider** to a range of **1** to **120** frames.

The pose information is now saved in the Visor under the Poses folder.

2 Create a clip of your kicking performance

Select your Trax panel layout to aid in organizing your workflow.

- In the Trax Editor, select **Create** → **Clip** – □ and reset to the default settings with the **Use Time Slider Range** option.
- Select **Create Clip**.

Note: A clip is created and placed in the Trax Editor. This clip is an instance of the main source clip.

---

3 Import the alternate performance clip *melvinFlop.ma*

Another clip has been created for you that includes an alternate ending to the kick.

- Select **File** → **Import Clip...** from the Trax Editor menu.
- Select *melvinFlop.ma* in the *Clips* directory.
- Press **Import Clip**.
- In the **Visor** tab for **Unused Clips,** select and **MMB-drag** the imported *melvinFlop* clip to the *Melvin* character track.
- **RMB** and deselect the **Enable box** to temporarily disable the *melvinFlop* clips while you prepare the kick clip.

4 Split the kicking performance into two parts

The imported clip also includes the walk up to the can. You will trim the end of the kicking performance and the beginning of the falling performance by first splitting the clips into two pieces.

- Play up to the point where Melvin has reached the extreme pose of his kick, frame **65**.
- Select the *melvinKick* clip, **RMB-select Split Clip**.

  This will cut the clip into two clips at the current time.

- Select the new clip named *melvinKickEnd* that begins at frame **65** and ends at frame **120**. **RMB** and deselect **Enable** to **disable** this clip.

5 Split the melvinFlop clip into two parts

Now align and split the alternate performance clips.

- In the Trax timeline, **LMB-drag** the *melvinFlop* clips to a position in alignment with the *melvinKick* clips starting at frame **1**. The track will expand to provide room for the overlapping clips.

- With the current time at frame **65**, select and **Split** the melvinFlop clip.

- **Disable** the start clip using the previously discussed technique.

Playback the animation so that the character kicks the can and falls down.

6 Blend between the two clips

Now that the animation has been converted to clips, the timing and movement can be easily manipulated.

- **Shift-select** *melvinKickStart* and *melvinFlopEnd* clips.

- Select **Create → Blend – ❑**.

- Select **Ease-In-Out** as the interpolation type.

This will create a blend between the two clips. You can now move the clips apart or with an overlap and the blend will smooth out the motion.

7 Experiment with timing and duration of the motion

By pushing the end clip forward in time you can create an overlapping blend that will expedite the kick, slip, and fall.

Delaying the end clip so there is a gap between the clips will create a hesitation in the kick and fall. The blend holds it together so there is not a stop in the motion.

Scale the clips to change timing and duration.

OPTIMIZATION

There are several options that can optimize feedback when setting up the animation of a character.

Display optimization

Geometry can be viewed at many levels of accuracy. By selecting the geometry and then pressing **1**, **2**, or **3** on the keyboard, you can select between coarse, medium, and fine display accuracy. This will not affect how the geometry is rendered, only how it will display. There are several options under the Display menu that affect the performance of Maya's display.

NURBS smoothness

Under the **Display** menu you will find a sub-menu for **NURBS Smoothness**. These options control how NURBS surfaces are displayed.

- **Display** → **NURBS Smoothness** → **Hull** displays the selected geometry in the crudest form. From the option box you can adjust the coarseness of the hull display. By default, this display type is not mapped to a keyboard key but **Ctrl+1** is as good as any if you are setting your own hot keys.

- **Display** → **NURBS Smoothness** → **Rough, Medium, and Fine** are as you would expect and are selected by pressing the **1**, **2** or **3** keys on the keyboard. The option box for each of these allows you to decide whether you want this mode to affect the selected object or all objects.

- **Display** → **NURBS Smoothness** → **Custom** is a user defined setting for display smoothness. There are many customizable settings in the options box allowing for almost infinite combinations to suit your needs.

Fast interaction

Display → **Fast Interaction** enables the user to interact with the scene more quickly by temporarily changing the resolution of the geometry while the scene is being manipulated, then switching back to the higher resolution after the scene has settled. This setting will also improve playback of animation in the timeline, but be prepared for some degraded looking geometry.

Animation preferences

In **Window** → **Settings/Preferences** → **Preferences**, the **Timeline** section has a few settings that will influence the way Maya playsback your animation. In the **Playback** section you have options to change:

Update View

Update the Active panel or All panels

Looping

Determines the Looping method

Playback Speed

Free – Maya will play every frame regardless of frame rate settings

Normal – This setting forces Maya to playback at the frame rate that is set in the **Options** → **General Preferences Units** section. Video frame rate is 30fps and 24fps is for film.

Half /Twice – Maya plays back at half or twice the specified frame rate.

Other – Maya will playback at a user defined percentage of the specified frame rate.

In the **Settings** section you have options to change:

Time - Maya can playback at a wide range of frame rates.

Performance options

None – Changes made in the Animation Editors are not reflected in the scene until the Transport Controls are used or the Current Time indicator is moved.

Delayed – Changes made in the Animation Editors are not reflected in the scene until the mouse action is completed by releasing the button.

Interactive – This is the default setting. Scenes update as changes are made to the keys and curves in the editors.

Summary

In this section, the character has been put through some more testing. Now that the character is skinned, it is important to make sure that the skinned surfaces are performing correctly and that the rig is animatible. Understanding the animation process and Maya's animation toolset for animating includes the use of in-betweens and Breakdown keys. The animation process usually will involve a blocking process and then cycles of refinement until the performance is as good as the schedule permits.

Your character has also been created with a Character Set to aid in organizing the attributes of the character. A typical fully articulated character can contain hundreds of attributes that will need to be keyed. Trax is a great tool for working with this level of complexity and being able to mix and match and edit character performances in a non-linear and non-destructive manner. Optimization is also important for maintaining a character that is animatible. Work to keep the character light so the animator is not waiting for the character to move. Realtime performance is always what the character rigger is striving for and what the animator will demand.

Chapter 10
Summary

11 **Rigid Skinning**

In this chapter, you will explore Rigid Skinning techniques. While Smooth Skinning binds CV's or deformer components to multiple joints and influence objects, Rigid Skinning binds these components to only one joint. The components are then weighted to provide smooth interaction. The use of flexors and other layers of deformers then work to control the skin deformation. You will use a number of techniques in combination for skinning Melvin's skin to the skeleton.

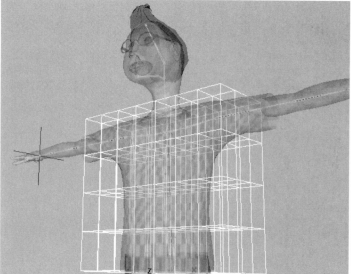

Lattice bound to the bones

In this chapter, you will learn the following:

- Skinning surfaces to bones;

- Binding surfaces through lattices to the bones;

- Combining direct and indirect skinning;

- Creating partitions and skin set organization.

Before skinning Melvin, you will experiment on some practice joints. You will run through some short examples in binding skin geometry to joints in preparation for Melvin.

In this chapter, you will look at Bind Skin and lattices. Lattices offer a great way to get smooth, generalized skinning around areas that can be more tedious if skinned directly, such as the shoulders or the area where the legs meet.

BIND SKIN

Bind Skin is probably the most common technique of binding geometry to skeletal joints. With Bind Skin, the geometry is divided into clusters based on proximity to the nearest joint. As the joints in the skeleton move, the clusters are in turn transformed.

A cluster can be thought of as a "smart" set. The vertices of the surface are put into a set where they can be weighted, or receive percentage effects from the cluster node. Unlike a set, a cluster is also pickable in the modeling windows. Weighting and membership will be discussed in the following chapter.

Bind Skin example

1 Create a cylinder to act as a skin

- Select **Create** → **NURBS Primitives** → **Cylinder**.
- **Scale** and **Rotate** the cylinder to a horizontal position.
- In the Channel Box, set the **Spans** and **Sections** to **8**.

2 Draw skeleton joints

- Select **Skeleton** → **Joint Tool** and create **3** joints to form an arm with an elbow.

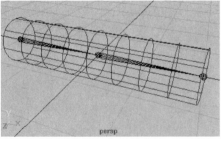

Cylinder and joints

3 **Bind the cylinder to the joints**

- Select the skeleton, then **Shift-select** the geometry.

- Select **Skin → Bind Skin → Rigid Bind**.

4 **Test the movement by rotating the middle joint**

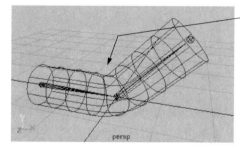

Pay attention to how the elbow bends and folds

The Bind Pose

Once a skin is bound to a skeleton, Maya remembers the pose that the character was in when it was bound. This is useful when you are testing poses and want to return to the starting pose. To get back to the Bind Pose, select the skeleton then select **Skin → Go To Bind Pose**.

The Bind Pose is only stored for a joint if a cluster is created for it, so it is good practice to bind the entire character at one time.

Detaching skin

If you have bound skin that you no longer want bound, you can detach the skin. Do this by selecting the geometry to detach, the skeleton, and **Skin → Detach Skin**.

BIND SKIN WITH A LATTICE

A lattice is another type of deformer that works in a more general manner. A lattice is a bounding box with points that will deform the geometry sitting inside the lattice. The benefit of using a lattice is that you are dealing with a lesser number of control points.

Binding a lattice example

In this exercise, you'll take the method from above a step further. For this technique, you'll create a lattice deformer for the cylinder and bind the lattice to the skeleton.

1 **Create a cylinder to act as a skin**

- Select **Create → NURBS Primitives → Cylinder**.

Disabling Nodes

Whenever IK or joints are driven by constraints or expressions, the **Go To Bind Pose** button will not immediately work. To make it work, you can select **Modify → Disable Nodes → IKSolvers, Constraints**. Toggle off the control of any nodes that may prevent you from reaching the *Bind Pose*. Don't forget to **Enable All Nodes** to animate with the controls you've created.

- **Scale** and **Rotate** the cylinder to a horizontal position.
- In the Channel Box, set the **Spans** and **Sections** to **8**.

2 Apply a lattice to the cylinder skin

- Select the cylinder.
- Select **Deform** → **Create Lattice** – ❐ and set the following:

   STU divisions for the lattice to **8**, **2**, and **2**.

Note: Translating any of the lattice points in component mode deforms the cylinder.

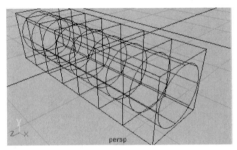

Lattice on cylinder

3 Create 3 arm joints inside the cylinder

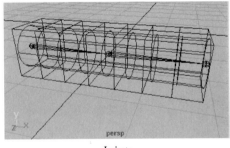

Joints

4 Bind the lattice to the joints

Make sure that the geometry is not selecting when binding the lattice to the joints.

5 Test the movement by rotating the elbow joint

In shaded mode, compare the elbow bend of the basic Bind Skin with that of the lattice skin that you just created.

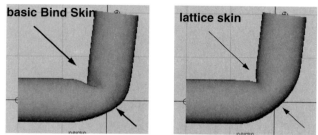

Binding options compared

You will see that the skeleton deforms the lattice which deforms the cylinder. This technique produces a more generalized skinning than the basic Bind Skin which should provide smoother deformations. You'll be using this technique to get a smoother skinning deformation for Melvin's shoulders and where his legs meet.

SETS

A set is a collection of objects or components. For example, a set might include geometric objects, NURBS, CV's, polygonal vertices, lattice points, polygonal facets, or other items. Any item you can select can be in a set.

Maya uses sets for all sorts of functions. You'll use them to divide and organize Melvin's various parts (skin, skeleton, lattice, etc.) to make the skinning process easier. Organizing the components into sets for selection is an important method for efficient workflow.

Partitions

You can also use set organization to aid in controlling group membership. By putting your sets into a *partition*, you can ensure that the member components are *exclusive* to each set. That is, you remove the possibility for overlapping membership between surface points, CV's, lattice points, or whatever component you are working with. This is especially important when skinning. For example, we will divide up Melvin's shirt components for Rigid Skinning with direct (bound to joints) and indirect (bound to lattices which are bound to joints) binding.

- **left sleeve** - shirt sleeve bound to skeleton (direct)

- **right sleeve** - shirt sleeve bound to skeleton (direct)

- **shirt_lattice** - shirt deformed by lattice and lattice bound to skeleton (indirect)

Partitions
An example of partitions at work are the layers you use in Maya. Layers are sets that belong to the layer partition. Geometry can only be on one layer. The partition keeps the sets organized so that the geometry is not on more than one layer.

By using partitions, you can ensure that you do not bind parts of the shirt that are in two of these sets at the same time. This would result in double transformation where a CV or object component gets moved twice, once by the joint, and once by the lattice.

Note: Dual or multiple membership of geometric components will result in double transformations following Bind Skin.

This dual membership can be corrected after the Bind Skin operation, but is much easier if everything is organized beforehand. By creating a partition, then creating sets of skinning groups within the partition, you will maintain exclusivity of geometric and deformer components.

SKINNING MELVIN

The workflow for skinning Melvin's shirt and shorts consists of combining skinning methods. Below are the key steps to complete this task:

1. Create sets for the selected components
2. Create the lattices for the shirt
3. Import the wrap for the shorts
4. Create the lattice point sets
5. Create a skeleton set
6. Select the sets
7. Bind Skin

Quick Sets

Quick Sets differ from sets in that they are used to quickly organize a group of objects into a selection group. The **Edit → Sets → Make Quick Select Sets** function does *not* create sets under a partition and thus, they are *not* exclusive.

Creating a skinSets partition

You need a partition to place your skin sets in. Again, this helps you avoid overlapping Set Membership and aids with selection.

Tip: Sets can have overlapping membership but sets in a partition will not have overlapping membership.

---

1 Open an existing file

- Open the scene file *Melvin_08_handControls.mb*.

2 Create a partition called skinSets

- Select **Create → Sets → Create Partition – ❏**.
- Enter *skinSets* in the **Name** text field and click **Apply and Close**.

3 From the Relationships Editor, display the Partition Editing section

- Select **Window** → **Relationship Editors** → **Partitions...**

  The *skinSets* partition should be listed in the Partition Editor. If you select the folder for "skinSets" there should be no sets or objects highlighted in the right-hand side.

Adding geometry to sets

For both Melvin's upper torso (his shirt) and his pelvis region (his shorts), you will create deformers to act as indirect objects for binding skin. Before you do this, you'll create sets of the geometry points that the lattice will deform. This is an important step for working with objects that will be bound with lattice or wrap deformers and straight Bind Skin. By organizing Melvin's geometry into exclusive sets before skinning, you'll save time by eliminating the need to edit the membership after skinning. You could potentially skin up Melvin and avoid double membership, but this can be very tedious and sometimes won't be completely accurate.

To skin the lattice for the torso and the geometry outside the torso, you would need to select:

- The lattice

- The shirt sleeve CV's that are not affected by the lattice

After going through this workflow a few times, you'll appreciate the fact that partitions help with exclusivity and thereby avoid dual membership.

Dividing geometry into sets

You will create sets for the shirt, head, arms, legs, and shorts. The shirt will be divided into two sets:

- *shirtBodySet;*
- *shirtSleevesSKINSet;*

and the rest of Melvin's sets:

- *shortsWrapSKINSet;*
- *shirtLatticeSKINSet;*
- *legsArmsSKINSet;*
- *neckSet;*
- *headSKINSet;*
- *skeletonSKINSet.*

Tip: Notice that some of the names end with *"SKIN."* These will be the sets
that you will bind to Melvin's skeleton. The other sets will be deformed by
a lattice and you don't want to bind those CV's. Rather it's the lattice that
is deforming them that you want to bind.This naming technique makes
the selection in the Set Editor much easier.

Because the sets will contain specific vertices in surfaces such as the shirt,
you need to divide the geometry into parts based on those vertices. For this
process you will work and select in Component mode. Following is a
diagram displaying the breakdown of the sets you will be creating.

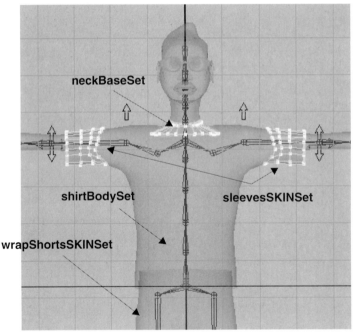

Shirt and shorts

1 Select vertices for the set

- Set the component mode Pick Mask options to **Select** only **Poly
  Vertices**.
- Select the vertices of both shirt sleeves.

Tip: Avoid having vertices of one contiguous edge in two sets. When deciding where to cut off the membership for the shirt sleeves, select a few edges down from the shoulder so you have about 3-4 rings of vertices going up from the end of each sleeve.

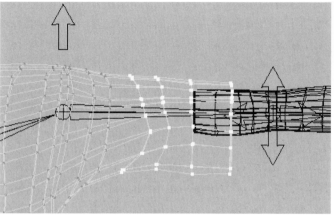

Selected vertices for left sleeve

2 Create a set for the shirt sleeves

- Select **Create → Sets → Set – ❏** and enter *shirtSleevesSKINSet* in the **Name** text field.

- In the **Add to a Partition** section, toggle on **Only if Exclusive**.

  Notice the Partition pull-down menu is now highlighted.

- From the **Partition** pull-down menu, select the **skinSets** partition.

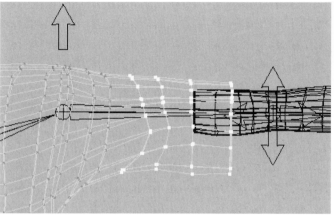

Create Set Options

- Press **Apply and Close**.

You have now added this portion of the shirt geometry to the skinSets partition. You can easily select these CV's by selecting the set in the Set Editor and **Edit → Select Set Members** from the Relationships Editor **Edit** menu.

As you add more sets to this partition (with **Only if Exclusive**), Maya will warn you if you try to add a set with overlapping components.

Tip: If you use **By Making Exclusive**, Maya will sort out the Set Membership for you. If another set in that partition contains any overlapping members, they will be pulled out of their set and forced into the new one.

---

3 Create a shirtBodySet and add it to the skinSets partition

With the sleeve's vertices selected, you can quickly select the body CV's by holding down the **Shift** key and marquee **LMB-dragging** across the shirt, toggle selecting the shirt body CV's.

- **LMB-Shift-Drag** select the shirt to toggle select the body vertices.

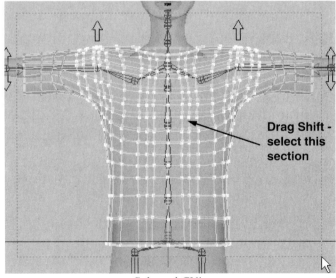

Drag Shift - select this section

Selected CV's

Select Modes

Shift-select toggles your selection.

Ctrl-select removes from the selection.

Shift-Ctrl-select adds to the selection.

Use these different selection modes whenever possible to improve your workflow.

- Select **Create → Sets → Set** – ❏ and enter *shirtBodySet* in the **Name** field.
- Add the set to the skinSets partition.
- Click **Apply and Close**.

4 Save your work

Tip: To remove a set, select the set in the Relationships Editor and select **Edit → Delete Highlighted** from the Set Editing Edit menu. Or, with **show sets** selected in the Outliner you can select and backspace delete sets.

Creating arm and leg sets

1 Create sets for the arms and legs

- Repeat the above steps to create the armsLegsSKINSet.

  Use the Outliner to select both arms and both legs. You aren't picking individual CV's here - pick the objects themselves.

Creating head and neck sets

For this chapter, you'll divide Melvin's head into two sets.

- **neckBaseSet** - base of Melvin's neck (for the shirt lattice)

- **headSKINSet** - Melvin's head (which will get the basic Bind Skin)

1 Create a set for Melvin's neck

- Make the MelvinNonDeform layer invisible

- Create a set for the base of Melvin's neck, called *neckBaseSet*, which includes the two rows of vertices at the base of the neck.

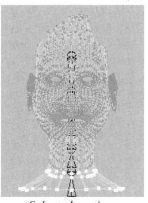

Selected vertices

- Add *neckBaseSet* to the *skinSets* partition.

- Create a set for the rest of the head, including the ears. The eyeballs, lids, teeth, and glasses will be parented and do not need to be skinned. Name the new set *headSKINSet* and put it into the *skinSets* partition.

    Shift-drag-select the head with the *neckBaseSet* CV's selected to toggle your selection.

Selected vertices

Creating skeleton sets

In the same way that you created sets for the geometry, you'll create a set for the skeleton. You don't have to create this set, but this will aid in the selection of all the objects that will go into the Bind Skin operation.

You can go through and select all the necessary sets in one place - the Set Editor. Selecting the objects in the work area can get quite messy and can require multiple attempts with a greater chance of error.

1 Create a set for the skeleton

- Select the *back_root* joint.

- Create a new set called *jointsSKINSet* and add it to the *skinSets* partition.

- Open the Set Editor and verify that the following list of sets appear in the *skinSets* partition.

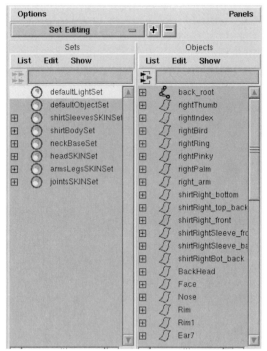

Relationships Set Editor

Skinning with lattices and wraps

The indirect skinning methods provide a generalized skinning that allows for smoother deformation when the joint is moved. Using lattices to Bind Skin is a useful technique for areas that are difficult to skin, such as the shoulders. Here the lattices will create a smoother deformation when the shoulder rotates and is easier to weight and control with Set Driven Key due to the fewer control points.

Creating the upper torso lattice

You'll set up a lattice around the mid-section of Melvin's upper torso. This lattice will be bound to the skeleton underneath. Because you've already created skin sets, you can easily select the CV's where you'll apply the lattice by selecting the sets in the Set Editor.

1 Select the shirtBodySet and neckBaseSets

- Select **Window → Relationship Editors → Sets...**

- Select the *shirtBodySet* and *neckBaseSet* sets.

- In the Set Editor **Edit** menu, select **Select Set Members**.

2 **Create a Lattice for the body and the neck**

- Select **Deform** → **Create Lattice** – ❑.

- Click **Reset** to return to the default values, then enter the following:

  Enter **8**, **5**, and **4** for the **S**, **T**, and **U resolution**;

  Select **Center Around Selection**;

  Select **Group Base and Lattice together**.

- Click **Create**.

- Label the lattice *shirt_lattice*.

Tip: The higher the resolution of this lattice, the smoother the resulting deformation, but it will also take longer to compute and assign weight.

Shirt lattice

Creating the shorts wrap

Now you will set up a wrap deformer for Melvin's shorts. The goal is to have more general control over the shorts' patches. This makes weighting and other tasks simpler.

1 **Create a wrap deformer for the shorts group of surfaces**

- Select **File** → **Import** and select *Melvin_wrapShorts.mb*.

  This is the low resolution "stand-in" object that you will apply the wrap deformer to.

- **Ctrl-select** the *shorts* geometry group and the *wrapShorts* objects from the Outliner.

- Select **Deform** → **Create Wrap**.

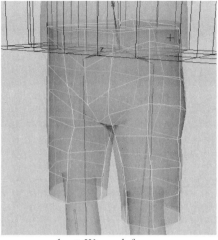

shortsWrap deformer

2 Create a set for the lattice and wrap objects

- **Ctrl-select** the *shirt_lattice* object and the *wrapShorts* object from the Outliner. Make sure the base objects are not selected.

- Select **Create** → **Sets** → **Set** → ❐, and name the set *latticeWrapSKINSet* and add this to the skinSets partition.

Binding lattices and skin to joints

Now you'll bind the lattice and wrap objects to your skeleton along with the other geometry that has been grouped into the sets of the skinSet partition. After you've built the sets using the partition's exclusivity properties, it is easier to select the component groupings—especially when they belong to the same object, like the shirt. This exclusivity goes a long way in ensuring that surface points and lattice components do not inadvertently end up in more than one joint cluster which can lead to double transformations when you move your character.

1 Binding "SKIN" sets to the skeleton

Now you'll select all the sets with "*SKIN*" in the name to Bind Skin.

- In the Relationships Editor, Set Editing section, select all the sets to Bind Skin. Assuming everything was named correctly, this will be any set that has "*SKIN*" in its name.

  Be sure that none of the geometry deformed by the lattices or the wrap is selected! These are already being transformed by the lattices.

- In the Edit menu for the Set Editor, choose **Select Set Members** to select the objects and components contained within the sets.
- Select **Skin** → **Bind Skin** → **Rigid Bind** – ❐, and set the following:

  Bind to **Complete Skeleton**;

  Color Joints to **On**;

  Bind Method to **Closest Point**.
- Press **Bind**.

Note: The **Closest Joint** option binds the skin to the closest point. The **Color Joints** option applies the same colors to the joints that are used to distinguish the membership of the skin that belongs to that joint.

---

2 Test the results

Test the results of this Bind Skin by moving the *back_root* joint and translating the wrist and ankle locators. Pay attention to the deformations around the shoulders and legs.

3 Save your work

Summary

Rigid Skinning was the original type of skinning included in the earliest versions of Maya. Although Smooth Skinning offers many advantages to Rigid Skinning; Rigid Skinning is still an important deformation tool. Rigid Skinning has much faster performance and is still the preferred method for many situations. Indirect skinning using lattices and wrap deformers can create very flexible characters. Rigid Skinning a complex character will also benefit from having an organized approach that includes the use of sets and partitions. Maya's use of exclusive sets in a partitioned rationale can help prevent skinning problems such as Double Transformation of surface components. In complex Rigid Skinning setups that make use of indirect skinning methods, the chances for skinning problems is great. These are virtually eliminated when you organize your character's skins into partitioned sets.

12 Set Membership

You've now bound all of Melvin's skin (lattices and geometry) to his skeleton. You will now look at making the deformations look better by weighting CV's and editing Set Membership.

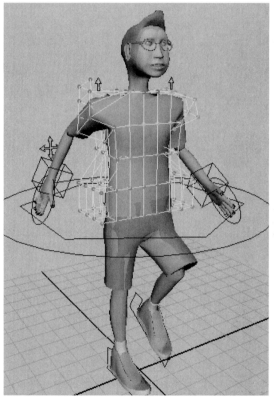

Testing membership

In this chapter, you will learn the following:

- How to weight CV's;
- How to edit Set Membership.

CV WEIGHTING

As mentioned earlier, CV's can be weighted in clusters to get differing amounts of deformation.

Adjust cluster weights on a cylinder example

1 Create a cylinder

- Select **Create** → **NURBS Primitives** → **Cylinder**.

2 Make the cylinder into a cluster

- With the cylinder selected, select **Deform** → **Create Cluster**.

3 Weight the CV's in the Component Editor

- Select **Window** → **General Editors** → **Component Editor...**

- Switch to component mode.

- Select the bottom row of CV's.

- In the Component Editor, switch to the **Weighted Deformers** tab, then press **Load Components** to display the CV weights.

- Change their weight to **0**.

- Replace the selection with the next row of CV's above and press **Load Components** again.

- Set their weight to **0.33**.

- Select the next row above and set their weight to **0.66**.

- Select the top row of CV's and make sure that their weight is at a value of **1**.

4 Test the new weights by rotating the cluster in X, Y, or Z

5 Test the new weights by scaling the cluster in X or Z

This shows how CV weights in a cluster can vary the deformation and create bending, twisting, and/or tapering effects.

Tip: Delete construction history to make the deformation permanent. This can be a good modeling technique.

EDITING SET MEMBERSHIP

Once you've bound the skin and lattices, you need to check the CV membership to ensure that each CV is only in one set and that each is in the appropriate set. As soon as you start to translate/rotate the joints, you will notice if any CV's are in the incorrect set.

Tips for editing Set Membership

- Watch for CV's that end up in more than one set. This results in double transforms. Using partitions can help to avoid this.

- It is better to add CV's to the desired joint rather than removing them from the undesired joint. When you add them to a new joint, they are automatically removed from the original owner.

- Exaggerate the translation/rotation of the joint/bone when testing Set Membership. CV's with incorrect membership will become quite obvious.

- **Move** the root of the skeleton to check for correct membership.

- Take notes! Do a quick sketch of your character and take notes as to how you are dividing up the membership.

Editing Set Membership for the shirt lattice

You will be dividing Melvin's shirt lattice horizontally into slices which correspond directly with the back joints. There are some areas under the armpits that may need to be grouped with the upper arm joints instead of the back. The armpit area will likely require experimentation with grouping and weighting, and may possibly require some specialized bone structure to drive the motion of the shirt sleeves when Melvin drops his arms.

The following diagram shows Melvin's skeleton and shirt lattice. The lattice is the black grid.The dashed lines indicate how the membership should be edited. Note that the breakdown of memberships will differ from character to character. The regions are numbered to give you an idea of how the breakdown works:

> A - shoulder joints
>
> B - collar bone joints
>
> C - neck joint
>
> D - shoulder join joint
>
> E - back joints

Use the diagram only as a general guideline for editing which lattice points belong to which joint.

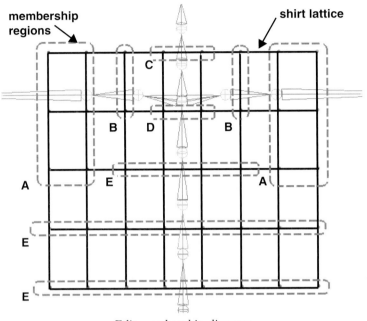

Edit membership diagram

1 Open a file

Open the file named *Melvin_11_rigidSkinned.mb*.

2 Edit the membership for the shirt lattice

- Select **Deform** → **Edit Membership Tool**.

  Notice that your cursor changes to a triangular shape to signify that you are now in a new pick mode. In the default pick mode, you can only select joints. When you select a joint, the CV's deformed by that joint will highlight. This is where you might see some obvious membership problems.

  Once you have selected a joint, you can **Shift-select** to *add* new CV's to the current set or **Ctrl-select** to *remove* CV's from the set.

- Select the joint where you want to edit the membership.

- **Shift-select** the CV's or lattice points you want to add to the current joint.

- Repeat for the other joints, continuing through the entire skeleton.

You may find that when the hands are at the side, the shoulders are not rounded but have sharp corners. Try editing the membership of some of the lattice points between the shoulder and the collar joint. It also may require the skin to be rebound after increasing the resolution of the lattice.

Tip: The joint colors can be edited to have more contrast. Use **Window** → **Settings/Preferences** → **Colors** to change the values of the user defined colors.

Editing Set Membership for the shorts wrap

This workflow is similar to the one above, except you are now editing the wrap deformer weights instead of the lattice point weights. Keep in mind that the best membership differs depending on the model, the skeleton, and the resolution of the deformer. Use the following diagram as a general guideline for editing the membership of the left side of wrapShorts deformer. Use the mirror image for the right side. There are two rows of vertices in the center of the shorts. Be careful not to group both of these vertices into the same bone: one should go with the corresponding left bone; and one with the right.

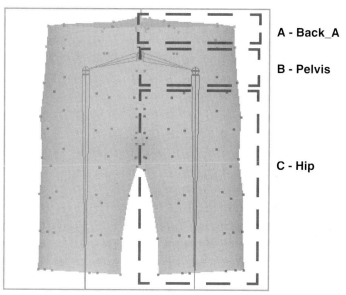

A - Back_A

B - Pelvis

C - Hip

Membership areas for left side of wrapShorts

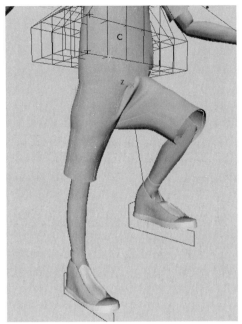

Testing the bending

- Add all the vertices at the bottom of the shorts to the correct hip joint.

Tip: In edit membership mode, **RMB-click** on a hull of the shorts geometry to select a whole row of CV's along an isoparm.

WEIGHTING LATTICE POINTS

When you lift Melvin's arms, notice that the shirt near the waist is pulled more than you want. If you change the weighting of the lattice points, you can control how much they affect the shirt.

Weighting the shirt lattice

Experiment with different lattice point weights to see how they affect the shirt when the character is moved. For Melvin's shirt, you want to decrease the weights of the lattice points controlling the shoulder joints and near the armpit to between 0.1 and 0.3.

Use the following chart below as a guideline for weighting the shirt's lattice points. Note that you only changed the weight of the lattice points that are deformed by the shoulder joints. This is easy to see when in component mode because Maya automatically colors the lattice points depending on what joint controls them.

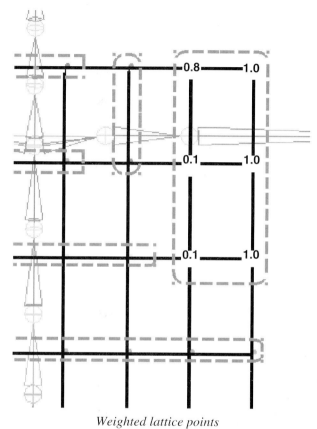

Weighted lattice points

Adjusting the weights of the shorts wrap (Optional)

You will need to taper the weights on the portion of the shorts lattice that is affected by the hip joints. This ensures that when Melvin's knee comes towards his chest, the shorts don't move through his belly.

You also want to crease the shorts around the belt line. You can do this if you taper the weights of the hip lattice points from 0 at the top, to 1.0 near the middle of the leg. See the following diagram for a general idea of how to weight the shorts lattice.

The best overall method to smoothing out the skin values is to use the **Deform → Paint Cluster Weights Tool.** This tool works similarly to the weight painting you did in the Smooth Skinning chapter. Make sure you are smoothing the weight values on the wrap deformer since it is what is bound to the skeleton.

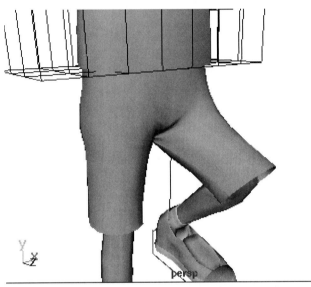

Smoothing applied near hip region of wrapShorts

Testing skinning with animation and poses

You haven't added any flexors or muscle control to the skinned character yet. Before doing that, you need to test the membership and weighting by putting Melvin into different poses. You should also consider setting some keyframes to verify that this skinning, membership, and weighting will prepare you to add flexors.

Below is a list of poses and animations to test the skinning:

- Move Melvin's hands to his hips - look at how the shoulders and armpits deform. In some cases, the membership and/or weighting might need to be adjusted to get the shoulders to round correctly and to crease the shirt under the armpits.

- Move Melvin's hands to his head. Don't forget to adjust the Pole Vector constraints.

- Make Melvin touch his right shoulder with his left hand. This is a very basic move, but it will display any skinning problems.

- Move Melvin into a hurdling pose.

- Move Melvin into a crouched pose, checking to see how the geometry deforms around his waist.

- Set up another walk cycle.

While testing Melvin's movements, you might find that you want to go back and re-skin him with the joints in slightly different places. You also may want to consider different resolutions for the lattices on his shirt and shorts. If possible, you'll want to get fairly decent deformations - otherwise it will be even harder to fine-tune the skinning when you start adding flexors.

Exercise

Work on the weighting for the shirt, shorts, hands, and fingers. You can use the file named *Melvin_12_rigidWeighted.mb*.

Summary

In this chapter, you learned the importance of working with Rigid Skinning membership and weighting. This part of skinning can be tedious and time consuming so learning to work quickly and efficiently is important. Having preset poses in extreme positions should be used to keep consistent balances of weighting and membership. In the next chapter, you will see how flexors and other deformers can be used to enhance the deformation. Be prepared to come back and revisit your membership and weighting choices. This is an iterative process.

13 **Flexors**

Now it's time to fine-tune the Rigid Skinning that you started in Chapter 11. Currently, Melvin's skin looks like a rubber suit and there are areas where the deformation needs to be either smoothed or controlled with more detail.

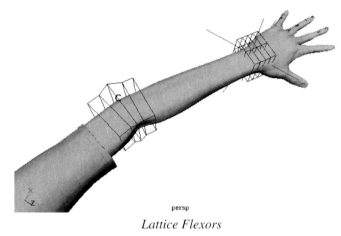

Lattice Flexors

In this chapter, you will learn the following:

- How to add a lattice flexor to a joint;

- Adding lattice flexors to bones;

- Fine tuning the lattice flexor;

- How to work with sculpt flexors;

- How to add sculpt flexor to bones;

- How to fine tune the flexor with SDK;

- Adding a cluster flexor to Melvin's right elbow;

- How to fine tune the cluster flexor with the manipulator and the Component Editor.

FLEXORS

When you Bind Skin with the Rigid Bind option, you will get fairly smooth deformations in most areas. But in certain regions, where the joints rotate significantly (elbows, wrists, knees, ankles, etc.), you will need to add flexors to smooth out the deformations. In addition to smoothing out the deformations, flexors have some preset attributes that allow you to create realistic effects in characters - such as bulging biceps and creasing/rounding elbow joints. Lattice flexors have a generalized control on the skin. The two other flexor types (sculpt and cluster) provide different levels and types of skinning control. They will be discussed in the following chapters.

One thing to note is that flexors can only be used with skin bound with the Rigid Bind command. Smooth bound skin will not be affected by flexors.

Lattice Flexors

Lattice flexors are almost identical to lattice deformers. The differences are:

- Lattice flexors are controlled by and parented to a joint.

- Lattice flexors have pre-defined attributes to control how they fold and bulge the skin.

Lattice flexors are ideal for smoothing skin around joints like elbows and knees. An advantage to using lattice flexors is that the underlying geometry they smooth doesn't have to be high resolution to get satisfactory results. In addition to smoothing, lattice flexors can also wrinkle skin and create muscle definition, depending on whether they are added to a joint or a bone.

By default, lattice flexors are created with several preset attributes. You can also set up a Set Driven Key on the lattice points to fine-tune the deformation.

Lattice Deformers vs. Lattice Flexors

The best way to see the difference between lattice deformers and lattice flexors is to look at them in the Hypergraph.

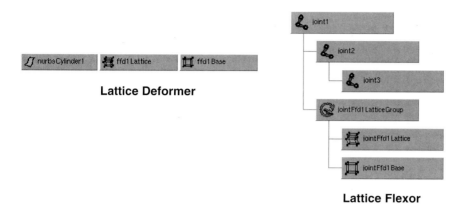

Lattice Deformer

Lattice Flexor

Lattices in the Hypergraph

When you create a lattice flexor, a *jointFfd1LatticeGroup* is created under the *LatticeFlex_joint* as its child. This group is made up of a *jointFfd1Lattice* and a *jointFfd1Base*.

- The *jointFfd1Lattice* is what actually deforms the geometry.

- The *jointFfd1Base* is what stores the base position where the deformation starts.

The *jointFfd1LatticeGroup* looks like a regular lattice parented to the joint, but it also has some special attributes specific to deforming geometry bound to a joint.

Creating a lattice flexor on a joint vs. a bone

When the flexor is created on the "bone," the flexor is parented to the currently selected joint. If it is created on the "joint," it is parented to the parent joint of the currently selected joint.

There will also be different pre-set attributes depending on whether the flexor is created on the "joint" or the "bone". The following attributes are created for joint lattice flexors. If any of these attributes are changed when the elbow is bent, a pseudo-Set Driven Key will be created. When the elbow is rotated back to its bind pose, the attributes will return to their default settings. The attributes will be driven by the joint on which the flexor was created. In other words, a bone flexor created for a bicep will be driven by the rotation of the elbow, not by the rotation of the shoulder.

The following table contrasts the attributes that are created:

Joint Flexor	Bone Flexor
Creasing	Bicep
Rounding	Tricep
Length In	Length In
Length Out	Length Out
Width Left	Width Left
Width Right	Width Right

Joint Flexor vs. Bone Flexor

Selecting LatticeGroup

To easily select the latticeGroup, select the lattice in the work area, then click the up arrow to select the node just above the lattice.

Create flexor options

Most of the options for flexors are the same as options for the deformer type flexor but a couple are different. One option is bone or joint flexor. The other is **Position the Flexor**. This selects the group node above the lattice and the base after creation so that they can be translated, rotated, or scaled without deforming the geometry.

Note that the flexor can be transformed at a later time by selecting the *jointFfdLatticeGroup* which contains both the lattice base and the lattice.

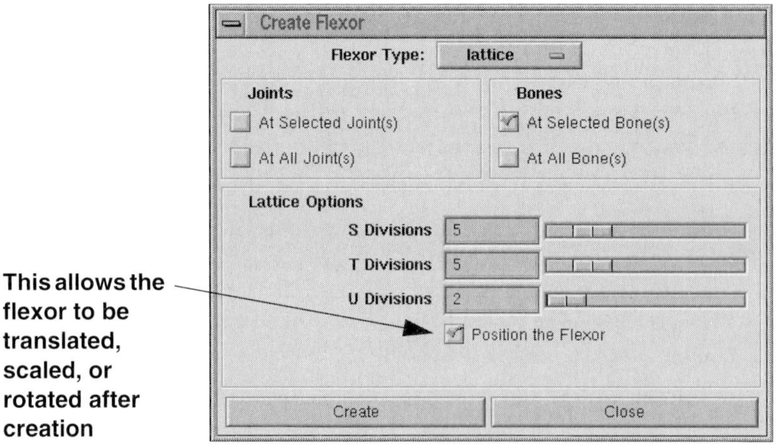

This allows the flexor to be translated, scaled, or rotated after creation

Flexor Options

LATTICE FLEXORS FOR MELVIN'S ARMS

Fine-tuning Melvin's skin with flexors can be a tedious, trial and error process depending on how "tuned" you want the skin to be. You will work through some of the basics of getting skin to behave in a desirable manner. The best approach is to tweak the skin in areas where it folds and bends, such as elbows, wrists, knees, and ankles.

The Bind Skin function from the previous chapter will give you a good starting point. Flexors help take the skinning to the next level of realism. In addition to skin folding, you'll explore ways to bulge skin to mimic real muscles and bones.

When the elbow is bent, the elbow folds into itself and you lose any sense of an underlying skeletal structure. Use a lattice flexor to help this area crease and round out a little bit at the tip of the elbow.

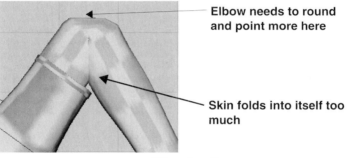

Elbow needs to round
and point more here

Skin folds into itself too
much

Elbow bending

You will use a combination of flexors to get the desired behavior for the elbow. It is important to understand Maya's ability to combine multiple flexors/deformers on a single piece of geometry because it is really helpful for tuning the skin to the correct shape. In later chapters, you will look at how to combine multiple flexors to solve the elbow problems.

Tip: Always add flexors when the skeleton is in its bind pose.

---

1 Open an existing file

- Open the file *Melvin_13_readyForFlexors*.

2 Add a flexor to the left elbow

From the bind pose, add a **Lattice** flexor to the elbow joint.

- **Select** the *left_elbow* joint.

- Select **Skin** → **Edit Rigid Skin** → **Create Flexor...** and set the following:

  Flexor Type to **lattice**;

  Joints to **At Selected Joints**;

  Lattice Options to **(S=2, T=5, U=2)**;

  Set **Position Flexor** to **On**.

- Click **Create**.

3 Position the flexor

- Position and scale the flexor so that it surrounds the elbow area as shown below:

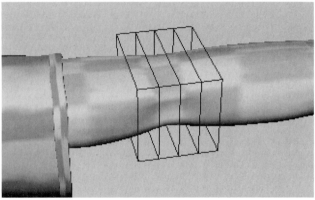

Lattice on elbow

- Label the flexor *left_elbowLatticeFlexor* and the group node above *left_elbowLatticeGroup*.

4 Adjust the parameters of the flexor

Bend the elbow, then adjust the flexor parameters to get the crease and roundness to look correct.

- Select *left_armControl* and translate until the elbow is bent at about **90-120** degrees.

- **Select** *left_elbowLatticeFlexor* and adjust the following attributes. Experiment a little, then test the results by bending the elbow.

These are some approximate values that work well for rounding the elbow:

Creasing to **1**;

Rounding to **1.5**;

Length In to **-1.25**;

Length Out to **-1.25**;

Width Left to **-0.5**;

Width Right to **-0.5**.

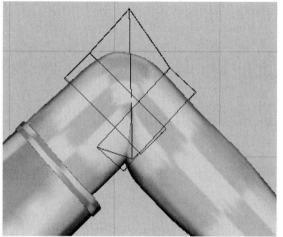

Bent flexor

Forearms

You can use a lattice flexor to smooth out the deformations caused when the forearm is twisted. Currently, if you rotate the wrist/forearm, the deformation is a little harsh and needs to be tapered down the length of the forearm.

1 Add a lattice joint flexor to the left forearm joint

- Add a lattice joint flexor to the *left_forearm* joint with the following setting:

  T Divisions to **6** to **8**.

  Set **Position the Flexor** to **On**.

- Position the flexor, scaling it along the length of the forearm, as shown in the following figure:

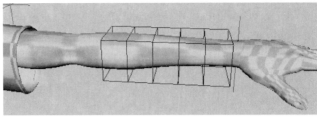

Forearm lattice

- Name it *left_forearmLatticeFlexor*.

2 Test the flexors

- To judge how the forearm flexor smooths out the deformation, select the *left_armControl* and twist the wrist joint (which drives the forearm joint's rotate x).

3 Repeat for the right forearm

Note: A similar approach can be used for the wrists.Sculpt Flexors.

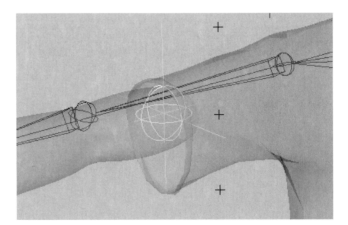

4 Save your work

SCULPT FLEXORS

Sculpt flexors are best used to bulge a character's skin (e.g. biceps, triceps, tummies, etc.). You will get the most effective results if you use them to deform more general areas. In order for sculpt flexors to be successful in detailed areas, such as deformation around the elbow, they need to collide with a lot of isoparms/vertices.

Before adding sculpt flexors to Melvin's right arm, we'll look at how Sculpt Deformers work in Maya. Once you understand the basic concept of Sculpt Deformers, using them as flexors will be very similar.

Basic Sculpt Deformers

A Sculpt Deformer is similar to a collision object for CVs, lattice points, and poly vertices. This deformer is located at **Deform** → **Create Sculpt Deformer**. There are three types of Sculpt Deformers:

Stretch - this is the default and the most commonly used mode for flexors and other deformations. There are two parts to the Sculpt Deformer when created in stretch mode:

> **Sculpt Sphere** - This defines the area of the sculpt object's force field. This deformer shape is always elliptical. It will attempt to keep CVs, lattice points, and/or poly vertices outside.

> **Sculpt Origin** - This defines the direction in which the Sculpt Sphere will be deformed. This deformer shape is a Locator. Moving it around in relation to the Sculpt Sphere and the deformed points will change the direction of the deformation. By default, this shape is created in the middle of the Sculpt Sphere.

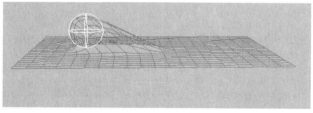

Sculpt

Flip - This mode is similar to Stretch, except that the Sculpt Origin is automatically hidden and parented to the Sculpt Sphere, so that it will always stay inside the Sculpt Sphere.

Project - This literally projects the deformed CVs, lattice points, and/or poly vertices onto the Sculpt Sphere.

Sculpt Flexors

Sculpt flexors are almost identical to Sculpt Deformers. This deformer is located at **Skin** → **Edit Rigid Skin** → **Create Flexor....**

The differences are that when the sculpt object is created with the Create Flexors window:

- the Sculpt Sphere and corresponding origin automatically get parented to the selected joint:

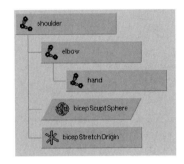

- The Sculpt Sphere automatically deforms a certain section of CVs depending on what joint is selected.

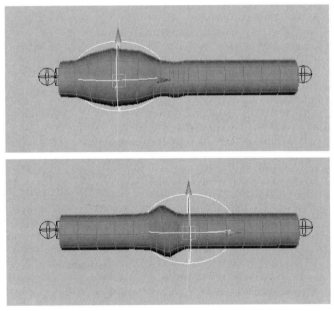

Sculpt

Sculpt flexors are best used on parts of the body where there are plenty of CVs, lattice points, and/or poly vertices to intersect with. They are best used on biceps, triceps, stomachs, and other large general areas. Trying to use them on detailed areas will require that you increase the resolution of the deformed object - otherwise, you will see the deformed object "pop" as the points snap onto and then off of the Sculpt Sphere.

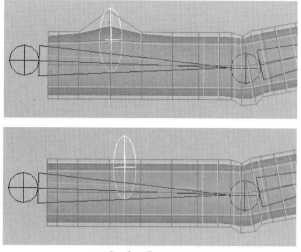

Sculpt flexor

Using Set Driven Key, you can make the Sculpt Flexor deform and bulge based on the rotation value of the elbow joint.

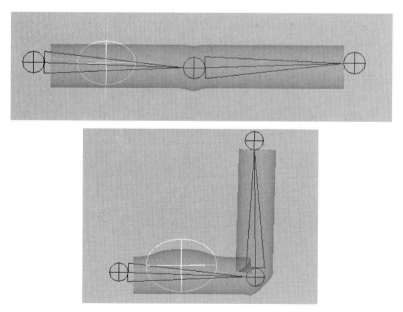

Sculpt effect

SCULPT FLEXOR FOR MELVIN'S ARMS

You'll use a sculpt flexor for Melvin's right bicep. Ultimately, the sculpt objects needs to be parented to the shoulder joint but deform the skin between the shoulder and the elbow - so it is important how this flexor is created.

1 Open an existing file

- Open the file *Melvin_13_readyForSculpts.mb*.

2 Add a sculpt flexor to the shoulder bone

- Return to bind pose.
- **Select** the *right_shoulder* joint.
- Select **Skin** → **Edit Rigid Skin** → **Create Flexor...** and set the following options:

    Flexor Type to **sculpt**;

    Dropoff Type to **None**;

    Mode to **Stretch**;

    Inside Mode to **Even**.

- Press **Create**.

3 Position and scale the Sculpt Sphere flexor

Position and scale the Sculpt Sphere flexor so that its default size is inside the bicep area.

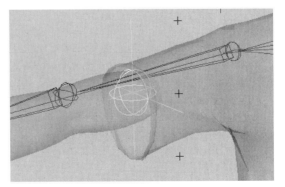

Sculpt object

- **Select** the *sculptSphere* and the *sculptStretchOrigin* and **scale** and **translate** until they are just under the skin where the bicep would be.

- Label the two flexor objects *right_shirtSculptSphere* and *right_shirtStretchOrigin*.

4 Save your work

Setting up the biceps bulge

Although Melvin's biceps are obscured by his t-shirt, you can add a little deformation using the sculpt object. Using Set Driven Key, animate the scale and position of the Sculpt Sphere with the rotation value of the elbow joint.

1 Create Set Driven Key for biceps

- In the Set Driven Key window, **select** the *right_elbow* **RotateY** attribute as the Driver and the *right_shirtSculptSphere* **Translate** and **Scale** attributes as the Driven object.

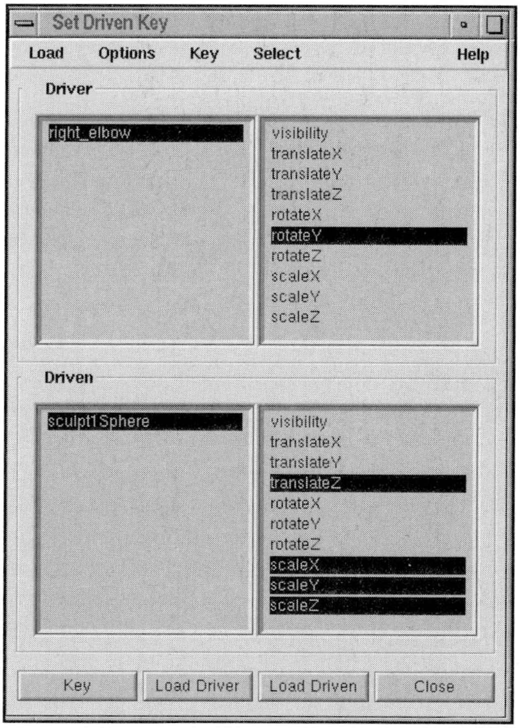

Set Driven Key window

- Set a key with *right_elbow* joint at its rest (bind) pose and sculpt sphere at its current (small) position and scale.

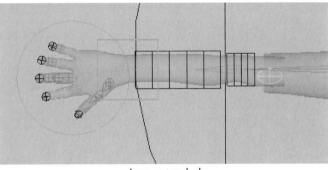

Arm extended

- In the Set Driven Key window, click **Key**.
- Set a key with *right_elbow* joint bent in a **90-120** degree bend in the **Y-axis** and the *sculptSphere* **translated** and **scaled** to bulge the shirt a little.

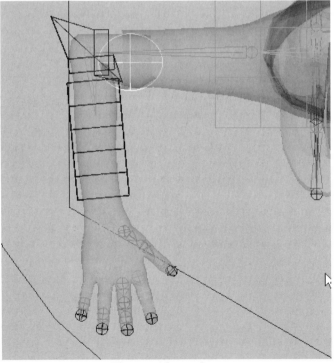

Flexor with arm bent

2 Save your work

BASIC CLUSTER FLEXORS

Cluster Flexors provide more localized control than a lattice flexor, allowing you to set the individual deformation percentages (weights) of all the CVs that are affected by the flexor. Maya's joint Cluster Flexors have a manipulator that provides fast workflow for defining the upper and lower *bounds* of the flexor's influence.

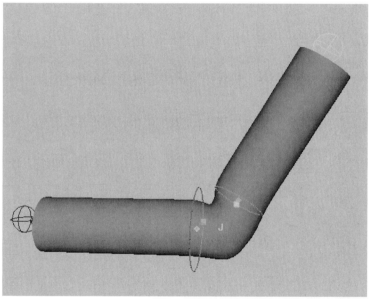

Cluster Flexor

By selecting the elbow joint and selecting **Modify → Transformation Tools → Show Manipulator Tool,** the 3D manipulator will be displayed. The **t** hotkey will also carry out this function.

- The rings designate the upper and lower *bounds* of influence on the flexor. By middle mouse dragging the center diamond, these *bound* positions can change. These values can also be changed in the Attribute Editor.

- The radius of the rings can be changed by middle mouse dragging on the diamond at the edge of the ring. This will change the percentage/weights.

The manipulator changes can be seen if you open up the Component Editor. You will notice the weights respond accordingly when the manip's rings are translated. The manipulator provides a quick way of setting the upper and lower *bounds*.

Note:	To save the selected components in the Component Editor while selecting the joint cluster in the viewport, turn off **List** → **Auto Update** in the Component Editor.

Cluster Flexor For Melvin's right elbow

Following is the workflow for creating a joint cluster on Melvin's right elbow.

1 Open an existing file

- Open the file *Melvin_13_readyForClusters.mb.*

2 Create the flexor on the elbow

- **Select** the left elbow joint.
- Select **Skin** → **Edit Rigid Skin** → **Create Flexor...** and set the following:

    Flexor Type to **jointCluster**;

    Joints to **At Selected Joint(s)**

- Press **Create**.

    You should see the letter "**J**" at the joint, representing the joint cluster.

3 Manipulate the values on the flexor

- **Select** the elbow joint and **rotate** it to about **-90** degrees in **Y**.

Note:	You may need to disable IK handles to rotate the joint.

- **Select** the joint the flexor is on. This will automatically select the joint Cluster Flexor.
- **Select** the **Show Manipulator Tool**.

Tip:	Visualizing the flexor effects can be easier in shaded mode.

- Change the manips to see the effect and to make Melvin's elbow look good in a bent pose. You will likely want to bring the *bounds* closer together to get a more shapely elbow.

How it works

The name jointCluster can be misleading, because a new cluster is not created. This type of flexor affects the clusters on either side of the joint (in this case of the elbow and shoulder). Changing the upper/lower bound or value affects the weighting of the two clusters on either side of the joint.

You will have to switch between the inputs for the elbow and shoulder clusters in order to edit the values in the Channel Box. It is important to know that the lower bound on the shoulder cluster is the upper bound of the flexor, and the upper bound on the elbow is the lower bound of the flexor.

The Cluster Flexor can be a good choice for making finger knuckles. There are a lot of knuckles to setup and a Cluster Flexor looks pretty good by default. If the scene is not a close up of the hand you, might not have to do any other work. A Cluster Flexor does the job with less overhead, keeping your scene cleaner as well.

Exercise

Now that you have seen all of the different flexor types, finish adding flexors to Melvin wherever necessary. Use your judgement as to which type you like best for each situation. If you're unsure, take time to experiment.

Summary

Flexors are Maya's deformers specially designed for Rigid Skinning. They employ the Maya deformers, Lattice, Sculpt, and Cluster. Each flexor type has its inherent advantages and limitations so experimentation here is needed. The Cluster Flexor, for example, is a great way to even out the skinning of the character's fingers. The Cluster Flexor is fast in its performance so you can apply them liberally. Access the flexor controls by selecting the joint then pressing the **t** key. The manipulators will let control the operation on both sides of the joint, but remember flexors are driven by the joint's rotation so you must test the extreme positions of the joint.

14 Blend Shape

Blend Shape is a deformer type that lets you use several target shapes to drive a base shape. The tool creates controls for each of the target shapes that can be edited and animated to control the look of the base shape.

In this chapter, you will use Blend Shape to add some bulging to Melvin's calf. You will duplicate his existing leg, then sculpt the new surface to show the bulging. Blend Shape will then be used to create the blended deformation between the bulge target and the original leg. The value of the blend can then be animated using Set Driven Key so that the rotation of the knee joint animates the bulging.

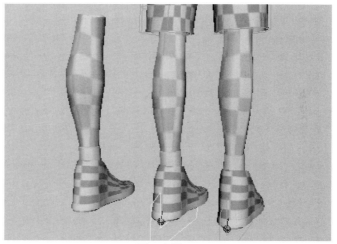

Blend Shape

In this chapter, you will learn the following:

- How to set up a Blend Shape muscle bulge;
- How to work with the deformer order;
- How to use Set Driven Key with a Blend Shape.

BLEND SHAPE

Blend Shape is a powerful morphing tool. You can build several shapes and use Blend Shape to link them together. Blend Shape will create sliders so you can have smooth transitions between shapes after you put keyframes on the sliders.

In the most basic sense, a Blend Shape consists of two things: the *target* shape(s) and the *base* shape. It's easy to understand the basics of the Blend Shape by examining how Maya executes the Blend Shape function.

When executing a Blend Shape, Maya looks at the changes between the base and the target shapes. The value of the Blend Shape (which ranges from 0 to 1) is a percentage of how much of that difference will be added to the base shape.

Make a calf muscle bulge

This is the procedure to make the calf muscle bulge.

1 Open an existing file

- Select **File** → **Open**.
- Select the file *Melvin_14_calfNoBulge.mb*

2 Duplicate the left leg

- Select the *leftLeg* geometry.
- Select **Edit** → **Duplicate**.
- Rename the new leg *L_calfBulge*.

3 Move it to the side

- Unlock *L_calfBulge's* Translate X channel.
- Translate it to the side of the original leg.

4 Model the calf bulge

- Select the leg.
- Press **F8** to go into component selection mode.
  Make sure that the selection mask is set up to only pick CV's.
- Pull CV's on the leg surface to make the calf appear bulged.

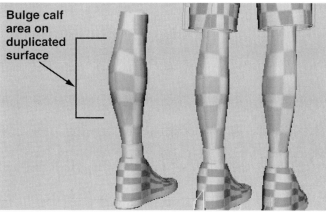

Bulged calf

5 Create the Blend Shape

- Press **F8** to go back into object selection mode.
- Select the *L_calfBulge* geometry followed by the original leg geometry.

Tip: When defining a Blend Shape the base shape must be selected last.

- Select **Deform** → **Create Blend Shape** – ❑. In the Option window, set the following:

  Name to *leftCalfBulge*.

- Press the **Create** button.

6 Test the Blend Shape

- Select **Window** → **Animation Editors** → **Blend Shape...**

This will open up the Blend Shape Editor which has a slider for controlling the bulge of the calf.

Blend Shape Options

Listed below are some of the options available on the Blend Shape Tool.

Envelope

This is a scale factor for the slider. A value of 2 will double the effect of the slider, 0.5 will make it half and 1 will invert the effect.

Origin

This can be either *Local* or *World*. Local means the change takes place relative to the base shape. World will cause the blend to move from the position of the base to the position of the target.

For Blend Shapes of this nature you will generally want to use *Local*. You can compare the effects in the Attribute Editor.

In-Between

In-Between will chain targets together. If it is set to *on*, a slider could change from a frown, to a face at rest, to a smile. If the smile were the base, the selection order would be frown, default, and then smile.

(Cont'd on next page)

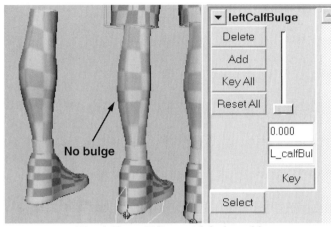

Blend Shape Editor with bulge of 0

- Move the vertical slider up to **1** and the calf will bulge.

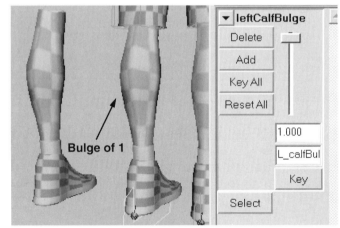

Blend Shape Editor with bulge of 1

Tip: You can also access the Blend Shape by clicking on the *leftCalfBulge* input node in the Channel Box and changing the value of the *calfBulge* field. This attribute is accessible through the Attribute Editor as well.

This method for a muscle bulge is quite effective. It not only lets you control the amount of bulge but also lets you create a very specific shape. For example, an arm will bulge differently if it is lifting a pencil vs. a computer monitor.

Deformer order

By default, the Blend Shape deformer, when applied to a skinned surface, will be placed correctly before the skin cluster deformation. But, you may find that other operations result in deformers in the wrong order.

An example of a Blend Shape deformer that is not in the proper order will have the following behavior:

- Deform the leg to a bent position then invoke the Blend Shape deformer by adjusting the Blend Shape deformer.

- The Blend Shape will deform the leg back towards its original position with a bulged calf.

If you switch the deformation order around, so that the Blend Shape is executed first, the leg will still get bent, but it gets bent *after* the Blend Shape deforms the leg.

Try this with your newly setup leg:

1 Rotate the knee backwards

- Set the Blend Shape back to **0**.

- **Rotate** the knee backwards.

  You may need to disable IK Handles.

2 Bulge the calf

- **Move** the vertical slider up to **1** and the calf will bulge

  You should see the leg geometry bulge and not move off the bone and into the position that the Blend Shape was created in. This would happen when the clusters from the Bind Skin operation affect the leg and then the Blend Shape is applied last, which in this case would be incorrect.

3 Reorder the deformers

- **RMB-click** on the leg geometry and, from the pop-up menu, select **Inputs → All Inputs**.

- This opens up a window that shows you a list of the deformers currently affecting this surface.

Blend Shape Options

(Cont'd)

Check Topology
Check Topology *off* will allow you to Blend Shapes with different numbers of vertices. When turned *on*, it will return an error stating that the shapes have a different vertices count.

Delete Targets
Delete Targets will delete the targets after the Blend Shape has been created. Once created, the targets are not needed, so this can result in improved performance.

It is a good idea to save a copy of your targets somewhere in case you need to use them later to make adjustments.

Blend Shape Control

Listed below are some of the options available in the Blend Shape Control window.

Select

This will select the Blend Shape so that it can be controlled through the Channel Box or manipulated in the Dependency Graph.

To delete a Blend Shape, select it with this button and then delete it.

Key

This will allow you to key the current value of the slider at the current frame.

New

This will create a new Blend Shape much like using the **Deform → Create Blend Shape -** ❐. Pick the targets, followed by the base, and press the **New** button.

New targets can be added to an existing Blend Shape with **Deform → Edit Blend Shapes → Add -** ❐.

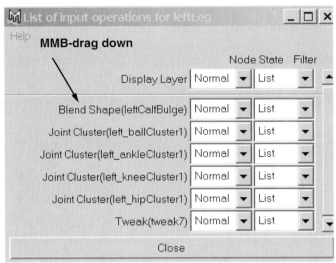

List of deformers

- **MMB-drag** the *Blend Shape* to the bottom of the list. This reorders the deformers.

Reordered deformers

4 Bulge the calf

Now things should be working as expected.

Blend Shape integration

The Blend Shape control window is a good tool for controlling the deformation, but you don't want to have to go there every time you want the corrective blend to occur. The window is designed for more complex blends like facial animation, and isn't designed to be used effectively in cases like the calf bulge.

You will integrate the bulge with the rotation of the ankle using Set Driven Key. To drive the *Blend Shape* with SDK, you'll do the following:

1 Load the Driver

- Open the Set Driven Key window with **Animate** → **Set Driven Key** → **Set** – ❑.
- Select the *left_ankle rotateZ* attribute.
- Press **Load Driver**.

2 Load the Driven

- Press **Select** in the Blend Shape window to make it the active object.
- Select the *L_calfBulge* attribute as the **Driven** object.

3 Set a driven key in the unbent position

- With the *left_ankle rotateZ* and *leftCalfBulge* attributes selected, press **Key**.

4 Set a driven key in the bent position

- **Rotate** the *left_ankle* **60** degrees on X.

Note: You may need to disable the IK solvers to rotate the ankle joint.

- Set the *leftCalfBulge* to a value of **1**.
- With the *left_ankle rotateZ* and *leftCalfBulge* attributes selected, press **Key**.

5 Test the ankle rotation

- As the ankle rotates you should see the calf bulge.

6 **Save your work**

USING BLEND SHAPE WITH OTHER DEFORMERS

Deformers that are based on objects such as the Wire Deformer can be driven with Blend Shape to create a hierarchy of deformation and control. Wire Deformers can be used in many ways, such as making waves on an ocean or creating wrinkles on a face. In this chapter, the Wire Deformer and *Blend Shape* tools will be used to further enhance the behavior of Melvin's clothing. This will also correct the problem of Melvin's shorts intersecting his legs.

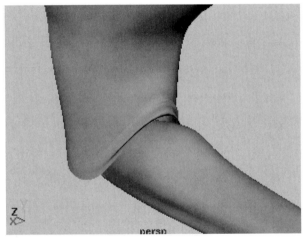

Creating wrinkles with the Wire Deformer

Wire Deformers

Wire Deformers are curves that influence a surface. A relationship is defined between a curve and a piece of geometry. As the curve is transformed, or its shape changed, it will be reflected on the surface.

Deforming Melvin's shorts cuff

When Melvin bends his leg at the knee, he will eventually bend it far enough to cause his calf to intersect with the cuff of his shorts. One way to fix this is to deform the cuff of the shorts with a Wire Deformer so the cuff bunches up where it meets the back of his leg.

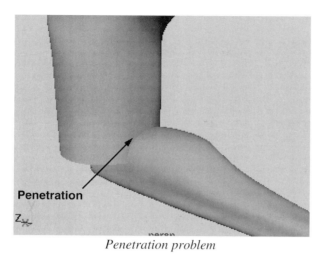

Penetration problem

The Wire Deformer can then be changed with a Blend Shape and controlled with SDK so that the shorts are affected gradually as the knee bends.

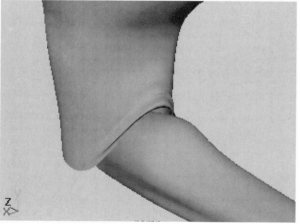

Corrected wrinkle

Create a Wire Deformer on the shorts

The first step in this process is to create a Wire Deformer for the shorts.

1 Open an existing file

- Select **File → Open**.
- Select the file *Melvin_14_calfBulge.mb*.

2 Turn on Wireframe On Shaded

- Select **Shading** → **Shade Options** → **Wireframe On Shaded**.

3 Draw a curve on the shorts

- Snapping to edges on the shorts surface, draw a CV curve down the back of the left pant leg.

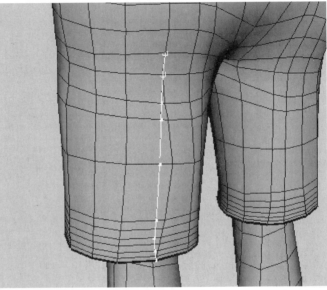

Curve down pant leg

- Name the curve *wireCurveBase.*

4 Duplicate the curve

Since you will use Blend Shape later to change the shape of the curve, it should be duplicated so that you have an untouched curve to work with.

- **Duplicate** the curve *wireCurveBase* and move it beside the shorts.

- Rename the curve *wireCurveTarget.*

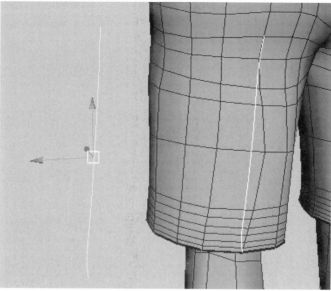

Moving the wireCurveTarget beside the shorts

5 Create a Wire Deformer

- Select the shorts surface.
- Select **Deform** → **Wire Tool**.
- Press **Enter**.

    This will define the shorts as the surface where the wire will be added.

- Select *wireCurveBase* to define it as the wire that will affect the shorts.
- Press **Enter**.

    The curve is now a wire for the shorts surface.

6 Change the wire shape

- **Rotate** the *left_knee* in X to Melvin's maximum bend position.

Note: You may need to disable IK in order to rotate the knee.

- Select *wireCurveBase* and press **F8** to change to component mode. You may want to turn hulls on in the Pick Mask as a visual guide.

- **Move** the CV's up in **Y** and back and forth in **Z** to create a bunched up look as shown below. X-Ray mode may help while you do this.

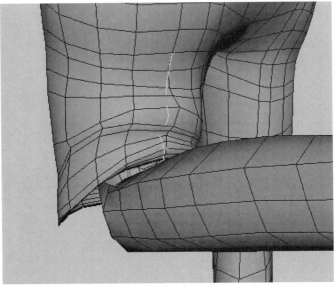

Deforming the wire

As you move the CV's you should see the surface change, so that you can get a better idea of how to shape the curve. You can also select multiple CV's and scale them. You can use the up and down arrow keys' *pickwalk* function to walk through the individual CV's.

7 Refine wire attributes

You may find that the wire is not affecting a broad enough area of the surface. You can adjust wire specifics in the Attribute Editor.

- Select the *shorts* surface.

- Open the Attribute Editor and select the *wire1* tab.

- Decrease the value of the **Dropoff Distance** to have the wire affect more of the surface. A value of **0.75** should work well.

8 Reorder deformers

Since Melvin was bound to the skeleton before setting up this Wire Deformer, the deformer order may need to be changed. The default behavior is to put added deformers before the skin cluster deformers. If this is not what you are experiencing, here is what to do:

- **RMB-click** on the shorts geometry to get the popup menu and select **Inputs** → **All Inputs**.

- MMB-drag the wire down in the list so that it is evaluated before the *Wrap*.

9 Save your work

Controlling a Wire Deformer with Blend Shape

Now that the Wire Deformer is applied to the shorts, a Blend Shape can be added so that the shorts can easily be changed from non-deformed to the deformed version. SDK will also be added so that bending the knee will control the Blend Shape.

You will continue working with the same file:

1 Create a Blend Shape with the two curves

- Select the *wireCurveTarget* first and the *wireCurveBase* curve second.

- Select **Deform** → **Create Blend Shape** – ❑, and set the following:

   Blend Shape Node to **L_shortsCuff**.

2 Drive the Blend Shape with Set Driven Key

- Select **Animate** → **Set Driven Key** → **Set** – ❑.

- Select the *left_knee* joint and load it as the **Driver**.

- Select the L_*shortsCuff* Blend Shape node from the Blend Shape Editor and load it as the **Driven**.

3 Set a driven key in the unbent position

- Select *left_knee* **RotateX** and *shortsCuff* **wireCurveTarget** attributes.

- Verify the **wireCurveTarget** value is set to **0**.

- Press **Key**.

4 Set a driven key in the bent position

- **Rotate** the *left_knee* back to **0**.

- Set the **wireCurveTarget** to a value of **1**.

- Press **Key**.

5 Test your knee rotation

As the knee rotates, you should see the shorts bunch up.

6 Save your work

7 Repeat for the other side

Summary

Blend Shape is such a powerful deformer in Maya that it is used for many things. Blend Shape uses a target - base approach where there can be many targets but one base shape. If you want to Blend Shape a collection of surfaces, they must appear in the same hierarchy from targets to base. Deformation order is important when dealing with Blend Shapes. By understanding that skinning is a deformation, and applying a Blend Shape to a skinned surface, you are layering deformations. Any time you are layering deformations you should be aware of what the intended order of this deformation is to be. In this last example, the Blend Shape is driving the Wire Deformer which is driving the skinned shorts. The ability to build up these layers of deformation is an incredible tool within Maya.

15 Facial Animation

In this chapter, you will set up and animate Melvin's facial deformation. Rigging the face is a task almost separate and equal to that of rigging the entire character.

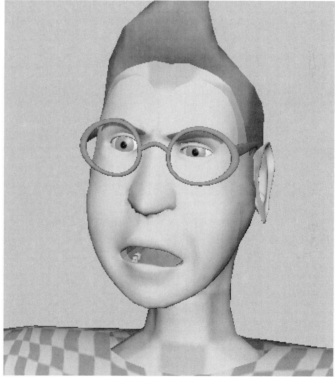

Melvin's face deformed

In this chapter, you will learn the following:

- Creating Blend Shape targets;

- Importing audio files into Maya's timeline;

- Working with phoneme facial poses to build lip-sync.

CHAPTER 15

FACIAL ANIMATION TECHNIQUES FOR LIP-SYNC

Facial animation for lip-sync can be broken down into some basic steps.

Phonetic breakdown

The soundtrack is analyzed on a frame-by-frame basis and a chart of a particular sound or part of a word is made. The type of sound or phonetic interpretation is noted and aligned with its location in time.

Target shapes

Once the dialogue has been charted, the necessary phonetic shapes need to be created. These shapes will work in conjunction with jaw movements and other facial animation techniques. Below is a simple chart of the basic vowel and consonant sounds:

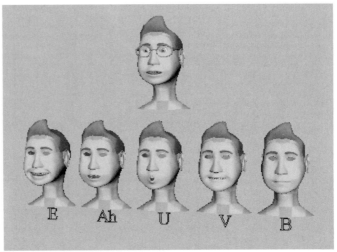

Basic vowel and consonant sounds

Basic keyframing

The basic timing of the character's movement will come from the soundtrack displayed in the timeline. You can use a simple mouth open and close to quickly establish a feel for the sequence.

Shape the mouth

Introduce Blend Shapes and other facial techniques to complete pronunciation of the syllables as charted. Accents are very important and generally will proceed the sound by several frames.

Whole face

The mouth is only one part of the speaking face. The audience will focus on the eyes if they are not distracted by bad lips and vice versa. Think of the whole head when animating.

This chapter can only provide a cursory overview of this very specialized form of animation. Some other tips include using motion study and, more importantly, a mirror to see how the face behaves when communicating. Test your animation back with sound and don't be surprised if you find your lip-sync is late. The general practice is to ensure the visual action proceeds the sound, sometimes by as much as 10 frames.

DIALOGUE SHAPES

Below is a simple chart of the basic vowel and consonant sounds. Use this as a guide to the phonetic breakdown. Vowels are usually the main emphasis, with the consonants *b, f, m,* and *l* the next most important. Accents are places where the character is making a bigger and slower movement. Pay attention to these accents and address them properly with the whole face.

Vowels

The three basic vowel shapes are:

"E"

As found in words like *he, see, tree,* and *believe.*

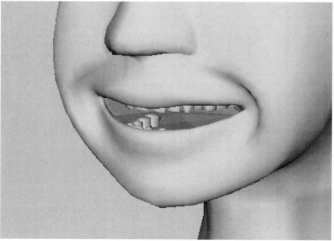

"E" vowel sound

"Ah"

As found in words like *alright, autumn,* and *car.*

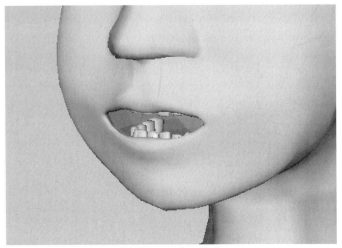

"Ah" vowel sounds

"U"

As found in words like *do, you, stew,* and *noodle.*

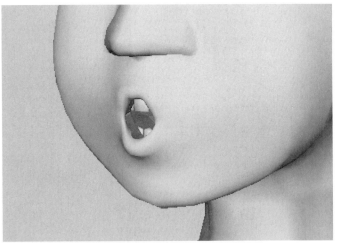

"U" vowel sounds

Consonants

The Primary Consonant Shapes are:

"V" and "F"

As found in words like *very* and *fabulous.*

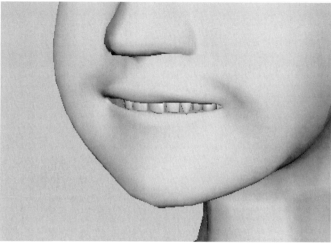

"V" consonant shape

"B" and "M"

As found in words like *Bee, mmm,* and *Princess.*

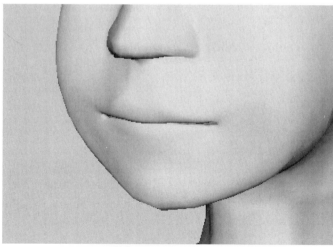

"B" consonant shapes

From these five basic shapes, you can create most key shapes for the initial blocking of the sequence. The tricky part is getting these shapes to transition properly, from one shape to the next, with the soundtrack. You will need to study how each word is formed and also how the mouth and face prepare for a word. The "P", for example, will require that the mouth closes and puckers before it opens to produce the sound. Many sounds do not come from the lips. Instead, they come from the throat through an open and static mouth. This is why Lip-Sync Animation does not look right on its own on a frame-by-frame basis. It must be viewed in real time with the sound. When in doubt, leave it out.

SETTING UP MELVIN'S HEAD

Blend Shape

Melvin's facial animation will be achieved principally through Blend Shape deformations. As you know, Blend Shape is a powerful morphing tool that allows you to build several target shapes and link them together. Blend Shape will create sliders so you can have smooth transitions between shapes after you put keyframes on the sliders.

1 The basic workflow that will be used here is:

- Weight the head's binding to the skeleton;

- Create Blend Shape targets;

- Apply Blend Shape;

- Do facial/lip-sync animation.

WEIGHTING MELVIN'S HEAD

Since Melvin's head was bound in the last chapter, all you need to do now is organize and weight the membership so that the skeleton deforms the head the way you want it to.

1 Open the scene file

- Open the file *Melvin_15_readyToWeight.mb*.

2 Organize the head's membership with the Edit Membership Tool

- Select the **Edit Membership Tool**, then select the joints in Melvin's neck and head to see how membership is distributed.

- Change the membership as necessary. Try to place entire rows of vertices with joints.

Note: The first two rows of vertices belong to *shirt_lattice* so they should be left alone.

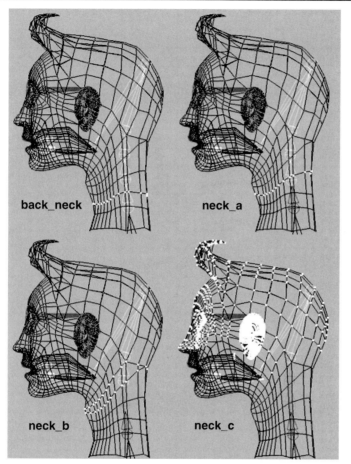

Membership for neck joints

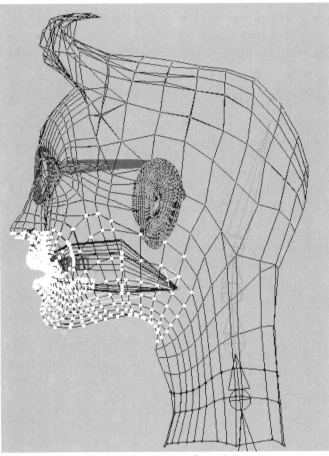

Membership for jawOpen joint

3 Rotate the neck and jawOpen joints to test the membership

- Rotate each of the neck joints on Z to test the deformation.
- Rotate the *jawOpen* joint to test the deformation of the mouth.

  The deformation in the neck should look pretty good, but may benefit from a little smoothing. The deformation in the face should be way off right now, with the entire face deforming when the jaw opens. You will correct that deformation in the next section.

4 Save your work

Painting the weight in Melvin's face

You will now paint the weights to correct the deformation in Melvin's face.

1 Pose Melvin's mouth

- It will be easier to edit the weighting if Melvin's face is in a posed position, so **rotate** *jawOpen* **-20** on **Z**.

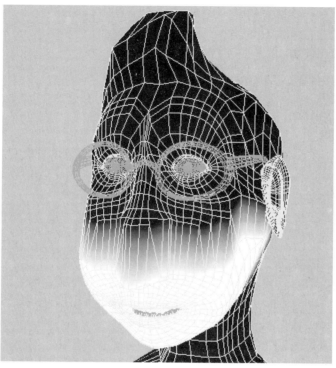

2 Set Paint Cluster Weight Options

- Select Melvin's head geometry.

- Select **Deform → Paint Cluster Weights Tool – ❑**.

- In the Brush section, set the **Radius U** to **0.1** and **Radius L** to **0.001**.

- In the Paint Attributes section, click on the List Of Paintable Attributes button and select **Cluster → jawOpenCluster1-weights**.

- Set the **Paint Operation** to **Replace**;

- Set the **Value** to **0.0**;

- In the Stroke section, make sure that **screen projection** is **Off**, and **Reflection X** is toggled **On**.

3 Remove weighting from the nose and upper face

You will now remove influence from the parts of the face that shouldn't be deformed by the rotation of the jaw.

- Paint in the nose and upper lip area to remove weighting from the *jawOpen* joint.

4   Scale the weighting in the upper face

- Set **Opacity** to **0.2**, **The Paint Operation** to **Scale**, and the **Value** to **0.5**.

- Paint in the area of the upper lip and cheeks to scale the weighting and even out the deformation.

5   Smooth the weight in the face

Once the deformation in the face is somewhat even, it should be properly smoothed out.

- Switch the **Paint Operation** to **Smooth**.

- Set **Opacity** to **0.5**.

- Click the **Flood** button repeatedly until the deformation throughout the face is fairly even.

Note: As always, painting the weights in Melvin's face will be an iterative process, requiring you to switch back and forth from Replacing, Adding, Scaling, and Smoothing values.

---

6   Remove some weighting from Melvin's upper lip

As a result of the flood smoothing, weight may have been added back to Melvin's upper lip area. If that is the case, you should now remove that weighting by replacing the values with 0.

- Set the **Opacity** value to **0.25**.

- Set **Value** to **0**.

- Paint in the upper lip area to replace the weighting value.

7   Rotate the jawOpen joint to test the deformation

- **Rotate** *jawOpen* on **Z** to test the deformation.

- Adjust the weighting as necessary.

8 Save your work

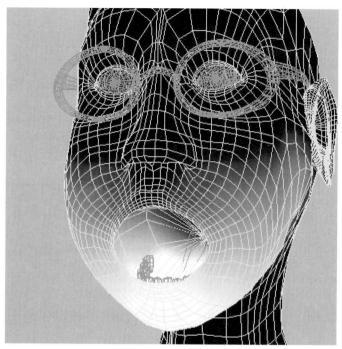

Adding a cluster to Melvin's cheeks

While the deformation in Melvin's face has been evened out, it lacks realism because the cheeks don't react properly when the mouth opens. You will now correct this by applying a cluster to Melvin's face that will scale the cheeks in as the jaw opens.

1 Apply a cluster to Melvin's face

- In the side view, select the vertices in the lower part of Melvin's face.

- Select **Deform** → **Create Cluster** – ❐.

- Toggle **Relative** to **On**.

- Click the **Create Cluster** button.

2 Name the cluster cheekCorrectionCluster.

3 Parent cheekCorrectionCluster to Melvin's skeleton

- With *cheekCorrectionCluster* still selected, parent it to the *skull_a* joint.

4 Correct the deformation order

Since there are now two separate deformers applied to the head geometry (the skeleton chain and the cluster), the deformation order must be corrected.

- **RMB-click** on Melvin's head.
- Select **Inputs** → **All Inputs**.
- **MMB-drag** *Cluster (cheekCorrectionCluster)* to the bottom of the list.

5 Pose Melvin's face

- **Rotate** the *jawOpen* joint **-20** on **Z**.
- **Scale** the *cheekCorrectionCluster* to **0.75** on **X**.

6 Paint the weights for the cheekCorrectionCluster

- Select Melvin's head geometry.
- Select **Deform** → **Paint Cluster Weights Tool** – ◻.
- Select *cheekCorrectionCluster.weight* in the Paint Attributes section.
- Use the **Replace** operation to remove all influence from areas, like the chin, that should not be affected by the cluster's scaling.

Note: Don't worry if you're not sure about which areas should, and should not, have influence. The weighting of this cluster can be adjusted anytime. Just get it basically correct for now.

- Switch the operation to Smooth and flood the influence to even out the deformation.

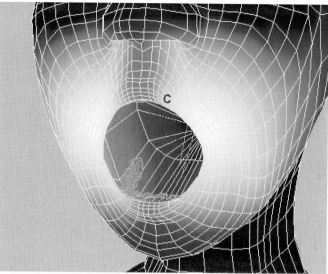

cheekCorrectionCluster weight

7 **Connect the joint to the cluster with Set Driven Key**
- Open the Set Driven Key Options window.
- Load *jawOpen:RotateZ* as the **Driver**.
- Load *cheekCorrectionCluster:ScaleX* as the **Driven**.
- Click the **Key** button.
- Rotate *jawOpen* back to **0** on **Z**.
- Set *cheekCorrectionCluster:Scale X* back to **1**.
- Set another key.

8 **Rotate jawOpen on Z to test the deformation.**

9 **Adjust the Set Driven Key curve to improve the deformation**

While Melvin's face looks better as you open the mouth, the deformation stops abruptly once the *jawOpen* joint reaches -20 on Z. You will now correct this by changing the Set Driven Key curve that was created for the cluster scale X value.

- Select *cheekCorrectionCluster*.
- Open the Graph Editor.
- Select **View** → **Frame All**.
- Select the key at **-20 / 0.75**.

- Change its value to **-40 / 0.5.**
- Rotate the *jawOpen* joint to test deformation.

10 Save your work

11 Experiment with the deformation

- Experiment with adjusting the Set Driven Key curve and the weighting of the *cheeksCorrectionCluster* to fine-tune the deformation.

CREATING BLEND SHAPE TARGETS

Now that Melvin's head is properly bound, you will create a series of Blend Shape targets to be used as the basis for Melvin's facial animation.

1 Open the scene file

- Continue working with your current file or open *Melvin_15_readyForTargets.mb*.

2 Duplicate Melvin's head

3 Name the duplicate head *E*

When Maya creates a Blend Shape node, it uses the name of each target shape to name the corresponding slider. Because of this, you should always give your Blend Shape targets concise, informative names.

- Name the duplicated head geometry, *E*.

4 Unlock "E"s channels

When a surface is bound to a skeleton chain, its transformation channels are locked to prevent the likelihood of double transformation. The duplicated geometry will also have its channels locked, so they must be unlocked before you can do anything else.

- Select all of *E*'s transform channels.
- **RMB-click** one of the channels and select **Unlock Selected.**

5 Move "E" to the side

- Move *E* **-2** units along **X**.

6 Draw a curve along Melvin's lips

- Draw a CV curve along the inside of Melvin's mouth, using curve snapping to snap the CVs to edges.
- Name the curve *mouthWire*.

Note:	You may find it helpful to turn on **Wireframe on Shaded** shading mode while drawing the CV curve.

7 Close mouthWire

- With *mouthWire* selected, select **Edit Curves → Open/Close Curves - ❑**.

- Make sure that **Blend** is toggled **On**, the **Blend Bias** is set to **0.5**, and **Keep Originals** is toggled **Off**.

- Click the **Open/Close** button.

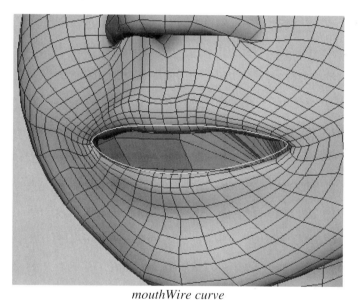

mouthWire curve

Note:	The mouthWire curve will be used to deform Melvin's mouth during the creation of the Blend Shape target heads. You may want to duplicate this curve and put it on a separate layer, or export it for retrieval later, so that you don't have to create a new curve for every target head.

8 Apply mouthWire as a Wire Deformer to the E head

- Select **Deform → Wire Tool – ❑**.

- Reset the Option window, then set the **Drop Off** value to **0.2**.

  Maya will prompt you to select a surface to be deformed.

- Select the *E* head and press the **Enter** key.

  Maya will prompt you to select a curve to be used as a wire.

- Select the *mouthWire* curve.

- Press the **Enter** key again.

9 Deform the mouthWire curve to deform the "E" head

- Move CVs on the *mouthWire* curve to reshape it, and Melvin's mouth along with it.

10 Adjust the wire settings as necessary

You may find it necessary to adjust the settings for the Wire Deformer to refine the deformation.

- Select the *E* head geometry.

- In the Channel Box, select the *wire* Input.

- Experiment with the **Drop Off** value.

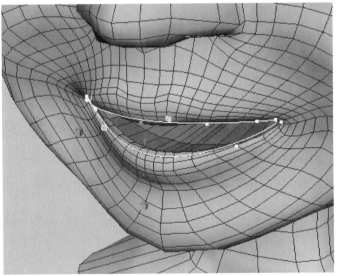

CVs for mouthWire scaled back

Note: You can adjust the degree to which a Wire Deformer is applied to a surface, on a global level, by adjusting the Envelope attribute. Using the virtual slider to adjust the **Envelope** value between **0** and **1** is an excellent way to evaluate the effects of the Wire Deformer on the surface.

Note:	You may find it easier to control the wire deformations applied to the face if you deform the *mouthWire* curve with a lattice.

Note:	While deforming the "*E*" head, you may find it helpful to duplicate a set of Melvin's teeth and put them inside the *E* mouth as a reference so that you don't produce deformations that result in teeth sticking out through the lips or cheeks.

11 Delete history from the head

Once you are happy with the shape of the target head *E*, you should remove its history to lock the deformations into place.

- Select *E*.
- Select **Edit → Delete By Type → History**.

12 Label the head with templated text

- Select **Create → Text – ❑**.
- Enter *E* in the text field.
- Click the **Create** button.
- **Move** and **Scale** the text so that it is clearly visible just below the head.
- With the *E* text selected, select **Display → Object Display → Template**.

13 Continue producing target shapes

- Repeat steps two through twelve to produce the target shapes you think you will need.

  The phonemes E, Ah, U, V, B/M, and a few eye expressions (eyebrows raised or scrunched up) are a good starting point for facial animation.

APPLYING THE BLEND SHAPE

You will now set up the actual Blend Shape deformation system. While there are several approaches to this, you will use a relatively simple yet flexible approach that uses separate Blend Shape nodes for phonemes, eye expressions, and general facial poses. An additional head target will be used to help deal with deformation order issues between the multiple Blend Shape nodes and the binding.

1 Open the scene file

- Continue working with your own scene file if you have created all of the necessary target shapes, or open the scene file named *Melvin_15_withTargets.mb*.

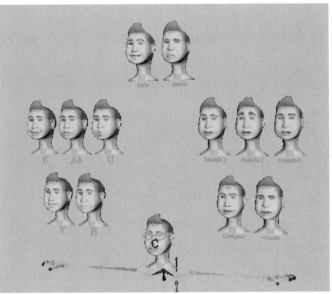

Melvin's target heads

2 Create a "buffer" target for the Blend Shape

Rather than placing all of the target heads in a single Blend Shape node, they will be organized by type. Separate Blend Shape nodes will be created for phonemes, eye expressions, and general facial poses.

- Select the original head geometry *head*.
- Duplicate it and unlock its transform channels.
- Translate it **4** units on **Y**.
- Name this new head *buffer*.

3 Create a Phonemes Blend Shape node

You will now start creating Blend Shape nodes. Rather than applying them to the original *head* geometry, they will be applied to the *buffer* node, which will eventually be connected to the *head*.

- Select the *E, Ah, U, V* and *B* targets.
- **Shift-select** the *buffer* head.
- Select **Deform → Create Blend Shape – ❒**.

- In the **Basic** section, name the Blend Shape node *Phonemes*.
- In the **Advanced** section, select **Parallel** from the **Deformation Order** field.
- Click the **Create** button.

4 Create an Eye Expressions Blend Shape node

- Select each of the Frontalis, Corrugator, and Occulis targets.
- **Shift-select** the buffer head again.
- Create another Blend Shape node, named *Eye Expressions*, with the same deformation order.

5 Create a General Face Blend Shape node

- Select the Smile and Frown targets.
- Create another Blend Shape node named *General Facial*.

6 Connect *head* and *buffer* with Blend Shape

Now that Blend Shape nodes have been created for all of the target shapes, you will create a Blend Shape node to connect the buffer target to the head geometry.

- Select *buffer* then **Shift-select** *head*.
- Select **Deform** → **Create Blend Shape** – ❐.
- Name this Blend Shape node *Deformation Buffer*.
- Select the default deformation order.
- Click the **Create** button.

7 Test the Blend Shapes applied to the *buffer* geometry

- Select **Window** → **Animation Editors** → **Blend Shape...**
- Find the *Phonemes* node and turn up the *E* slider from **0** to **1**.

  You should see the *buffer* head change shape to match the *E* target.
- Experiment with the slider values for the phonemes, eye expressions, and general facial Blend Shapes to see how they affect the *buffer* head.

Note: Right now the buffer head is changing shape, while the original bound head is doing nothing because the Deformation Buffer Blend Shape value is at 0.

---

8 Set the Deformation Buffer value to 1

- Find the Deformation Buffer Blend Shape and set the buffer slider's value to **1**.

9 Lock the Deformation Buffer value

Since this node's purpose is strictly to prevent deformation order conflicts between the other Blend Shape nodes and the skeleton, its value can be locked to prevent accidental editing.

- **RMB-click** in the value field for the buffer slider and select **Lock Attribute**.

10 Test the Blend Shape again

- Experiment with the other Blend Shape sliders again. Melvin's original bound head should now deform properly.

11 Correct the deformation order for *head*

- **RMB-click** on the original head geometry and select **Inputs → All Inputs**.

- **MMB-drag** Blend Shape (Deformation Buffer) down to the bottom of the list.

12 Save your work

Integrating joint control into the Blend Shape window

The Blend Shapes are now setup, and the face is bound and weighted. To improve animation workflow, a slider will be added to one of the Blend Shape nodes that will control the opening of the jaw. Currently, you would have to switch between keyframing the facial Blend Shapes and rotating the jaw to animate Melvin.

1 Create a single CV curve

- In the front view window, place a CV beside the buffer head with **Create → CV Curve Tool**.

- Rename the curve *jawOpenControl*.

2 Add the curve to the Phonemes Blend Shape

- Select the *jawOpenControl* curve then shift-select the *buffer* head.

- Select **Deform → Edit Blend Shape → Add – ❐**.

- Toggle **Specify Node** to **On**.

- Select *Phonemes* from the list of Existing Nodes.

- Toggle **Check Topology** to **Off**.

- Click **Apply and Close.**

  A new slider is now added to the Phonemes Blend Shape. The slider will do nothing at the moment but it will be made functional using SDK to control the jaw.

3 Create a Set Driven Key between the jaw and the Blend Shape

- Open the Set Driven Key window.

- Load the *jawOpen* joint's rotate Z as the **Driven.**

- In the Blend Shape window, click on the **Select** button for the Phonemes node to make it the active object.

- In the Set Driven Key window, load *Phonemes: jawOpenControl* as the **Driver.**

- Set a driven key with the *jawOpenControl* slider at **0** and the *jawOpen* joint rotated to **0** on **Z.**

- Set another key with the *jawOpenControl* slider at **1** and the *jawOpen* joint rotated to **-30** on **Z.**

Note: While it will probably never be necessary to rotate the *jawOpen* joint -30 on Z, it's always better to set your extreme poses beyond what you will ever need. If you find that you do in fact need to open the mouth more, you can always edit the animation curve for the joint in the Graph Editor.

---

4 Save your work

Melvin's head is now ready for animation.

ANIMATING FACIAL DEFORMATION WITH BLEND SHAPE

You will now use Blend Shape to animate the deformation of Melvin's face.

Animating the lip-sync

Work through these steps to create some lip-sync animation on Melvin.

1 Open the scene file

- Continue working with your present scene or open the file named *Melvin_15_readyForLipSync.mb.*

2 Change your panel layout to include the Blend Shape window

- Select **Panels** → **Layouts** → **Two Panes Side By Side.**

  Maya should now display two windows, a perspective window and another view.

- In the window other than the perspective window, select **Panels** → **Panel** → **Blend Shape.**

3 Save this layout

- Select **Panels** → **Saved Layouts** → **Edit Layouts...**
- Click on the **New Layout** button.
- In the Name field, enter persp/Blend Shape.
- Press the **Enter** key.
- Click on the **Close** button.

  Now you can select this panel layout anytime you need to just by selecting it from the Saved layouts menu.

4 Import an audio file

In the `~/maya/projects/melvin/sounds/` directory, you will find an assortment of dialogue passages. Search this directory for an appropriate dialogue track.

- Select **File** → **Import.**
- Select *Ill_Be.aiff.*
- Click **Import.**
- Load the sound file by **RMB-clicking** in the timeline and selecting **Sound** → **Ill_Be.aiff.**

  The waveform will appear in the timeline. To hear this in playback, you must set the **Playback Speed** to **Real Time** in your animation preferences.

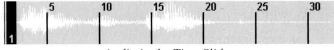

Audio in the Time Slider

5 Hide unnecessary geometry

- Hide everything except Melvin's head to help improve interactive performance.

Interactive performance is critical when doing all character animation, including facial animation. If the computer is sluggish while you scrub through the Time Slider, it will be difficult to judge the timing of the sound.

6 Keyframe Melvin's eye expressions

When doing lip-sync animation, it is generally a good idea to do the actual lip movement last. Animating the eyes and head movement first helps to set the context for the lip movement which reduces the likelihood of over-animated, or "chattery" mouth action.

- Go to frame **1**;
- Click on the **Key All** button for the Eye Expressions Blend Shape node;
- Go to frame **5**;
- Set the Corrugator value to **0.7**;
- Click the **Key All** button;
- Go to frame **10**;
- Click the **Key All** button again;
- Go to frame **16**;
- Set **Corrugator** to **0**;
- Set *Front_R* and *Front_L* to **1.0**;
- Set *Front_C* to **0.5**;
- Click the **Key All** button;
- Go to frame **25**;
- Click the **Reset All** button;
- Set **Corrugator** to **0.5**;
- Click the **Key All** button.

7 Playblast the animation

8 Refine the eye expressions

- Go to frame **25**.
- Set the **Occulis** value to **0.5** and set a key.

Note: It is not necessary to set a keyframe for the Occulis value before frame 25 because one was already set in the last step when the Key All button was clicked at frame 1.

---

9 Adjust Melvin's general facial expression

- Go to frame **1**.
- Set the **Frown** slider in the *General Facial* node to **0.5**.

10 Playblast the animation

11 Animate the jaw movement

Now that Melvin's facial animation is roughed in, you can move on to his mouth.

- Go to frame **1**;
- Click the **Reset All** button for the *Phonemes* node;
- Set a key for *jawOpen*;
- Go to frame **5**;
- Set *jawOpen* to **0.2** and set a key for it;
- Go to frame **8**;
- Set **jawOpen** to **0** and set a key for it;
- Go to frame **12**;
- Set *jawOpen* to **0.1** and set a key for it;
- Go to frame **15**;
- Set *jawOpen* to **0** and set a key;
- Go to frame **20**;
- Set *jawOpen* to **0.3** and set a key for it;
- Go to frame **25**;
- Set *jawOpen* to **0** and set a key for it.

12 Save your work

13 Animate Melvin's phonemes

Melvin's animation is falling into place. Now you can start working with the phonemes.

- Go to frame **5**;

- Set a key for the **B slider** at **0.0**;
- Go to frame **10**;
- Set **B** to **1.0** and set a key for it;
- Go to frame **12**;
- Set **B** to **0.7** and set a key;
- Go to frame **15**;
- Set **B** to **1.0** again and set a key;
- Got to frame **20**;
- Set **B** to **0.0** and set a key.

14 Playblast the animation

15 Refine the phoneme animation

- Go to frame **10**;
- Make sure that the **E slider** is set to **0.0** and set a key for it;
- Go to frame **12**;
- Set **E** to **0.25** and set a key for it;
- Go to frame **15**;
- Set **E** back to **0** and set a key for it.

16 Playblast the animation

17 Refine the phoneme animation one more time

- Go to frame **15**;
- Make sure that **V** is at **0** and set a key for it;
- Go to frame **20**;
- Set **V** to **0.6** and set a key for it;
- Go to frame **25**;
- Set **V** to **0** and set another key.

18 Fine-tune the animation

Now that the timing and basic poses for Melvin's facial animation is roughed in, it is time to refine the animation by adjusting curves in the Graph Editor.

- Select the *Eye Expressions* node by clicking on its **Select** button.
- Open the Graph Editor.
- Display and select the curve for **Occulis** in the Graph Editor.

- Change its tangent type to Flat.

19 Playblast the animation

20 Save your work

21 Playback the animation as it progresses

Continue experimenting with the curves in the Graph Editor and playblasting the animation. As you work with the character, it is advisable to make playblasts frequently and early on. This feedback is necessary to anticipate how the flow of the motion is occurring. Avoid the temptation to apply keys on every frame in an effort to pronounce every little nuance and syllable. A good rule of thumb in facial animation is "less is more". Try to animate your character's faces with as few keys as possible.

MORE FACIAL SETUP TECHNIQUES

This section will look at setting up different aspects of the face, including:

- Using clusters for eyelids;

- Aim constraints to control the eyes;

- Spline IK applied to the tongue.

EYELIDS

Eyelids are folds of skin that are pushed together to cover the eyeball. They have thickness and generally have a seamless transition from the cheek. One method of creating and animating the eyelid is to model your character with this feature in mind.

This example uses separate eyelids as lofts that were generated from isoparms on Melvin's eye socket. This example starts after the eyelid is built.

1 Open the Scene file

- Open the scene file *Melvin_15_readyForLipSync.mb*.

2 Cluster the eyelid

- Select the vertices in the area of Melvin's left upper eyelid.

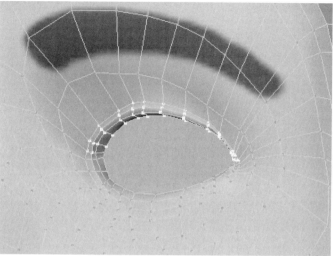

Selected vertices for upper eyelid cluster

- Create a cluster for these CVs by selecting **Deform** → **Create Cluster** – ❑, and set the following:

    Mode to **Relative.**

3 Name the cluster Left_upperEyelidCluster

4 Move the pivot of the cluster

- Select the cluster, then press the **Insert** key to select the pivot manip tool.
- Translate the pivot manip back to the center of the eye.
- Press the **Insert** key again.

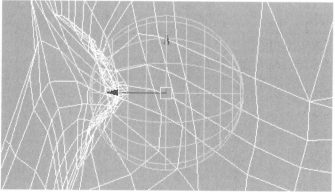

Moved cluster pivot

5 Rotate the cluster to test

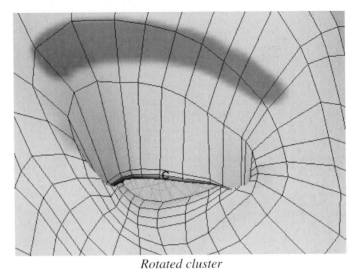

Rotated cluster

6 Paint the weights for the eyelid

Currently, the eyelid deformation is incorrect because all of the vertices in the eyelid have the same weighting in the cluster.

- Select Melvin's head geometry;

- Open the **Paint Cluster Weights Tool** window;

- Select the *left_upperEyelidCluster* from the list;

- Use the various Paint operations to edit the weighting of the cluster so that the lower edge lines up with the midpoint of the eyeball.

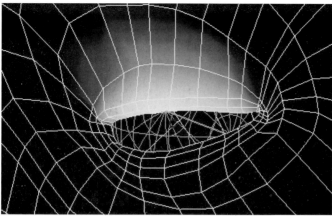

left_upperEyelidCluster's weighting

Note: You may find it easier to edit the weighting of the vertices at the corner of the eyelid by using the Component Editor rather than the Paint Weights tool.

---

7 Add any necessary vertices to the cluster

As you adjust the cluster's weighting, you may find that some vertices that should have been included in the cluster have been left out. If this happens, simply use the **Edit Membership Tool** to add the errant vertices to the cluster.

8 Rotate the cluster to test deformation

As you adjust the weighting, you should periodically rotate the cluster to see how the cluster is deforming the eyelid.

9 Correct the deformation order

Open the list of Inputs for Melvin's head and drag Cluster(*Left_upperEyelidClusterCluster*) so that it is second from the bottom of the list.

10 Parent left_upperEyelidCluster to the skull_a joint

11 Save your work

12 Repeat for the bottom eyelid and the right eye

The same procedures can be applied to the bottom eyelid and then again for the upper and lower eyelids for the right eye.

Add control to the eyelids

Eyelid control will be incorporated into the Eye Expressions Blend Shape node in the same way that the jaw control was added to the *Phonemes Blend Shape* node.

1   Draw two single CV curves beside the buffer head

2   Name the curves left_eye and right_eye

3   Add the target curves to the Eye Expression Blend Shape node

- Select both *left_eye* and *right_eye* curves, then **Shift-select** the *buffer* head.

- Select **Deform** → **Edit Blend Shape** → **Add** – ❐.

- In the **Add Blend Shape Target** option window toggle **Specify Node ON** and select *Eye Expressions* from the list of Existing Nodes.

- Click the **Apply** and **Close** button.

4   Create a Set Driven Key for the eyelids

- Set **Use Set Driven Key** to connect the *Left_Eye* and *Right_Eye* Blend Shape sliders to the **RotateX** of the two left eye clusters.

- Set keys with the **Left_Eye** at **0** and the eyelids open.

- Set keys with the **Left_Eye** at **1** and the eyelids close.

- Repeat for the right eye.

Note: The eyelids will probably look best in the closed position if the upper eyelid is rotated further than the lower lid. Try rotating the upper lid to 45 degrees on X, and the lower lid to -25 degrees on X for the closed position.

Tracking history of the face

The eyelids are an integral part of the face and eye socket. As you apply deformations to the face, you will want the eyelids to track with these deformations which could be created from a Blend Shape target. To get the eyelids to track, you could include these objects into the Blend Shape target so that they get deformed as well.

Another method is to parent the eyelids to the eyeballs. This keeps the eyelid and eyeball as separate structures that are not part of the Bind Skin. They are parented to the joints and do not participate in Blend Shape deformations. This way, the eyes maintain their shape as the skin moves around them.

They look more solid, but you have to make sure that the skin deformations do not interpenetrate the eyes too obviously.

EYEBALL ORIENT CONSTRAINTS

Aiming the eyeballs can be obtained by Orient Constraining their orientation to a locator. This locator can then be placed in the scene and animated to guide the character's attention from a single point.

- **Group** the eye to itself. This ensures that the eye moves as a unit and it will make the local axes line up with the world so that the eyes do not move strangely when the constraint is added.

- **Orient Constrain** these groups to a **locator**.

- **Group** the locator under the character.

The face will often change shape in relation to how the eyes are looking. If the eyes are looking down, the lower eyelids will sink back while the upper eyelids and supporting structures will pull down. The opposite is true for when the eyes look upward.

It may seem subtle, but when it is missing from your facial setup, your face will seem that much more lifeless.

MELVIN'S TONGUE WITH IK SPLINE

A critical part of believable lip-sync is the tongue. Many phonemes such as the "th" in the "the" word involve a very visible upturned tongue against the upper front teeth.

The tongue could be included in the Blend Shape or you could use IK spline like you did on Melvin's back. You can create a tongue from a sphere, create joints for it, bind the skin, and add IK spline.

1 Open an existing file

- **Import** the file *melvinTongue.mb*.

   This is the geometry and skeleton.

2 Run SplineIK through the Joints

Use the default settings for Spline IK.

3 Add clusters to the splineIK

- Add two relative clusters to the splineIK curve's CVs at the tip of the tongue and in the middle of the tongue.

- **Parent** the clusters under the SplineIK curve.

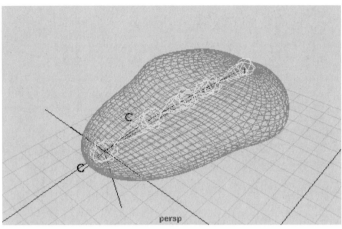

Skeleton for the tongue

4 Bind the tongue geometry to the tongue skeleton

- **Bind** the tongue to the skeleton.

5 Parent the tongue skeleton to Melvin's skeleton

Melvin's skeleton chain is grouped under an extra Transform node named *tonguegroup* to help prevent double transformations in the tongue. When parenting the tongue skeleton to Melvin's *jawOpen* joint, make sure that it's the *tonguegroup* node that gets parented.

- Select the top joint of the tongue's skeleton chain, *tonguechain*.

- Press the up arrow key to pick walk up to the *tonguegroup* node.

- **Shift-select** the *jawOpen* joint.

- Select **Edit → Parent.**

Controlling the tongue is now a matter of selecting either of the clusters and translating or rotating them to position the tongue.

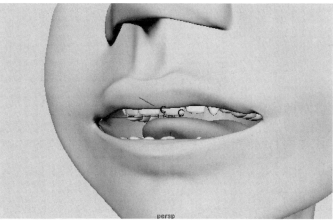
Tongue control

Summary

This chapter covered some techniques for specific facial areas such as the eyes, mouth, and tongue. The main goal is to get the base head to a pose that can be duplicated for use as a Blend Shape target. Using various deformers is useful to create these poses. Blend Shape targets can also be deleted once a Blend Shape has been created, but it is a good idea to keep them in case you need to go back and adjust or edit such a pose.

A Quarternions

Following are some insights into Maya's implementation of quarternion rotation interpolation.

WHAT ARE QUARTERNIONS?

Quarternion evaluation is different than Maya's default method of Euler space based rotation or angular interpolation.

Flipping

With Euler based evaluation of rotational values, Maya internally calculates the rotational path without respect to the shortest possible solution in world or local space. The shorter path often times is the correct or logical path for an object to rotate, especially for character or animal movement. This can create the case where an object's rotation is calculated to take the long way around. This can appear as a "flip" in the objects rotation.

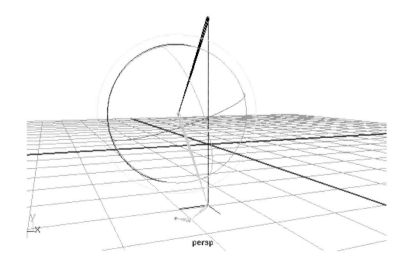

Imagine a series of joints controlled by an Inverse Kinematic chain. Let's say a joint in the chain has current rotational values of:

<< 300, 0, 0 >> at **frame 10** where a keyframe has been made on the IK handle.

The IK handle is then positioned to a new location and keyframed at **frame 20**.

The intended value on the joint at **frame 20** is equivalent to:

<< 10, 350, 0 >>

Maya is presented with several ways to get to this target value on the joint by way of IK solving:

It could **rotate -390 degrees** in **X** and **+350 degrees** in **Y**.

These are large rotations, however.

The joint could also achieve the same ultimate position by **rotating +70 degrees** in **X** and **-10 degrees** in **Y**.

Which solution is intended? Did the user intend for such a large rotation or were they more interested in the most natural possible solution? Typically in nature (as in muscle driven bone rotations in animals), the shortest path or easiest solution requiring the least amount of energy is preferred. Quarternions follow this type of interpolation - the shorter path by default.

Quarternion evaluation works in +-180 degree values. It does not directly keep track of an objects spin or revolutions. (0, 360, 720...) values are kept normalized to a 360 degree range. -180 to +180, and a solution that involves the shortest path is invoked. Think of a path or arc along the surface of a sphere which represents the intended rotation of an object.

Gimbal Lock

Also with Euler - angle interpolation each angular curve (X,Y, Z) is calculated separately and the result is combined to form the ultimate angular orientation. This can lead to a logical, yet undesirable path of rotation. Gimbal Lock is just such a side effect where an axis appears to not be involved in the rotation because the Euler - angle based interpolation has established an alignment between two complementary axes.

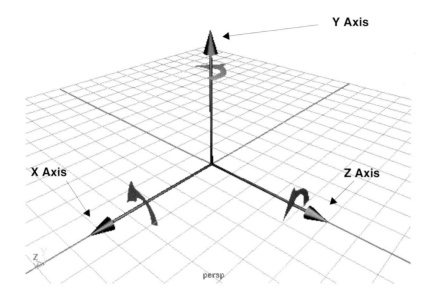

If you rotate to a position where the Y-axis overlaps the X-axis, a subsequent Y rotation can appear to be a negative X rotation. These can fight against each other and result in a loss of degree of freedom (DOF) during interpolation and interaction, cancelling out an axis' role in the arc ball manipulation of the object.

Quarternion interpolation can alleviate these problems but also has its own limitations. Because Quarternion interpolation is achieved by calculating from all 3 axes, you are prevented from editing or manipulating a single axis or degree of freedom independently.

The display of Quarternion curves is also different in the Graph Editor. Euler space uses an open range of values which appear logically in the Graph Editor, which has an open range as well (0 -> very large positive and negative numbers). Quarternion curves, which have only values normalized between -180 and +180, do not fit the Graph Editor's format as well. For this reason, you may see display of Quarternion value and tangent in this context.

How to use Quarternions

You have three ways to work with rotation curves in Maya:

- Independent Euler-Angle Curves;

- Synchronized Euler-Angle Curves;

- Synchronized Quarternion Curves.

Quarternions can be used by either establishing them as the default manner for Maya to handle rotational evaluation or they can be selected and changed to the other types from the Graph Editor menu using the **Curves→ Change Rotation Interpolation** menu.

Tip:	When changing curve interpolation type, be sure to select the curves in the **Outliner** portion of the **Graph Editor**. Also note that if you change from Euler to Quarternion and then back to Euler, the original Euler tangency is maintained.

To set the different interpolation types as the default:

- Under **Window → Settings/Preferences → Preferences...**
- Select the **Keys** Category.
- Set the **Rotation Interpolation** new curve type default, as desired.

Note:	Quarternion curves do not have tangency control as of Maya4.0. They are created as linear or step type interpolations only.

Tip:	Typically, a user would only use Quarternions when they need to. Usually, when they are encountering flipping or working with rotational data that is historically prone to interpolation and evaluation problems. Import of motion capture data is typically best handled with Quarternion interpolation.

Constrained animation and camera animation are other areas that are vulnerable to the effects of Euler - angle interpolation flipping and Gimbal Lock. Rigid body and dynamic simulation animation can also lead to flipping and rotational problems that can benefit from Quarternion interpolation.

B Alternate Feet

Following are some alternative solutions for animating and controlling a character's foot.

IK AND FK COMBINATION FOOT

This method creates Inverse Kinematics from the hip to the ankles, but requires Forward Kinematics for the ankle rotation and the bending of the toe.

Skeleton setup

The skeleton for this method is similar to the one used previously in this book, except it has no heel joint.

1 Create the legs and feet of the skeleton

- Starting with the hip, place 5 joints (hip, knee, ankle, ball, toe). Draw the knee in a bent position.

2 Move the legs into position

- Move Melvin's leg to his left side.

- Mirror these joints for the right leg.

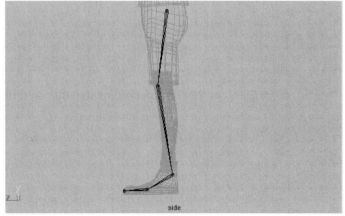

Leg setup

Setting up Single Chain IK

Set up a Single Chain solver between the hip and the ankle of each leg.

1 Set up an SC solver between the hip and ankle

- Select **Skeleton** → **IK Handle Tool** – ❐ and make sure **ikSCsolver** is selected.

- Select the *left_hip* to establish the starting point of the IK chain and then the *left_ankle* to establish the ending point of the IK chain.

  Note that an IK chain with joint effector is automatically created. The end effector is the transform position of the IK handle.

2 Repeat for the right leg

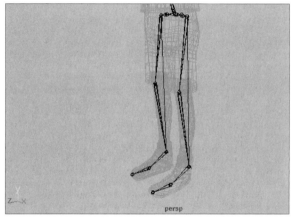

IK from hip to ankle

3 Label the IK handles

- Label the IK handles *left_legIK* and *right_legIK*.

Parenting the IK and Orient constraints

Note that if you select the IK handle and rotate its Y axis, the leg rotates with it. By parenting this handle to another object you can have two levels of control:

- Y- rotating the parent object will rotate the leg

- Y- rotating the IK handle will allow the knee to point in a different direction than the foot. You can use this second level of control when Melvin bends down.

Once this parenting is complete, you want the foot to point in the same direction as the locator. Using an Orient constraint on the ankle joint, the foot's rotation will be the same as the locator.

Parenting the IK

First you'll create locators to serve as parent objects for the IK handles, then you'll repeat the process for the other leg.

1 Create a locator and place it near the left ankle.

- Select **Create** → **Locator**.

- Move the locator to the ankle.

- Scale the locator bigger to make it easier to select later.

- Label the locator *left_ankleLocator*.

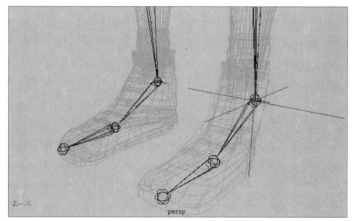

Locators on ankles

2 Parent the IK handle to the locator

- In the Outliner, select *left_legIK*.

- **Ctrl-select** the *left_ankleLocator*.

- Select **Edit** → **Parent** from the main menu.

3 Repeat for the right leg

- Name the locator *right_ankleLocator*.

4 Orient constrain the ankle joint to the locator

To make the foot rotate with the locator, you'll use orient constraints.

- In the Outliner, select the *left_ankleLocator*.

- **Ctrl-select** the *left_ankle* joint.
- Select **Constrain** → **Orient** from the main menu.

5 Repeat for the right leg

You should now be able to select either ankle locator to move the ankle and rotate the foot and leg.

Bending toes and twisting the knee

For more realistic character motion, the toes should bend when a character walks. To manually animate toe-bending, you would select the ball joints and rotate them for each step the character takes. Instead, you'll streamline the animation workflow by adding an attribute to the ankle locators. Then you'll use this attribute to drive the bending of each toe.

Adding attributes

You'll create two attributes, **bendToe** and **kneeTwist**, that will be used to drive the *x*-rotation of the ball joint and the *y*-rotation of the IK handle.

1 Add an attribute to the locator at the ankles

- Select *left_ankleLocator*.
- Select **Modify** → **Add Attribute** and set the following:

  Data Type to **Float**;

  Attribute Type to **Scalar**.

  Name the attribute *kneeTwist*.
- Click **Add**.
- Add another attribute to the locator called **bendToe**.

2 Connect the kneeTwist attribute to drive the rotation

- Select **Window** → **General Editors** → **Connection Editor...**
- In the Outliner, select *left_ankleLocator*.
- In the Connection Editor, click **Reload Left**.
- In the Outliner, select *left_legIK*.
- In the Connection Editor, click **Reload Left**.
- In the left column of the Connection Editor, click **Knee Twist** and in the right column, click the **Rotate** folder, then click **RotateY**.

You have now created a connection between the **KneeTwist** attribute and the **RotateY** attribute. When you adjust **KneeTwist**, you are actually rotating the leg IK - and thus offsetting the leg rotation from that of the foot.

3 Connect the bendToe attribute to drive the ball joint

- Select **Window** → **General Editors** → **Connection Editor...**
- In the Outliner, select *left_ankleLocator*.
- In the Connection Editor, click **Reload Left**.
- In the Outliner, select *left_ball* joint.
- In the Connection Editor, click **Reload Left**.
- In the left column of the Connection Editor, click **BendToe** and in the right column, click the **Rotate** folder, then click **RotateX**.

  You have now created a connection between the **BendToe** attribute and the **RotateX** attribute. When you adjust BendToe, you are actually rotating the *left_ball* joint thus bending the toe.

4 Repeat for the right ankle

Now you can animate everything below the waist by selecting either of the ankle locators, foot placement, ankle rotation, and toe bending.

ALTERNATE LEG IK SETUPS

Here you'll use the Rotate Plane (RP) IK solver for Melvin's legs and arms. The difference between this solver and the Single Chain (SC) solver is that the RP solver provides a way to control the direction the knees and elbows will point. This is achieved by using a special aiming constraint called a Pole Vector. You will use locators as the Pole Vector constraints and animate them as needed to control the aiming of the knees and elbows.

Rotate Plane IK

You will set up a Rotate Plane solver between the hip and the ankle of each leg. The RP solver is the default IK solver.

1 Set up an RP solver between the hip and ankle for each leg.

- Select **Skeleton** → **IK Handle Tool** – ❏ and make sure **IkRPsolver** is selected.
- Select the *left_hip* to establish the starting point of the IK chain and then the *left_ankle* to establish the ending point of the IK chain.

- Notice that an IK chain with joint effector is automatically created. The end effector is the transform position of the IK handle.

2 Repeat for the right leg

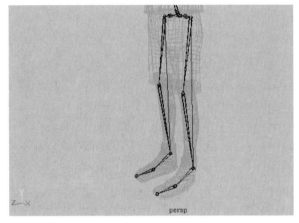

Leg setup

- Label the IK handles *left_legIK* and *right_legIK*.

Point and Orient constraints - legs and feet

To help control motion, Maya offers several constraint options - point, orient, aim, and Pole Vector. Constraints limit the motion of the constrained entity based on the type of constraint. Before you add the constraints, you'll create locators to control multiple keyframeable attributes with one entity (the locator).

At each ankle, you'll create locators to constrain both the position of the IK handles and the rotation of the foot. You'll point constrain the IK handles to the locators and orient constrain the ankle joints to the locators. An added benefit of the point constraining is that it will set up a pseudo "sticky-type" anchor for the feet. The benefit of this approach will become apparent when you start to animate and pose Melvin.

Adding constraints

You'll set up point constraints at each ankle to constrain the position of the IK handles to the locators. You'll work on one leg, first creating the locators, then adding the constraints. Then you'll repeat the process for the other leg.

1 Create a locator and place it near the left ankle

- Select **Create → Locator**.

A cross-hairs appears at the world origin.

- **Translate** the locator to the ankle. You do not have to be precise in your positioning of the locator.
- **Scale** the locator bigger to make it easier to select later.
- Label the locator *left_ankleLocator*.

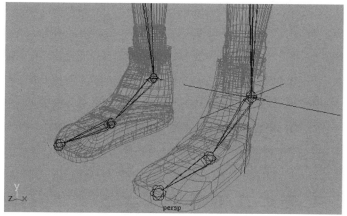

Control for the feet

2 Point constrain the locator to the IK handle

- In the Outliner, select the *left_ankleLocator*.
- **Ctrl-select** *left_legIK*.
- Select **Constrain** → **Point** from the main menu.

3 Orient constrain the locator to the ankle joint

- In the Outliner, select the *left_ankleLocator*.
- **Ctrl-select** the *left_ankle* joint.
- Select **Constrain** → **Orient** from the main menu.

4 Repeat steps1-3 for the right leg

- Name the locator *right_ankleLocator*.

You should now be able to select either ankle locator to move the ankle and rotate the foot.

Pole Vector constraints - knees

The Rotate Plane solver includes a constraint to control which plane the RP solver will work in. This constraint is the Pole Vector constraint. It's a great way to visually determine which direction the knees will point.

Adding Pole Vector constraints

You'll add Pole Vector constraints to Melvin's knees. (This constraint is also useful for elbows.)

1 Create a locator for each leg and place it out in front of each knee

- Label these locators *left_KneeLocator* and *right_KneeLocator*.

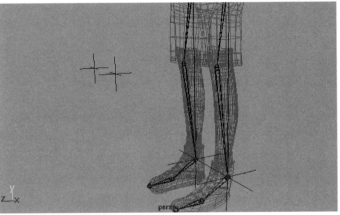

Constraints for the knees

2 Pole Vector constrain these locators to the IK handle of each leg

- In the Outliner, select *left_KneeLocator*.
- **Ctrl-select** *left_ankleIk*.
- Select **Constrain** → **Pole Vector** from the main menubar.

  Notice a line is drawn between the *left_KneeLlocator* and *left_hip* where the *left_legIK* begins.

- Repeat for the right leg.

Parenting the Pole Vector locators

You'll want these Pole Vector locators to travel with your character when you animate. There are several places to parent these locators depending on the preference or the needs of the shot. Since you want these Pole Vector locators to travel with the character when you animate, you'll parent them to the skeleton. There are several places to parent these locators, but you'll parent them to the root because this covers most of the general poses for the animation.

1 Parent the Pole Vector Locators to the root of the skeleton

- In the Outliner, **MMB-drag+drop** *left_kneeLocator* and *right_kneeLocator* over *back_root* joint.

There are several other places you could parent these Pole Vector constraints for the knee, depending on the behavior you want or the needs of the shot. These include hip joints, ankle or ball joints, or keyframe by hand.

INDEX

Novice/New to 3D

Looking for a better understanding of 3D space and the concepts and theory behind working in Maya? Want a highly visual tour through 3D space? Try *The Art of Maya*, a full-color illustrated guide to working in 3D or get hands-on experience through one of our Maya Beginner's Guide DVDs. The Maya Beginner's Guides provide you with a step-by-step, highly visual guided learning experience to help you understand how to animate, render and create dynamic effects in Maya.

Intermediate

Transitioning to Maya from another 3D package? Looking to improve your general skills when using Maya? Choose from our Learning Maya family of books. Explore Maya through theoretical discussions, step-by-step instructions and with helpful instructor-led chapter overviews - the Learning Maya books are must-have reference materials for any Maya user. Delve deeply into *Character Rigging, Modeling, Rendering, Dynamics, MEL,* and *Maya Unlimited Features*.

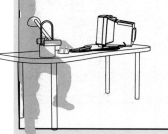

Want to Learn More?
Visit
www.alias.com/store
and check out our books and training materials.

Step 1

Step 2

Step 3

Advanced

Are you a seasoned Maya user looking for time and money saving tips and techniques? Want to understand how your industry peers have successfully solved their production problems? Select from our extensive selection of Maya Techniques™ DVDs and learn from pros like Jason Schleifer (Weta Digital, Dreamworks/PDI); Tom Kluyskens (Weta Digital); Erick Miller (Digital Domain); Paul Thuriot (Tippett Studio) and more.

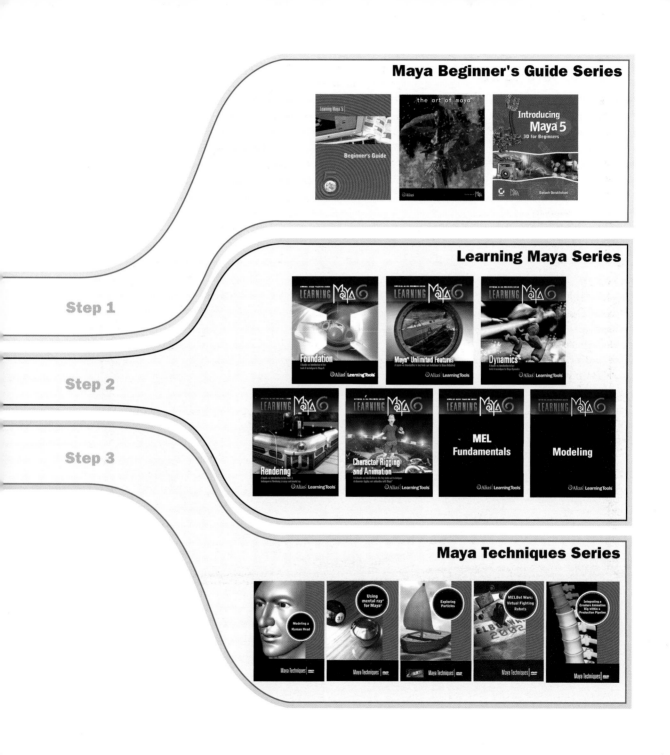

Maya Beginner's Guide Series

Learning Maya Series

Step 1

Step 2

Step 3

Maya Techniques Series

OFFICIAL ALIAS TRAINING GUIDE

LEARNING Maya 6™

Maya® Unlimited Features

available now for $59.99 US

Learning Maya 6 | Maya Unlimited Features is your key to learning Maya Unlimited quickly and easily. Get hands-on experience with the innovative tools and powerful techniques available in Maya Unlimited through project-based lessons. You'll learn to create Maya Fluid Effects, work with Maya Cloth, create Maya Fur effects and make long hair and dynamic curves.

To purchase Alias | Learning Tools visit:
www.alias.com/store

CHARACTER RIGGING
AND ANIMATION

Credits:

Content Developers: Bill Dwelly, Lee Graft, Cory Mogk, Rob Ormond, Damon Riesberg

Copy Editor: Erica Fyvie

Technical Editors: Lenni Rodrigues, David Haapalehto

Cover Design: Louis Fishauf

Cover Image: Leon Vymenets

Production Manager: Carla Sharkey

Product Manager: Danielle Lamothe

Indexing: Bob Gundu

DVD Production: Roark Andrade, Julio Lopez

A special thanks goes out to:

Mike Ahmadi, Matt Baer, Corban Gossett, Deion Green, Rachael Jackson, Kevin Lombardi, Robert MacGregor, Vivien May, Cathy McGinnis, Jason Schleifer, Michael Stamler, Marcus Tateishi, Lisa Williamson

The material contained herein (the "Copyrighted Material") is copyrighted ©2004 Alias Systems, a division of Silicon Graphics Limited ("Alias") and is protected by national and international intellectual property conventions and treaties. All rights reserved. Unauthorized reproduction, display, use, exhibition or broadcast of the Copyrighted Material is prohibited and may result in severe criminal and civil penalties.

THE COPYRIGHTED MATERIAL IS PROVIDED "AS IS". ALIAS DOES NOT WARRANT THAT THE COPYRIGHTED MATERIAL WILL MEET YOUR REQUIREMENTS, WILL BE ERROR-FREE, OR THAT THE CONTENT OF THE COPYRIGHTED MATERIAL IS ACCURATE OR COMPLETE. ALIAS MAKES NO WARRANTIES, EXPRESS, IMPLIED OR ARISING BY CUSTOM OR TRADE USAGE RELATING TO THE COPYRIGHTED MATERIAL, AND WITHOUT LIMITING THE GENERALITY OF THE FOREGOING, TO THE EXTENT PERMITTED BY APPLICABLE LAW, SPECIFICALLY DISCLAIMS ANY IMPLIED WARRANTIES OF TITLE, NON-INFRINGEMENT, MERCHANTABILITY OR FITNESS FOR A PARTICULAR PURPOSE. IN NO EVENT SHALL ALIAS AND/OR ITS AFFILIATES, PARENT COMPANIES, LICENSORS OR SUPPLIERS BE LIABLE FOR ANY DAMAGES WHATSOEVER ARISING OUT OF OR RELATED TO YOUR USE OF THE COPYRIGHTED MATERIAL.

© Copyright 2004 Alias Systems, a division of Silicon Graphics Limited. All rights reserved. Alias is a registered trademark and the swirl logo, the Maya logo, MEL, and Learning Maya are trademarks of Alias Systems, a division of Silicon Graphics Limited in the United States and/or other countries worldwide. Maya is a registered trademark of Silicon Graphics, Inc. in the United States and/or other countries worldwide, used exclusively by Alias Systems, a division of Silicon Graphics Limited. SYBEX and the SYBEX logo are either registered trademarks or trademarks of SYBEX Inc. in the United States and/or other countries. All other trademarks, service marks, trade names or product names mentioned herein are property of their respective owners.